TOM AIKENS COOKING

TOM AIKENS
COOKING

EBURY
PRESS

TO LAURA, WHO HAS SHARED SO MUCH WITH ME, AND FOR ALL THE SUPPORT SHE HAS GIVEN ME

First published in Great Britain in 2006

1 3 5 7 9 10 8 6 4 2

Text © Tom Aikens 2006
Food photography © John Lawrence-Jones 2006
Reportage photography © Alexander Webster 2006
Cover photograph © Angela Moore 2006 used by kind permission
of Elle Deco Magazine.

Tom Aikens has asserted his right to be identified as the author
of this work under the Copyright, Designs and Patents Act 1988.

Ebury Publishing
Random House, 20 Vauxhall Bridge Road, London SW1V 2SA

Random House Australia (Pty) Limited
20 Alfred Street, Milsons Point, Sydney, New South Wales 2061,
Australia

Random House New Zealand Limited
18 Poland Road, Glenfield, Auckland 10, New Zealand

Random House South Africa (Pty) Limited
Isle of Houghton, Corner Boundary Road & Carse O'Gowrie,
Houghton, 2198, South Africa

Random House Publishers India Private Limited
301 World Trade Tower, Hotel Intercontinental Grand Complex,
Barakhamba Lane, New Delhi 110 001, India

The Random House Group Limited Reg. No. 954009
www.randomhouse.co.uk

A CIP catalogue record for this book is available from
the British Library.

Editor: Susan Fleming
Project Editor: Gillian Haslam
Designed by: www.jpcreative.co.uk
Props stylist: Penny Markham

ISBN: 0091910013
ISBN-13 (from January 2007): 9780091910013

Papers used by Ebury Press are natural, recyclable products
made from wood grown in sustainable forests.

Printed and bound in China

CONTENTS

INTRODUCTION

I spend most of my time in the restaurant kitchen, making quite complicated and creative dishes, so when I'm at home I prefer to cook and eat more simply. I like things like salad, fresh fruit and a good steak sandwich; toasted tea cakes with melted butter and honey; fish cooked simply with lemon, olive oil and a few herbs; or a nice roast with all the trimmings on a Sunday, followed by rhubarb crumble and custard. The recipes in this book are therefore a combination of what I cook professionally and what I like to cook and eat at home: some are simple, to be achieved in less than half an hour, and some are more complex, which might take at least a couple of hours to bring together.

Because of this, I decided to lay the book out largely according to ingredients, rather than having the more traditional structure of starters, main courses and desserts. Basically, I take a simple, usually seasonal ingredient and then use it to come up with a range of dishes from easy to more challenging. This, I thought, would also help to encourage you to think on your own — to use a recipe as a base and then adapt it to create something else. This will also inspire confidence because, above all, I want to get you cooking.

Cooking is a fun, loving and light-hearted thing to do. There is no need to get stressed, as many people do, when it comes to preparing a meal. You will never have to spend all day slaving away in the kitchen. You may be incredibly busy, and think that convenience foods are the easiest option, but I'll show you that they're definitely not. Some of the dishes here can be cooked very quickly, and even if a stew takes 1½ hours, you don't have to watch it all the time, which leaves you free to concentrate on other tasks (or pleasures).

This book is for everyone who loves food and wants to get more out of their shopping, ingredients and cooking, whether you're a complete beginner or quite advanced.

OUR FOOD CULTURE

We British as a nation seem to eat to live, not live to eat (which is what's said about the French). In any other European country, there are food markets virtually daily countrywide, and you will see people chatting away about the food they buy — about how good this cheese is or how fresh those vegetables are from the man next to the butcher. Sadly, it rarely happens here, and I think it's because we are just not educated enough about food. We seem to care more about our status and looks than we do about what we put in our mouths. It's generally acknowledged that more than half the British population are eating a less than adequate diet, mostly because they are too busy — or lazy — to buy and cook sensibly, even on a budget.

As a result, the food industry has stepped in with an array of microwaveable readymeals – something you wouldn't ever see in a European food shop. These readymade dishes — mostly eaten on the lap in front of the television — are destroying the family set-up and the structure of the home. (They're also much more expensive than buying and cooking fresh food.) To me, home and family revolve around the kitchen table – cooking, tasting, eating, talking, sharing and airing problems. I remember vividly the family meals my mother cooked when I was growing up — she even made the bread. Nowadays, though, family life is slowly being eroded because of convenience, time and money.

What is even more upsetting is that we seem to have forgotten how to cook. We can make cars, invent microchips that can run entire transport systems, but some of us in this country cannot even boil an egg. That's a frightening thought. Neither are we educating our children enough about how important food and eating is, about how health depends on good food. For me, cooking and eating well is a way of life.

SHOPPING

It's all about how we shop. Once we would have shopped several times a week for fresh food. Today, we live in a supermarket culture, and we bulk-buy once a week. Most of us shop in supermarkets because it is convenient. Why would we want to spend the time going to different places when we can get it all under one roof? The prices are cheaper too, and they never seem to run out of certain foods. But this year-round availability comes at a cost, particularly to British seasonal foods and to British farmers. Once strawberries would have been a yearly treat at Wimbledon time, but now they are flown in all year round from places like South America. What this does to the environment is another question altogether, but it eats into the British farming economy — how can they compete? — and doesn't do us consumers much good either. Fruits from abroad, for instance, are picked under-ripe, packed, stored in the dark while travelling to hinder ripening, then reach the supermarket shelves, possibly some two weeks later. All this inevitably affects the taste of the fruit, but also its nutrient content, and you'd be better off taking some vitamin pills instead. If supermarkets really stuck to the seasons, the shelves would be empty for part of the year.

And that's why I want to encourage you to buy fresh foods, foods that are in season, preferably foods that are organic, and foods that are British. The flavours and nutrients will be far superior, and you will be helping local producers. Small food shops still survive — just — and you should buy as much fresh food as possible from them. Farmers' markets are on the increase too,

which is good news — and also echoes the sociability and appreciation of foods which are so much part of European food culture. And, happily, some of the supermarkets are now making an effort in the way they produce their foods — and reducing the packaging which damages the environment. (We must have the highest amount of packaged foods in Europe, mostly because of our readymeals and convenience foods.) If we all cooked at home more, we'd all be doing something for the planet too. Supermarkets are also beginning to encourage local farmers and sell local and organic produce, which is great.

A WELL-COOKED SIMPLE MEAL CAN BE JUST AS GOOD AS AN EXTRAVAGANT DINNER.

Many of us think shopping is a bit of a chore, but I think it can be exciting, especially at a farmers' market. Depending on the season, there's always something new and interesting on display. I like wandering from stall to stall, seeing what is best, and mentally picturing what I could make with it. You may well say that as I am a chef, I inevitably have a knowledge and creative experience you might lack. But, armed with a few ideas from this book, you too could shop in a similar way. And don't ever take a shopping list with you. Without one, you will have a sense of freedom, and when you see something you like, you will be inspired, possibly to try something you might not have tried before.

I WANT TO ENCOURAGE YOU TO BUY FRESH FOODS, FOODS THAT ARE IN SEASON, PREFERABLY FOODS THAT ARE ORGANIC, AND FOODS THAT ARE BRITISH.

We all have different resources and incomes, but the primary rule is always to buy within your means. Set yourself a budget to spend every week if possible. You don't ever have to go mad with glamorous ingredients: a well-cooked simple meal can be just as good as an over-extravagant dinner — and can be more rewarding for all concerned.

COOKING AND EATING

Once you have changed the way you buy, you can also change the way you and your family cook and eat. Instead of readymeals or takeaways, buy and cook seasonal foods. Instead of chips, give them roast carrots or parsnips; instead of takeaway fried chicken, roast a chicken whole or in pieces; offer fruit or home-made biscuits instead of sweets.

Obviously what can be cooked depends on the time of year. Winter vegetables can be combined with cheaper cuts of meat for casseroles and braised dishes (good on a tight budget). The veg can be made into soups, or just plainly roasted with a bit of thyme or honey to accompany a roast joint. In summer, there is an abundance of choice in both veg and fruit. There are a multitude of possible salads, you can grill vegetables (perhaps on the barbecue), or, taking it further, you could make a pea mousse or cold pea soup, for instance. Gluts of veg or fruit can be preserved, and there are some ideas in this book.

When cooking, try to really think about what you are doing, rather than just following the instructions in a cookery book. At the beginning, you may indeed need those instructions, but as you progress, you will recognise that certain methods are the best so far as a particular ingredient is concerned.

With that basic level of knowledge, you can then adapt, change and possibly enhance — while there are certain food combinations that work, and accepted methods of cooking, there are never any real restrictions in cooking apart from your own ability. You may make mistakes at first — we all do! — but it's part of the learning curve. After a while, you may even want to add something to one of my dishes, which is not dissimilar to what a chef does — continually being creative and using one's imagination.

My recipes have been designed to help you do just this. Some of the more complicated ones consist of several elements: you may choose to use just one of those elements with a simple steak or fish fillet; or you might want to combine a couple of elements from different recipes to create a completely new and unique dish.

WHEN COOKING, REALLY THINK ABOUT WHAT YOU ARE DOING, RATHER THAN JUST FOLLOWING THE INSTRUCTIONS.

Whatever you do, never forget that people may come and go, but food is here to stay, whether being re-invented or just the family meal. Treat it with respect and love, and then you will see the true benefits.

MY STORY

I wanted to be a chef from a very early age, probably because my grandfather and father were in the wine trade, and we would often go to France. All I was really interested in eating there was chips, or steak and chips, and not a lot else. My mother and father would happily tuck into frogs' legs and snails, but my twin brother Robert and I would cringe at the very thought. But what did make an impression on both of us was the people of France, their very real love affair with food, and how food brought them together. In the markets you could see how excited they were about food — smelling it, touching and squeezing it — and just being there was great fun for me.

When we were sixteen, my brother and I applied to Norwich City College Hotel School. I remember having a very bad interview and I think they only let me in because I was a twin. But being very determined, I thought, I'll show you. I believed in myself implicitly, and I think I have shown them. I found something I was good at, something that I loved, and I completed a two-year Advanced Catering Diploma in 1989.

My first job was as a commis chef at the Mirabelle in Eastbourne. I then went to London. Getting a job there was extremely hard, as there weren't many good restaurants, certainly few that I would want to work in, and there were many more chefs than there were positions.

The first place I experienced was David Cavalier's on Queenstown Road, Battersea. At first I worked for nothing as a stageaire (a trainee), which involved long days and nights, from six in the morning until midnight. David was a great chef, and he valiantly put up with me and my many mistakes. Eight to twelve weeks later, a position became available and I began work as a chef. It was hard, but fun, and I learnt a lot in some five or six months. The only problem was sharing a flat with my twin brother who worked straight shifts in another restaurant: this meant he had every night off and was having fun with friends. In comparison, I was working 18 hours a day, and arriving home early in the morning just as he was getting in from a night out.

Work had become a lot harder now, as I had been made responsible for the veg section, and now I got shouted at for the mistakes I made, which I thought was unfair. So I decided to walk out one night without telling anyone (a lot of people did, so I thought it was normal). David and his wife Sue persuaded me back a few days later, and I shall never forget some of his words: he said that to get anywhere in life you had to work harder than anyone else in the kitchen, and you have to learn to take a few bawlings. It would all pay off in the end, he said, and that advice has stayed with me ever since.

I REMEMBER HAVING A BAD INTERVIEW AT COLLEGE AND I THINK THEY ONLY LET ME IN BECAUSE I WAS A TWIN. BUT BEING VERY DETERMINED, I THOUGHT, I'LL SHOW YOU. I BELIEVED IN MYSELF IMPLICITLY.

Some time later I moved to Tante Claire in Kensington to work with Pierre Koffmann, who was like a god to me. His two-star Michelin restaurant was staffed entirely by French people, both front of house and kitchen, bar one other chef, so it was quite daunting, as the French often seemed to hate the English. Employed as a commis on the larder, I learned to organise my day's work, the same every day, so I got into a routine. Being a chef is not just about being able to cook but about thinking logically about how you work. Once you establish a routine, you become consistent, and with that you get quicker.

After nine weeks there, I was in charge of the larder. After three and a half months, I moved to the fish section, and was completely over my head. I had not filleted a fish since college, so I was in trouble every day. But I got to grips with it and was soon filleting as quickly as Koffmann (who had incredible knife skills). When he was in a good mood, he would race me prepping the fish!

I eventually worked in all the sections in the kitchen and the great man's passion and drive rubbed off on me. While I worked there, the restaurant gained a third Michelin star. After I left, I would drop in now and again to say hello and once Mr Koffmann treated me to an eight-course lunch, a lovely way of saying thank-you without saying thank-you. As I was wearing ripped jeans and a T-shirt at the time, I got strange looks from the other diners as the dress code was normally jacket and tie.

After this I went into a real madhouse, Pied à Terre in Charlotte Street. The chef, Richard Neat, although brilliant and full of passion, was a total nutball. The way he worked and handled the kitchen was unbelievable — I had never experienced anything quite like it, and probably never will again. It was if we were all his enemies, and he drove me and the others to despair

and madness. The adrenaline kept us on our toes, and Richard's colourful vocabulary did the rest.

But I loved the food, and the great guys in the team. We were like a small family: me with one other chef on the stove, Richard, and then one or two others on pastry. We all had to muck in where we could. I used to fix fridges and stoves when they didn't work, and did any painting that needed to be done. What Richard and proprietor David Moore achieved there was remarkable, and I respect them both for that. Richard's cooking had a good effect on me: working under that pressure really makes you focus, and quickens your reactions. And of course it was Richard who gave me the chance to work at the three-star Michelin restaurant Joël Robuchon in Paris.

I consider this the pinnacle of my career. But one thing I had always dreamed of was to open a restaurant with my twin brother Robert. Before I started work at Joël Robuchon, he visited me in France along with my mother and father, and told me that he had taken a job in the Point Restaurant in upstate New York, in the Adirondacks. My dreams were shattered. I cried the day he told me: his decision broke me in two, as he was me, and I was him, and we should have been together. Only twins will understand this, because it's as if you have lost your very soul.

But I had to get over it and get on. And it was like a dream to be in one of the best restaurants in the world, working as a chef de partie on meat. It was a crazy place but the cooking was amazing, as was the loyalty of the brigade. There were the same number of chefs as there were customers, some 60 in all.

IT WAS LIKE A DREAM TO BE WORKING
IN ONE OF THE BEST RESTAURANTS IN
THE WORLD.

You weren't allowed to talk at all during service, but simply listen to the orders being called in. If you ever missed anything, you were in trouble, as you couldn't go and look at the checks. Lunch finished at 3pm, and we then spent an hour cleaning down before a break of 15–20 minutes. When we finished in the evening it was the same routine, an hour or so of cleaning. The primary thing I remember from that time is the splitting headaches from not enough sleep. But what we all learned seemed to make it bearable.

Working in Paris was great too. I had the weekends off, so I would spend most of my time just walking around the streets, visiting markets and museums. I lived just down from the Gare du Nord in a tiny flat, and loved the French way of life. Laura, my girlfriend, would come over every other weekend to stay with me. This was one of the best times of my life, as I made so many friends and learned so much. But I had to leave, very sadly, after just over a year, as it was virtually impossible to live on my low salary, and M. Robuchon retired.

I then went to Rheims in Champagne to work at Gerard Boyères de Crayères, a very quiet hotel which seemed like heaven in comparison. While I was there, David Moore called to ask me if I would return to Pied à Terre as head chef, as Richard was leaving. I leapt at the chance, although I was sad to leave France. I shall never forget how happy Laura and I were there, and professionally, I gained enormously. I think every aspiring chef should go to work in France (or Spain): it gives them a unique insight into how professional European kitchens work, and invaluable experience.

I went to Pied à Terre as head chef at the age of 26. Looking back at what I accomplished at such a tender age, I would have to think seriously about whether I would do the same again. The pressure was incredible, as I was determined not to fail, and a lot of people assumed that I would fall flat on my face. It was hard

taking over from Richard, and with no reputation or recognition, it was very difficult to get staff. Neither had I any skills in running a kitchen or how to handle or manage people. Trying to cook the food I wanted with such a tiny brigade was a constant uphill battle. David Moore would even have to come down occasionally at lunchtimes to give me a hand.

I worked myself into the ground again, six days a week, eighteen hours a day. I seemed obsessed with work and achieving recognition. Pushing yourself to the limit all the time has a detrimental effect, and not being a great communicator, I took my anger out on others. I didn't recognise how much grief I was giving other people – and for what? Something marginally over-cooked or mis-seasoned? It all seems a bit silly now, but I thought that I was infallible. That time helped me to understand why Richard Neat had worked as he did.

Whatever happened at Pied à Terre, it gave me a reputation, and I was awarded two stars at the age of 26, a feat I don't think will ever be surpassed. I shall always be grateful to David Moore for giving me the opportunity of running Pied à Terre. I may have left under a cloud, but there was only one person to blame, and now I'm sure it was the best thing that could have happened.

I then went to work again for Pierre Koffmann as his head chef at the Berkeley Hotel for nine months, after which I worked in some private homes, and started to feel normal again. Getting out of restaurant kitchens was refreshing, as I had not stopped working since I was nineteen. I worked for Lady Weinberg who had great energy and enthusiasm, and then for Andrew Lloyd Webber, who had a wide knowledge of food and wine.

I MAY HAVE LEFT UNDER A CLOUD, BUT THERE WAS ONLY ONE PERSON TO BLAME.

Then a job came up with the Bamfords in Gloucestershire, one of the kindest, most loving families I have ever met. They had just started in the organic farming business: they had their own abattoir and they bred their own deer, cattle, sheep and chickens. I was brought on board as their chef, but as time went by I got more and more involved with the farming aspect. They later set up an organic farm shop in an old barn on their estate, for which I made products like soups and sauces, using ingredients that came from the farm. Working with the Bamfords and with their livestock and produce changed my whole outlook on food. I now source most of my meat and vegetables from farms, and yes, I still buy from the Bamfords.

But I was hungering to be back in a 'proper' kitchen again, and during my time with the Bamfords, Laura had been looking for a restaurant site. We hadn't had much success until she found an old pub called the Marlborough Arms in Chelsea. We bought it, Anouska Hempel did all the interior design, and we set about completely restructuring the whole building, which was lengthy, costly and a big gamble. Laura project-managed, whilst I was still working.

By then I had been out of the London restaurant scene for three or four years, which is a long time, and I occasionally doubted whether I could do it. But I believed I still had a lot to give in terms of cooking, and it felt so right. It would have been impossible without Laura, who gave me all the support I needed, and we finally managed to open the restaurant in April 2003. We were a great team, both very strong in our own fields: she in front of house organising, and me downstairs in the kitchen, barking orders. The restaurant was a huge success and we won a host of awards.

Yes, I am lucky to be where I am, but I have sacrificed a lot to reach that point, as must everyone who wants to be a chef and make it to the top. It is a very steep hill to climb, and getting there is demanding on oneself and one's family and friends. What I love about my job today is playing a role in inspiring other chefs. I may still work a hard kitchen, but those that work with me know they will learn and become better at their jobs because of it. When I see them leaving with the same motivation, commitment and drive as myself, I feel have done a good job.

IDEAS JUST COME TO ME, WHEN I AM WORKING, ON HOLIDAY, IN THE MIDDLE OF THE NIGHT.

CREATIVE UNDERSTANDING,
CREATIVE MADNESS

They say that creative minds are a little on the edge of madness. I myself have been called numerous things in my short life and career, and I could say, yes, perhaps I am a little strange in the head. But it is truly great to be different, and to be capable of creating something that is original and unique.

Who else, other than chefs, can create, make and choose so many options and directions? We are very lucky indeed. It is a skill to be able to cook, and that is something you can learn. But you cannot be taught to create and invent — these come from within — and there is a never-ending cache of ideas and dishes waiting to be discovered. The way in which an idea for a dish becomes realised varies from chef to chef. How I create is quite different, I think, from other chefs, as I don't look through books for inspiration. Ideas just come to me, when I am working, on holiday, or in the middle of the night. I first draw an idea on paper, which gives me the visual look, and then I chop and change it. Sometimes I can have a dish perfectly formed in my head and there is nothing I need do to it. At other times I will replicate the dish in my kitchen at home, or fine-tune it on the lunch menu.

For the way that food is presented and looks is yet another significant aspect of cooking, and it takes a long time to acquire your own unique style. Ten years on from being a head chef, I can say that I am finally happy with the style of food I produce and the way it looks. We chefs are very fussy and will always try to achieve the ultimate perfection, which is a difficult road. But it is the passion for and understanding of what we do that pushes us and keeps us focused. My work is a joy, it is my life, it keeps me happy. Who else can truly say that they love what they do? I have found my true vocation. It is not a job, more a feeling of belonging.

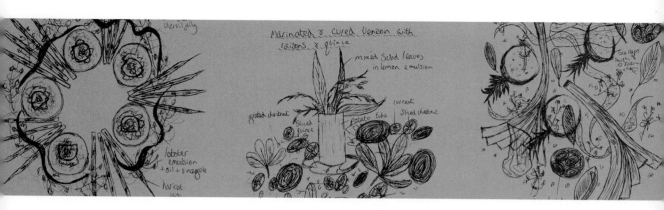

VEGETABLES CAN BE
AMAZING — ALL IT TAKES
IS A LITTLE IMAGINATION
TO TURN THE SIMPLEST
OF INGREDIENTS INTO
SOMETHING EXCITING.

We might not consider vegetables to be particularly inspiring, possibly because most of what we get nowadays is mass-produced, out of season, flown in from abroad, pre-washed, pre-packed and, as a result, often completely tasteless. Always try to buy seasonally, and from local suppliers, farmers' markets and farm shops. Organic vegetables are best. In this chapter I'll show you how to turn everyday vegetables into something special.

Many of the dishes here can be used as a garnish or as an accompaniment to another dish. In the instructions I often tell you to slice vegetables on a mandolin — if you don't have one, just slice very thinly using a sharp knife.

VEGETABLES

ARTICHOKES · ASPARAGUS · BEANS · BEETROOT · CABBAGE · CARROTS · CAULIFLOWER · CELERIAC ·
COURGETTES · FENNEL · LETTUCE · ONIONS · PARSNIPS · PEAS · POTATOES · SQUASH · TOMATOES

WHAT TO BUY

ARTICHOKES, GLOBE AND JERUSALEM

Artichokes of both varieties are wonderful, and can be used in so many delightful ways. They can be boiled, braised, baked, steamed, and roasted whole, and they can contribute to soups and salads. Baby globe artichokes can even be sliced and eaten raw. The acidity that they provide is great with roasted fish and scallops, and with cured and sliced cold meats.

ASPARAGUS

Asparagus is a uniquely seasonal vegetable that England and its farmers are well known for, and it's one we can be rightly proud of. It is associated with early to mid summer, and everyone looks forward to this time. But nowadays we can find asparagus in the supermarkets all year round, from far-flung corners of the world such as Peru or the USA. It won't taste as good as home-grown, and won't be as fresh. Buying asparagus out of season is bad for the well-being of our farmers and the stability and growth of business for the UK market. Basically, just don't do it.

BEANS

With beans in pods, it is always best to use fresh as opposed to dried for both taste and flavour. Borlotti beans are more widely available now, and their season runs from the beginning of October to the end of November. Broad beans come in from the end of May/beginning of June, and sometimes last through until August. If you wanted to keep borlottis for later, you could freeze them or dry them (the latter at airy room temperature, so long as they are on a wire rack).

BEETROOT

Beetroot is a winter vegetable that is great with meat and fish. It has always been a favourite of mine because it is so versatile. It can be eaten raw: it can be fried, baked, roasted, juiced, made into soups, jellies and tarts. Beetroot is a very cheap vegetable and

although it has been looked upon as a secondary vegetable, I assure you it has a lot going for it.

CABBAGE

Although the humble cabbage is cheap and looked down upon, it is a great vegetable to eat in the winter. It can taste terrible if it is just boiled and served plain, but again if you try to make it into a tasty dish, it can be a real treat.

CARROTS

Most people tend to shy away from carrots, as they don't immediately inspire one to turn them into something that could be deemed exciting. The problem is that most of us feel carrots are secondary vegetables, more often used in casseroles or as a complement to a Sunday roast, than as something special. But if you buy younger carrots with the green fern on, these will be a little sweeter and fresher in taste. Carrots are a truly wonderful vegetable, and they are very adaptable. And, yes, they are good for you!

CAULIFLOWER

This vegetable is available all year round but it is predominantly a winter vegetable, best from the middle of October onwards. There is nothing nicer than getting a fresh cauliflower straight from the ground, with crisp green leaves and a snow-white curd, and the best are always organically grown. There are so many things you can do with a cauliflower: make it into soups, sauces, pickles, beignets…

COURGETTES

Courgettes always remind me of spring and summer. There are many different varieties, shapes, sizes and colours of courgettes, and there are many different ways of cooking them as well. We can sauté, roast, grill, steam, deep-fry and marinate them, and although they are mostly made up of water, they still have a

unique taste and flavour, and can, very simply, be turned into something rather beautiful.

FENNEL

Fennel is a wonderful vegetable, with a complex and exquisite flavour. Aniseed comes to mind as well as tarragon when we crunch on a piece of fennel, which is obviously why it is mostly paired with fish as opposed to meat. It is such a versatile vegetable, and can so easily be adapted to many recipes: it can be eaten raw in a salad, used in a cold soup, or roasted. It is often overlooked, but I think it is probably because many people are suspicious of something which looks so curious, and which tastes so strong.

PEAS

Peas are another favourite vegetable of mine, because they herald spring, and an abundance of other spring vegetables, as well as the beginning of warmer weather. Try to buy the freshest peas you can, as the longer they are off the vine, the more their sugars will turn to starch. For that reason, there really is little point in buying peas grown in Africa.

PUMPKIN AND BUTTERNUT SQUASH

Pumpkins and other 'winter' squashes such as butternut appear in the autumn. These two vegetables are very similar in taste, and in the way that they cook. They can be boiled, but are much better simply roasted or used as the main ingredient in a delicious soup.

POTATOES

There are many varieties of potatoes, and there are as many ways of cooking them, in salads, soups, purées. Each variety has a different flavour and texture, and a different way of responding to cooking, which is why the potato is so versatile and adaptable. The potato plays a large part in our diet, and it can be used in conjunction with very simple or very extravagant ingredients. Potatoes are in season pretty much year-round. The best potatoes for baking are King Edwards and Maris Piper. Salad potatoes that can be boiled or steamed are Charlotte, Pink Fir Apples, Ratte and, of course, the Jersey Royal. For mash I use Desirée.

ROOT VEGETABLES

All root vegetables are at their best in the autumn and winter months, their natural season. Most root vegetables - such as onions, celeriac, parsnips, swede, turnip - are really best done simply: they can be boiled and puréed or mashed, or braised, made into soups and gratins. For some of them, roasting is the best way, as it brings out their natural sweetness.

SALAD LEAVES

See page 68 for my favourites and the dressings to go with them.

TOMATOES

Tomatoes are always associated with summer, even though we very rarely have enough sun to ripen them properly. But we still manage to grow so many different varieties, from the cherry, beef and plum, to the common English garden tomato. And thank goodness we have a lot of keen gardeners who still grow some of those magnificent heritage tomatoes like brandy wine and San Marzano. If you have ever had the chance to grow tomatoes, you will know that there is nothing more fantastic than picking your own and eating them warm, straight off the vine. Even the smell of the tomatoes when you walk into the glasshouse is amazing, the very smell of summer. However, having said that, the majority of the tomatoes we produce in this country are tasteless, watery and unripe, mass-produced for bulk, not flavour. Most of them are picked before they have ripened, and stored in the dark, so they don't reach the full taste and sweetness they would have if ripened in sunshine.

CHILLED ASPARAGUS SOUP WITH RICOTTA AND CHERVIL DUMPLINGS

THIS IS A VERY LIGHT AND REFRESHING WAY TO START A SUMMER EVENING MEAL.

MEDIUM ~ SERVES 4 ~ PREP 40 MINS PLUS COOLING TIME ~ COOK 30 MINS

16 large asparagus spears, washed

sea salt and black pepper

500ml white chicken stock (see page 155)

200ml double cream

50g unsalted butter

1 tsp caster sugar

1 large bunch fresh chervil, leaves picked, and finely chopped, plus a few sprigs to garnish

50ml olive oil

juice of 1 lemon

Ricotta dumplings

500g ricotta cheese

50g Italian 00 plain flour

1 egg plus 2 egg yolks

1 tsp chopped fresh chervil

1 Place a pan of water on to boil and season with salt. Take eight of the asparagus spears, break the tough ends from each and remove any ears that sprout from the sides. Discard the ends and trim the base of each spear into a point. Peel very lightly, then slice four of them very thinly on a mandolin. Keep all the trimmings for the soup. Firstly cook the asparagus slices in the boiling water for about 30 seconds, then plunge them into iced water. Cook the whole spears for about 2–3 minutes, and again put in iced water. Trim and chop the remaining eight asparagus spears finely.

2 In a large pan, bring the chicken stock and cream to the boil together. Heat up another pan on a medium heat and add the butter. When it has just melted, add the chopped asparagus, the asparagus trimmings, some salt and pepper and the sugar. Cover with a lid and cook for 3–4 minutes. Add the stock and cream mixture, bring to the boil and then add half the chervil. When cooled a little, purée in a blender. Pass through a fine sieve into a bowl over iced water to cool it down quickly. Add the remainder of the chopped chervil to the soup. Chill.

3 To make the dumplings, mix the ricotta with the flour, the egg and egg yolks, then add the chervil and some seasoning.

4 Bring a pan of seasoned water to the simmer, then take a teaspoon of the ricotta mix and push it off the spoon into the water with your finger. Do the same until you have used up the mixture. When the little dumplings rise to the top of the water, they are ready. Place into iced water to cool, but only for a minute, as they will fall apart if left too long in water.

5 Divide the slices of asparagus between four serving bowls with the oil, a little salt and some lemon juice. Pour the soup into the bowls, then add the blanched asparagus spears. Finally, drop in the ricotta dumplings. Garnish with the reserved chervil sprigs.

ASPARAGUS WITH SUMMER TRUFFLE AND WALNUT VINAIGRETTE

THE SUMMER TRUFFLES MAY SEEM A LITTLE EXTRAVAGANT, BUT THIS SIMPLE DISH MAKES A PERFECT STARTER ON A WARM DAY.

EASY ~ SERVES 4 ~ PREP 10 MINS ~ COOK 10 MINS

20 jumbo asparagus spears, peeled and trimmed (see page 20)

1 large frisée lettuce

sea salt and black pepper

1 tbsp white wine vinegar

4 eggs, cracked into 4 cups

1 recipe walnut dressing (see page 69)

2 small summer truffles, thinly sliced

1 Pick and wash the yellow leaves from the frisée lettuce, then spin dry in a salad spinner.

2 Place two large pans of salted water on to boil. Add the white wine vinegar to one pan for poaching the eggs. Cook the asparagus for 3–5 minutes in the un-vinegared boiling water until tender.

3 For the eggs, whisk the barely simmering vinegar water until you get a vortex. Drain off a little of the excess watery egg white from each cup, then drop the eggs into the water and poach for 4 minutes. Remove and drain.

4 Drain the asparagus, season with salt and black pepper, and then roll the spears in a tablespoon of the walnut dressing.

5 Place the frisée lettuce in a bowl with the truffles, and add a little dressing to bind the leaves. Season and then divide the asparagus between the plates. Put a poached egg on top of each, and arrange some lettuce and truffle around. Spoon a little dressing around the plates.

ASPARAGUS AND CHERVIL QUICHE

THE ASPARAGUS USED HERE IS WHAT IS KNOWN AS SPRUE; IT IS YOUNG, GREEN, AND VERY SPINDLY AND DELICIOUS. THIS SHORTCRUST PASTRY CAN BE USED FOR ANY OF THE OTHER SAVOURY TARTS THROUGHOUT THE BOOK.

EASY ~ SERVES 4 ~ PREP 40 MINS PLUS RESTING TIME ~ COOK 50–60 MINS

1kg green asparagus, peeled
350g mascarpone cheese
2 eggs plus 4 egg yolks
2g sea salt
a good pinch of freshly milled black pepper
4g chopped fresh chervil
8g chopped fresh chives
50g spring onions, trimmed and chopped
140g Parma ham, thinly sliced

Shortcrust pastry
400g plain flour
2g salt
200g cold butter, diced
1 egg, plus 1 egg yolk for brushing
iced water

1 To make the pastry, sift the flour into the mixer bowl with the salt, then add the diced butter. Turn the machine on to low and mix until the mixture is like fine breadcrumbs, about 1 minute. Then add the egg and then a little iced water until the dough comes together. It should not be too dry, otherwise it will just crumble when you roll it out. Wrap the dough in clingfilm and place in the fridge for 30 minutes.

2 Preheat the oven to 180°C/350°F/Gas 4, and grease and flour a 23cm quiche tin.

3 Roll out the pastry to a 5mm thickness, and use to line the prepared tin. Neaten the edges carefully. Line with a piece of foil, fill with baking beans (or pulses kept specially), and bake blind in the preheated oven for 20 minutes. Remove the baking beans and foil, and brush the base of the tart case with a little of the egg yolk. Cook for a further 5 minutes, then remove from the oven. Reduce the oven to 170°C/325°F/Gas 3.

4 Blanch the asparagus in boiling salted water for 3 minutes, then refresh in iced water for 2 minutes. Drain and dry well.

5 Mix the mascarpone, eggs and egg yolks, salt, pepper, chervil, chives and spring onions together. Arrange the asparagus spears in the tart case, pointing outwards and going around in a circle, then lay the ham in between them. Pour on the mascarpone mix, and bake in the oven for 25–30 minutes.

Note
Other herbs can be used in this recipe if chervil or chives are not available.

ROAST ASPARAGUS WITH PAN-FRIED DUCK EGGS AND GRILLED PANCETTA

THIS IS ANOTHER GOOD WAY OF EATING FRESH ASPARAGUS – PERFECT FOR A RELAXED SATURDAY BRUNCH.

EASY ~ SERVES 4 ~ PREP 10 MINS ~ COOK 15 MINS

20 jumbo asparagus spears, washed, peeled and trimmed (see page 20)
sea salt and black pepper
30g unsalted butter
50g duck fat

4 duck eggs
8 very thin slices pancetta (or smoked streaky bacon)
4 slices sourdough bread, 5mm thick

1   Bring a pan of salted water to the boil, then cook all the asparagus spears for 2 minutes. Place in iced water to cool. Drain and dry.

2   Heat a large frying pan, add and melt the butter, then add in all of the asparagus spears. Season and cook on a medium heat for around 5 minutes until evenly roasted.

3   Meanwhile, heat up another frying pan on a medium heat, and add the duck fat. Crack in the eggs, season, then add the pancetta. If the pan is not big enough, then place the pancetta under a preheated grill until crisp. Fry the eggs and pancetta until the eggs are how you like them, runny or well done.

4   Toast the sourdough bread on both sides. Pour the butter from cooking the asparagus on to the toast. Place the asparagus on top, then the bacon and lastly the egg.

ASPARAGUS WITH ASPARAGUS MOUSSE

YOU COULD MAKE THIS DISH MORE SUBSTANTIAL BY SERVING IT WITH SOME SMOKED SALMON OR SOME POACHED EGGS.

MEDIUM ~ SERVES 4 ~ PREP 30 MINS ~ COOK 20 MINS

20 large asparagus spears, washed, peeled and trimmed

sea salt and black pepper

1 small bunch of fresh chervil (or tarragon), leaves picked and half finely chopped

a little truffle oil

juice of 1 lemon

Asparagus mousse

250g asparagus, or about 5 large spears

25g unsalted butter, plus extra for greasing

3 eggs plus 2 egg yolks

200ml double cream

1 Prepare all the asparagus spears (see page 20). Chop the spears for the mousse finely, keeping them separate from the whole spears.

2 Bring a pan of salted water to the boil. Cook 12 of the whole asparagus spears in boiling salted water until tender, about 2–3 minutes, then remove and place in iced water. Slice the remaining whole asparagus spears lengthways very thinly using a mandolin: you should get 5–6 slices from each spear. Cook in boiling salted water for 10 seconds, then place in iced water to stop the cooking.

3 For the mousse, put a sauté pan over a low heat, melt the butter and add the chopped asparagus along with a tablespoon of water. Season, cover with a lid and cook slowly until soft, about 4–5 minutes. Place in the blender and purée until fine, then place in a bowl. Mix together the eggs, egg yolks and cream, then whisk and pass through a sieve on to the asparagus purée. Stir well and season.

4 Grease four dariole moulds (these are small, cylindrical moulds) with a little butter, and put a small piece of greaseproof paper in the bottom of each one. Put a steamer over a low heat.

5 Divide the asparagus mousse between the moulds, and place in the steamer. Cover with a lid and steam – they should take about 10–12 minutes. When they are ready they will be a little firm but will still wobble like a jelly.

6 Put the sliced and whole asparagus into the steamer for the last 2 minutes, then remove and place in a bowl. Add the chopped chervil, the truffle oil and lemon juice to taste. Season.

7 Unmould the mousses by carefully running a knife around the edges, and then turn out and place into the centre of four serving plates. Arrange the asparagus around, and sprinkle with the whole chervil leaves.

PICKLED CAULIFLOWER WITH MARINATED MACKEREL

THIS RECIPE CAN BE SERVED WITH FISH LIKE SARDINES AND RED MULLET AS WELL AS MACKEREL. IT'S ALSO GOOD WITH TUNA.

EASY ~ SERVES 4 ~ PREP 10 MINS PLUS COOLING TIME ~ COOK 10 MINS

1 medium cauliflower, cut into small florets

8 mackerel fillets, each sliced into three

8g fresh mixed herbs (chervil, dill, tarragon, chives), leaves picked

Cauliflower pickling liquor

100g shallots, peeled and sliced

50g caster sugar

10 black peppercorns

1 tsp coriander seeds

a sprig each of fresh thyme and tarragon

sea salt

400ml water

200ml olive oil

150ml white wine vinegar

150ml white wine

1 bay leaf

1 Place all the pickling liquor ingredients into a pan, bring to the boil and simmer for 3 minutes. Add the cauliflower, bring to a simmer, and cook for 4–6 minutes. The florets must remain a little crisp. Leave to cool in the liquor, then remove the cauliflower from the liquor and place in the fridge. Save the liquor.

2 Put the mackerel into a deep tray. Reheat the pickling liquor to a simmer and pour this on to the mackerel. Leave to cool, then store in the fridge.

3 Put some of the cauliflower on each plate with some mackerel and a little of the strained pickling liquor. Sprinkle the herbs over.

CAULIFLOWER SOUP WITH DILL GNOCCHI

THIS IS A GOOD WINTER DISH, WHICH COULD BE SERVED AS A STARTER OR MAIN COURSE.

CHALLENGING ~ SERVES 4 ~ PREP 30 MINS ~ COOK 2 HRS

800g trimmed cauliflower
sea salt and black pepper
1.2 litres milk
300ml double cream
vegetable oil for deep-frying
plain flour for dusting
1 recipe beignet batter (see page 32)
150g crème fraîche
½ bunch fresh dill, leaves picked, and finely chopped
1 recipe herb gnocchi made with dill (see page 66)

1 Cut 100g of the cauliflower into small florets, and blanch in boiling salted water for about 30 seconds.

2 Chop the remaining 600g cauliflower, and put in a pan with the milk, cream and a pinch of salt. Place this on a low heat and bring up to a very slow simmer. You don't want this to boil as the milk will catch on the bottom of the pan. Cook for about 20 minutes, purée in a blender, then pass through a fine sieve until smooth.

3 Heat the deep-frying oil to 180°C/356°F. Dust the cauliflower florets in a little flour then dip into the batter. Let any excess drain off, then deep-fry until golden, about 2 minutes. Drain well on paper towels, and season with salt.

4 Heat the soup gently, then add the crème fraîche, but do not boil. Add the dill. Reheat the gnocchi in a little of the soup. Place these into the bowls with the soup and, at the very last minute, the cauliflower beignets.

CAULIFLOWER AND GRAIN MUSTARD PUREE

YOU CAN USE THIS WITH FISH, SCALLOPS AND SMOKED FISH, OR EVEN AS A SOUP IF YOU THIN IT DOWN.

EASY ~ SERVES 4 ~ PREP 10 MINS ~ COOK 20 MINS

1 medium cauliflower, chopped
250ml double cream
250ml milk
1 tbsp grain mustard
sea salt and black pepper

1 Place the cauliflower in a pan and then add the cream and milk; the liquid should just cover the cauliflower.

2 Cook for 20 minutes until soft and then purée.

3 Pass through a sieve, then add the grain mustard, salt and pepper to taste.

SALAD OF PICKLED CARROTS AND CARROT VINAIGRETTE

THIS DISH HAS A NUMBER OF ELEMENTS, BUT NONE IS DIFFICULT. THE SALAD WOULD MAKE A GOOD STARTER.

MEDIUM ~ SERVES 4 ~ PREP 15 MINS PLUS MARINATING TIME ~ COOK 5 MINS

4 medium carrots with tops left on, peeled
16 baby carrots with tops left on, peeled
250g mixed salad leaves
200ml carrot vinaigrette (see page 65)
sea salt and black pepper

Carrot pickling mixture

300ml fresh carrot juice (from 8–10 medium carrots)
50g caster sugar
20 coriander seeds
a sprig each of fresh tarragon and thyme
10 black peppercorns
100ml each of water, white wine vinegar and white wine
250ml olive oil
5 star anise

Yoghurt dressing

200ml natural yoghurt
a small bunch fresh coriander, leaves picked
2 tsp clear honey
juice of 1 lemon
10g caster sugar

1 Pass the fresh carrot juice through a fine sieve. Place all the carrot pickling mixture ingredients into a pan and bring to a slow simmer. Check the seasoning.

2 Meanwhile, slice the medium carrots lengthways on a sharp mandolin as thinly as you can.

3 Put the baby carrots into the pickling liquor and cook for 3–4 minutes, then drop in the carrot slices and cook for 1 minute. Remove from the heat and leave the carrots to cool in the liquor. Depending on the size of the carrots, cook them as you like, but it is best to leave them crisp. I would nibble on one just to make sure. Leave in the liquor for a day before you use them, so they will take on the full pickled flavour.

4 For the yoghurt dressing, place the yoghurt in a blender with all the remaining ingredients, and purée for 30 seconds. Season to taste.

5 To serve, divide the salad leaves between four plates, arranging them in the middle of the plates. Dress with the carrot vinaigrette, and toss well. Place the carrots around, and then spoon the yoghurt dressing around the plate. Finish with some more carrot vinaigrette over the whole dish.

CARROT PUREE WITH STAR ANISE

HONEY ROASTED CARROTS WITH CUMIN

THIS WOULD HAPPILY ACCOMPANY SOME ROAST SCALLOPS OR A PIECE OF ROAST PORK BELLY.

SERVE THESE SWEET ROASTED CARROTS WITH EITHER ROAST OR BRAISED BEEF OR PORK.

EASY ~ SERVES 4 ~ PREP 10 MINS ~ COOK 15 MINS

EASY ~ SERVES 4 ~ PREP 10 MINS ~ COOK 20 MINS

300g small carrots, peeled and finely chopped

25g unsalted butter

2 sprigs fresh tarragon

3 star anise

200ml white chicken stock (see page 155) or vegetable stock, boiling

100ml double cream

juice of 2 lemons

4g caster sugar

20 finger-sized carrots, peeled

100ml olive oil

25g unsalted butter

a sprig of fresh rosemary

2 pinches sea salt

50g pale clear honey

1 tsp cumin seeds

juice and finely grated zest of 1 lemon

1 Melt the butter in a saucepan over a low heat, then sweat the carrots for a few minutes. Cover with a lid, and cook for 4–6 minutes more.

2 Add the tarragon, star anise, stock, cream, lemon juice and sugar, and cook until the carrots are soft, another 6–8 minutes.

3 Remove the star anise, and put everything else in a blender. Blend to a purée, then pass through a fine sieve. Warm through very gently when ready to serve.

1 Preheat the oven to 180°C/350°F/Gas 4.

2 Heat a large, heavy, ovenproof pan, and add the olive oil and butter. When just melted, add the carrots, rosemary and salt, then slowly cook over a medium-low heat until the carrots are golden in colour. This should take about 10 minutes.

3 Add the honey and cumin, and place in the preheated oven for 5 minutes. Add the lemon juice and zest, and reduce a little on top of the stove, about 2–3 minutes. It's best to leave the carrots with a little bite.

CARROT AND SAUTERNES JELLY

BALSAMIC GLAZED CARROTS

THIS COULD BE SERVED IN THE SUMMER AS A STARTER, ON ITS OWN OR WITH SOME POACHED SALMON, OYSTERS OR FOIE GRAS.

THESE ARE GOOD WITH ROAST DUCK OR CURED DUCK. USE THE SYRUP WITH OLIVE OIL AND LEMON JUICE AS A DRESSING.

MEDIUM ~ SERVES 4 ~ PREP 10 MINS PLUS COOLING AND SETTING TIME ~ COOK 10 MINS

EASY ~ SERVES 4 ~ PREP 10 MINS ~ COOK 20 MINS

800ml fresh carrot juice (use about 12 medium peeled carrots)

400ml Sauternes white wine

7 gelatine leaves, soaked in cold water

1 small bunch fresh tarragon, leaves picked

juice of 2 lemons

sea salt

caster sugar (optional)

20 baby carrots, peeled

100ml olive oil

5 star anise

2 sprigs fresh tarragon

300ml balsamic vinegar

1 Put the Sauternes into a pan, and boil to reduce by half, to 200ml.

2 Add the drained and squeezed gelatine leaves to the still warm reduced Sauternes, and stir occasionally until melted. Add the carrot juice and mix well, then pass through a sieve into a bowl. Place over iced water.

3 Place the tarragon leaves on top of one another on a board, and cut into neat squares. Mix these into the carrot jelly. Add lemon juice to taste, and salt: it may need a little sugar, depending on the sweetness of the carrots.

4 When the jelly has thickened up a bit, but not set completely, spoon into individual glasses and place in the fridge to set.

1 Heat a frying pan, then add the olive oil, star anise and whole peeled carrots. Slowly colour over a low heat for approximately 10–15 minutes.

2 Add the tarragon and balsamic vinegar, and cook a little faster until the vinegar has reduced and is thick and syrupy, coating the carrots. Use the syrup to go round the dish.

RAW FENNEL SALAD WITH ANCHOVY BEIGNETS

THE RAW FENNEL AND THE ANISE FLAVOUR OF THE FRESH TARRAGON ARE GOOD COMPLEMENTS TO THE OILINESS OF THE ANCHOVY. A GOOD STARTER OR LIGHT LUNCH. BEIGNETS ARE A TYPE OF DEEP-FRIED FRITTER.

MEDIUM ~ SERVES 4 ~ PREP 20 MINS ~ COOK 5 MINS

4 fennel bulbs

150ml olive oil

juice of 1 lemon

sea salt and black pepper

caster sugar

150g stoned black olives, chopped

1 bunch fresh tarragon, leaves picked, chopped neatly into squares (see page 31)

vegetable oil for deep-frying

30 anchovy fillets in olive oil, not brine

1 lemon, halved

Beignet batter

100g Italian 00 plain flour

50g cornflour

25g baking powder

about 250–300ml iced water

1 Slice the fennel bulbs very thinly on a mandolin, and then place in a serving bowl with the olive oil, lemon juice, a pinch each of salt and sugar and the chopped black olives. Add the tarragon, and toss.

2 For the beignet batter, mix the flours, plus the baking powder, with enough iced water to get a double cream consistency.

3 Heat the deep-frying oil to 180°C/350°F.

4 Toss 20 of the anchovy fillets in the beignet batter, and then deep-fry in the heated oil until crisp, approximately 2–3 minutes. Drain well on paper towels, then season with salt and pepper, and add a squeeze of lemon juice.

5 Add the remaining uncooked anchovies to the salad bowl, and mix very carefully to avoid breaking up the fillets. Place the hot fried ones on top, and serve straight away.

FENNEL GAZPACHO WITH BASIL AND BABY RED MULLET

THIS DISH CAN BE SERVED EITHER AS A STARTER OR MAIN COURSE.

MEDIUM ~ SERVES 4 ~ PREP 30 MINS PLUS COOLING TIME ~ COOK 20–25 MINS

4 fennel bulbs, finely diced
50g unsalted butter
sea salt and black pepper
juice of 3 lemons
300ml double cream
500ml white chicken stock, simmering (see page 155)

2 bunches fresh basil, leaves picked
4 little red mullet, filleted and pin-boned
extra virgin olive oil

1 Heat a medium pan on a low heat then add the butter. When melted, add the diced fennel, and season. Cover with a lid, turn the heat up a little, then sweat for 4–5 minutes. Make sure that it does not catch or colour. Add the juice of two of the lemons and reduce by half, then add the cream and remove the lid. Reduce this until it slightly thickens and then add the chicken stock. Bring to the boil, turn the heat down to a simmer, and cook for 5 more minutes. It is important not to overcook the soup, otherwise you will lose its essential freshness.

2 Place in a blender and purée, then pass through a fine sieve. Cool and check the seasoning; it may need a little more lemon juice. Chill.

3 Bring a pan of salted water to the boil then add three-quarters of the basil leaves. Cook for 2–3 minutes, then drain, keeping some of the water to help purée the leaves. Purée in a blender, but keep it as thick as you can; it should be nice and smooth. Then season and cool. Cut the remaining basil into fine strips.

4 Season the red mullet fillets with salt and pepper. Heat a non-stick frying pan, add a little olive oil, then fry the fillets for a couple of minutes on each side.

5 Remove and place in serving bowls. Pour the cold soup around, then spoon a little of the basil purée in the middle. Sprinkle with the chopped raw basil and a little extra virgin olive oil.

GRILLED FENNEL WITH GOAT'S CHEESE, PINE NUTS AND BLACK OLIVE OIL

YOU CAN USE ANY GOOD GOAT'S CHEESE IN THIS RECIPE, BUT YOU MUST HAVE A HARD CHEESE AND A SOFT CHEESE.

MEDIUM ~ SERVES 4 ~ PREP 45 MINS ~ COOK 40 MINS PLUS DRYING TIME

6 fennel bulbs
100g stoned black olives
15g unsalted butter
1 onion, peeled and very thinly sliced
a pinch of caster sugar
sea salt
1 tsp fresh thyme leaves

3 sheets filo pastry
350ml olive oil
60g hard goat's cheese, thinly sliced
60g pine nuts
200g mixed salad leaves
juice of ½ lemon
100g soft goat's cheese or goat's curd

1 Preheat the oven to 110°C/225°F/Gas ¼. Put the black olives on a tray, and dry out in the very low oven until they are semi-crisp, about a day. What happens is that they contract and reduce in size, thus intensifying the flavour. Remove from the oven, and leave to cool.

2 The next day, when ready to cook, preheat the oven to 180°C/350°F/Gas 4. Preheat the grill to medium as well.

3 Melt the butter in a small pan and add the onion, a little sugar and salt and the thyme leaves, then cook slowly until caramelised, about 15–20 minutes. Leave to cool.

4 Brush the three sheets of filo with about 50ml of the olive oil, then sandwich together, making sure that they are well pressed together. Put on a baking tray, and cut into eight equal pieces. Top with another baking tray (so the pastry layers remain flat), and bake in the preheated oven for about 10 minutes until golden brown. Remove from the oven and reduce the temperature to 170°C/325°F/Gas 3.

5 While the pastry is cooking, cut the fennel bulbs into three pieces each. Sprinkle with about 100ml of the olive oil and a little salt and then grill evenly on both sides. This should take about 10–12 minutes.

6 Smear the caramelised onion on to the baked pieces of filo and then place the slices of hard goat's cheese on top. Bake in the preheated low oven for 3–4 minutes to melt.

7 Place the pine nuts in a frying pan on a low heat and slowly dry-fry to brown. Place the dried black olives in the blender with 150ml olive oil and purée for a couple of minutes, then pass through a sieve.

8 Divide the fennel between four plates. Place the salad leaves into a bowl with the remaining olive oil, some salt and the lemon juice, and toss. Add a little pile to each plate, with two of the cheese tarts. Sprinkle on the soft cheese and browned pine nuts, and then drizzle over the black olive oil.

BROAD BEAN GAZPACHO WITH GOAT'S CHEESE EMULSION

THIS BROAD BEAN GAZPACHO CAN BE EATEN COLD, OR IT'S GOOD HOT TOO, WITH SOME GRILLED FISH. THE GOAT'S CHEESE EMULSION CAN BE USED AS A DRESSING FOR STURDY SALAD LEAVES.

MEDIUM ~ SERVES 4 ~ PREP 30 MINS PLUS COOLING TIME ~ COOK 10 MINS

400g podded, cooked and shelled broad beans

500ml white chicken stock (see page 155)

200ml double cream

juice of 1 lemon

sea salt and black pepper

a little pinch of caster sugar

100g soft goat's cheese or goat's curd

1 small bunch fresh chervil, leaves picked from the stalks, and chopped

50ml olive oil

Goat's cheese emulsion

100g soft goat's cheese or goat's curd

200ml olive oil

1 Reserve 150g of the broad beans for the garnish, and place the rest into the blender. Boil the chicken stock and cream together, then pour this on to the beans, and purée. Add the lemon juice and season with salt, pepper and sugar. Pass this through a fine sieve into a bowl over ice to cool the soup down. By stopping the cooking process, you keep the colour and freshness of the soup, and you don't want a stewed flavour.

2 For the emulsion, put the goat's cheese into the cleaned-out blender with 200ml olive oil and purée until it emulsifies. Season with salt and pepper.

3 Place the remaining whole broad beans into a bowl. Season and add half the chopped chervil and the olive oil.

4 Put the remaining chervil into the soup, and ladle this into four bowls. Divide the broad beans between the bowls, and crumble on the goat's cheese. Then spoon the goat's cheese emulsion around.

BORLOTTI BEAN CASSEROLE WITH PESTO

BROAD BEANS WITH OREGANO AND LEMON

THIS COULD BE SERVED WITH A ROAST LEG OF LAMB OR AS A SALAD.

EASY ~ SERVES 4 ~ PREP 20 MINS PLUS COOLING TIME ~ COOK 30–45 MINS

200g podded fresh borlotti beans

2 carrots, peeled and cut in half

2 onions, peeled and cut in half

1 x 50g piece smoked back bacon

a sprig of fresh thyme

10g basil cress or fresh basil leaves

Pesto (use the ingredients straight from the fridge)

40g fresh basil leaves

125ml olive oil

75g pine nuts

50g Parmesan, freshly grated

3g sea salt

1g freshly milled black pepper

1 Place a blender jug into the fridge or freezer for the pesto.

2 Put the beans into a fairly deep pan and then add the vegetables, bacon and thyme. Cover with water, bring to the boil, then simmer until tender, about 30–45 minutes. Leave to cool in the liquor.

3 For the pesto it is essential that all ingredients are kept at fridge temperature so the pesto will remain as green as possible. So, into the chilled blender jug, put the basil, olive oil, pine nuts, Parmesan, salt and pepper. Purée this to a coarse consistency and then chill.

4 Drain the beans well and shake off all the liquid. Place the beans in a bowl and add enough pesto to bind them together. Divide between serving bowls and then sprinkle with the basil cress.

SERVE THIS AS A LIGHT CANAPE. IT'S ALSO IDEAL FOR PICNICS: TAKE TOASTED BREAD WITH YOU, AND SPREAD IN SITU.

EASY ~ SERVES 4 ~ PREP 30 MINS ~ COOK 5 MINS

250g podded fresh broad beans

100ml olive oil

juice and finely chopped zest of 1 lemon

10 fresh mint leaves, ripped

1 tsp fresh oregano leaves

50g feta cheese, crumbled

sea salt and black pepper

4 slices sourdough bread

1 Cook the beans in boiling water for 2–3 minutes, drain then refresh in iced water for a couple of minutes. Drain again and shell them, removing the outer greyish skins.

2 Place the beans in a blender with the olive oil, lemon juice and zest, and just lightly blend until still coarse. Place in a bowl, and mix in the mint and oregano leaves, crumbled feta cheese and some salt and pepper.

3 Toast the sourdough bread and then spread with the broad bean mix.

BEETROOT PUREE

BEETROOT GRATIN

THIS INTENSELY FLAVOURED PUREE WILL BE GREAT WITH ANY GAME LIKE VENISON OR PARTRIDGE, AS WELL AS ROAST SCALLOPS.

THIS CAN BE USED WITH ANY SUNDAY ROAST AND WITH GAME WHEN IT IS IN SEASON.

MEDIUM ~ SERVES 4 ~ PREP 20 MINS ~ COOK 3–3½ HRS

EASY ~ SERVES 4 ~ PREP 50 MINS PLUS INFUSING TIME ~ COOK 35–45 MINS

600g beetroots
300ml fresh apple juice
100ml white wine vinegar
200ml port

3 medium beetroots
500ml double cream
3 garlic cloves, peeled and sliced
6g fresh thyme leaves
2 large white potatoes
sea salt and black pepper

Beetroot juice
10 medium beetroots

1 Preheat the oven to 170°C/325°F/Gas 3.

2 For the beetroot juice, peel the beetroots, then cut into quarters. Juice in a juicer, and pass this through a fine sieve. You should have about 500ml.

3 Wrap the beetroots individually in foil, then bake in the preheated oven for 2–2½ hours. Leave to cool in the foil for 15 minutes, so that they sweat, then unwrap and rub the skins off. Chop the beetroots finely.

4 Put the chopped beetroot, beetroot juice and the remaining ingredients into a pan and cook on a slow to medium heat until most of the liquid has evaporated, about 1 hour.

5 Place into a blender to purée, then pass through a fine sieve.

1 Preheat the oven to 180°C/350°F/Gas 4.

2 Put the cream, garlic and thyme in a pan. Bring to a simmer, then remove from the heat and leave to infuse for 10 minutes. Pass the mixture through a sieve, pressing well.

3 Peel the beetroots and potatoes, and slice on a mandolin, about 1–2mm thick.

4 In an earthenware dish or flat tray (about 2.5cm deep), start with a layer of cream then layer the vegetables in alternate layers, topping each one with a little cream, salt and pepper. Once built up, the gratin should be 1.5cm deep.

5 Bake in the preheated oven for about 35–45 minutes. To check if it's done, plunge a knife into the gratin – it should go through without resistance.

BEETROOT MOUSSE AND JELLY WITH DILL CREME FRAICHE AND CAVIAR

THIS DISH USES ALMOST ALL THE OTHER BEETROOT RECIPES! THE JELLY IS VERY LIGHT AND FULL OF FLAVOUR, AND GOES WELL WITH FOIE GRAS, CAVIAR, SMOKED SALMON AND MARINATED FISH SUCH AS SALMON AND MULLET. YOU CAN USE THE LIQUID JELLY AS THE BASIS OF A BEETROOT GRANITA.

CHALLENGING ~ SERVES 4 ~ PREP 20 MINS PLUS SETTING TIME ~ COOK 3½–4 HRS

250ml crème fraîche

a small bunch of fresh dill, leaves picked and finely chopped

1g salt

25g Sevruga caviar

Beetroot mousse

200g beetroot purée (see page 38)

2 gelatine leaves, soaked in cold water

100ml crème fraîche

50ml double cream, semi-whipped

Beetroot jelly

700ml beetroot juice (see page 38)

250ml port

2½ gelatine leaves, soaked in cold water

juice of 1 lemon

1 tsp caster sugar

1 To make the mousse, heat a little of the purée then add the drained and squeezed gelatine leaves and melt. When dissolved, pass this through a fine sieve then set over ice to chill. When almost set, mix in the remaining beetroot purée, the crème fraîche and cream, and then place in the fridge.

2 To make the jelly, put the port in a pan, and boil to reduce to almost nothing. Add the beetroot juice, bring to a simmer then skim off all the scum and simmer to reduce to 500ml. Add the drained and squeezed gelatine and pass through a fine sieve into a bowl set over ice. Add the lemon juice and sugar.

3 Chill four large glasses (such as martini glasses).

4 Pipe the nearly set mousse into the bottom of the four chilled glasses, and top with a layer of jelly. Stir the jelly left in the bowl every now and again so that it does not set.

5 Mix the crème fraîche with the chopped dill and salt, then pour half of this into the glasses. Top with about half of the remaining jelly and then set in the fridge for 10 minutes. Then add the rest of the crème fraîche and then the rest of the beetroot jelly. You want a layer of mousse, and two layers each of jelly and crème fraîche. Leave this to set in the fridge for another 10 minutes.

6 Put the caviar on top of each glass.

BEETROOT AND CREME FRAICHE SOUP

THIS IS A GOOD SOUP FOR SERVING IN WINTER, AND THE ADDITION OF SMOKED BACON GIVES IT THAT EXTRA FLAVOUR.

EASY ~ SERVES 4 ~ PREP 20 MINS ~ COOK 50 MINS

500g beetroot, peeled and cut into 1cm pieces
150ml vegetable oil
140g smoked bacon, cut into 1cm pieces
300g onions, peeled and cut into 1cm pieces
4g fresh thyme leaves, chopped
12g caster sugar

4g sea salt
2 tbsp lemon juice
1.25 litres white chicken stock (see page 155)
100ml crème fraîche

1 Place a large pan on a low heat, then add the oil and bacon. Cook slowly for 3–4 minutes until the bacon is golden brown, stirring now and again. Add the onion and thyme, and cook for a further 8–10 minutes with the lid on, stirring now and again. This will sweat and soften the onion without colouring it.

2 Then add the chopped beetroot, sugar and salt and cook with the lid on for another 10 minutes, still on a low heat. Stir the contents now and again so they don't stick or burn. Add the lemon juice and stock, turn the heat up to full and bring to the boil. Turn the heat down to a slow simmer, and cook for 25 minutes with the lid on.

3 Add the crème fraîche, turn the heat up to a simmer, and cook for 1 minute. Then turn the heat off and ladle the soup into the blender jug to half full. Purée for 2–3 minutes until very fine. Pass through a fine sieve into another pan. Do the same with the remainder of the soup. Heat gently to serve.

BEETROOT TARTE FINE WITH BEETROOT DRESSING

THIS FILO TART IS A GREAT DISH FOR VEGETARIANS, AND IT MAKES A NICE LIGHT ENTREE DISH AS WELL.

CHALLENGING ~ SERVES 4 ~ PREP 30 MINS ~ COOK 3 HRS

4 baked beetroot (see page 38), thinly sliced

3 sheets filo pastry

45g unsalted butter

4g fresh thyme leaves

sea salt and pepper

2 red onions, peeled and thinly sliced

100ml balsamic vinegar

200ml beetroot dressing (see page 68)

finely grated zest of 1 orange and 1 lemon

200g mixed salad leaves

Pickled beetroot

4 long beetroot

6 baby beetroot

300ml water

200ml beetroot juice (see page 38)

200ml white wine vinegar

200ml olive oil

40g caster sugar

2g salt

1 To make the pickled beetroot, peel all of the raw beetroots, then slice very thinly lengthways. Put all the remaining ingredients into a large pan, and bring to a simmer. Place the beetroot slices into the pickling liquor and cook for 3–4 minutes, then leave to cool in the liquor.

2 Preheat the oven to 180°C/350°F/Gas 4.

3 Place the three sheets of filo on some baking paper on a baking tray. Melt 20g of the butter, and brush some over the first sheet of filo. Sprinkle with a little of the thyme, then lay the second sheet of filo on top. Brush with more melted butter and sprinkle with a little thyme. Top with the third sheet of filo, butter and thyme, and season with salt and pepper. Put another sheet of paper on top, then the second baking tray on top. Bake in the preheated oven for 10 minutes until golden brown. Remove from the oven, and reduce the oven temperature to 170°C/325°F/Gas 3.

4 Place a pan on a medium heat and melt the remaining butter. Add the sliced onions, a little salt and half the remaining thyme leaves. Cook this for 10 minutes until the onion has a little colour and is softening. Add the balsamic vinegar, stir, then reduce down until the vinegar has virtually evaporated. Leave to cool.

5 Cut the baked filo into four. Spread each sheet with the vinegared red onion, then layer the sliced baked beetroot between the four. Brush with a little beetroot dressing, then sprinkle with the orange and lemon zest and remaining thyme. Put this in the preheated oven for 5 minutes.

6 While you are waiting, divide the pickled beetroot between four plates then add a little vinaigrette. Dress the salad leaves with a little dressing and salt. Put some of the leaves on each plate, then the tart on top, then the rest of the leaves.

FRESH PEAS WITH PEA SHOOTS, PEA MOUSSE AND PARMA HAM

THE COMBINATION OF PEAS AND HAM IS CLASSICALLY BRITISH, BUT HERE I HAVE GIVEN IT A SLIGHTLY DIFFERENT SLANT, SOMETHING I DO IN THE RESTAURANT.

EASY ~ SERVES 4 ~ PREP 15 MINS ~ COOK 15 MINS

600g podded fresh peas

caster sugar

sea salt

2½ gelatine leaves, soaked in cold water

200ml double cream, semi-whipped

1 small bunch fresh mint, leaves cut into julienne strips if large

lemon juice

2 banana or round shallots, finely diced

25ml olive oil

3 punnets pea shoots

8 slices Parma ham

Dressing

1 egg yolk

finely grated zest and juice of 2 lemons

caster sugar

200ml olive oil

1 Cook two-thirds of the peas in boiling water to cover for about 4 minutes with a large pinch of sugar and some salt to taste. Then drain and plunge into iced water, leave for a couple of minutes and drain. Leave whole, to one side.

2 Cook the remaining peas in the same way, this time retaining their cooking water. Place into a blender with 150ml of the cooking water, add the soaked gelatine and purée. Pass this through a fine sieve into a bowl, then chill. Stir from time to time and when nearly set add the semi-whipped cream and half of the chopped mint. Taste for seasoning: you may need to add a little sugar and a squeeze of lemon juice. Chill.

3 To make the dressing, place the yolk into a bowl with the lemon juice and zest, add a pinch of sugar and then whisk for 3 minutes. Slowly pour in the olive oil, adding a little water if it gets too thick, then season and add a pinch of mint.

4 Cook the shallots slowly in the oil, without letting them colour. Season with salt and pepper then, when they are soft, place in a bowl. Add the rest of the cooked peas and the rest of the mint plus a little dressing to bind them together.

5 Place some shallot and pea mixture on to each plate, then a spoonful of the pea mousse. Dress the pea shoots with the dressing, and place on the plates. Top with the Parma ham.

BUTTERED PEAS WITH SPRING ONIONS AND LETTUCE

PEA PUREE

THIS CAN BE USED AS A GARNISH WITH ANY FISH, EITHER GRILLED OR POACHED.

THIS CAN BE USED WITH ROAST SCALLOPS OR FISH, OR AS A SIDE DISH WITH LAMB.

EASY ~ SERVES 4 ~ PREP 20 MINS ~ COOK 10 MINS

EASY ~ SERVES 4 ~ PREP 25 MINS ~ COOK 10 MINS

500g podded fresh peas

sea salt and black pepper

2 large banana or round shallots, peeled and finely diced

50g unsalted butter

5 spring onions, thinly sliced

150ml white chicken stock (see page 155)

200ml double cream

1 tbsp each of chopped fresh parsley and chervil

1 soft English lettuce, cut into fine julienne strips

1 Cook the peas in boiling salted water for about 2 minutes, then refresh in iced water. Drain and dry.

2 Sweat the shallots in a pan in 25g of the butter until almost soft, then add the sliced spring onions. Cook for a couple of minutes, then add the chicken stock and cream. Bring to the boil and cook for 2 minutes, then add the peas.

3 Stir in the remaining butter, the herbs and lettuce strips, and serve.

500g podded fresh peas

sea salt and black pepper

caster sugar

150ml double cream

20g unsalted butter

1 tbsp chopped fresh mint

a squeeze of lemon juice

25g finely cut smoked bacon lardons

a little vegetable oil

1 Cook the peas in boiling salted water with a little sugar for 3–4 minutes until soft. Place in a blender with a little of the cooking water and blend until they start to purée.

2 Add the cream, butter, mint and lemon juice, then pass through a fine sieve into a small bowl.

3 Fry the bacon in the oil in a small frying pan until crispy, then drain on paper towels. Place on top of the purée. Warm through gently in a small pan before serving.

ROAST PARSNIPS WITH HONEY AND CUMIN

PARSNIP PUREE

YOU CAN COOK THESE EITHER ON THE HOB OR IN THE OVEN. THEY ARE A GOOD ACCOMPANIMENT TO PORK OR CHICKEN.

THIS PUREE IS IDEAL WITH YOUR SUNDAY ROAST, WHETHER BEEF, LAMB, PORK OR POULTRY.

EASY ~ SERVES 4 ~ PREP 10 MINS ~ COOK 20 MINS

EASY ~ SERVES 4 ~ PREP 20 MINS ~ COOK 30 MINS

8 medium parsnips, peeled and cut into batons, about 6 x 1cm

100ml vegetable oil

25g unsalted butter

2g sea salt

2 tbsp clear honey

a large pinch of cumin seeds

12 medium parsnips, peeled

500ml milk

500ml double cream

2g caster sugar

2g salt

1 Preheat the oven to 180°C/350°F/Gas 4.

2 Melt the oil and butter in an ovenproof pan, and add the parsnip batons and salt. Sauté until golden brown, turning, for about 10 minutes.

3 Add the honey and cumin seeds to the pan and turn the batons over. Place in the preheated oven for 10 minutes. Keep an eye on them so the honey does not burn.

1 Halve the parsnips, cut out and discard the centre core and then chop up the rest into 1cm pieces.

2 Place in a pan with the rest of the ingredients. Bring to a slow simmer and cook for 30 minutes until the parsnips are soft and the milk has reduced and almost disappeared.

3 Blend to a purée, then pass through a fine sieve.

MASHED SWEDE

CELERIAC MASH

THIS WOULD BE GOOD WITH BRAISED MEATS, SUCH AS LAMB OR BEEF — AND OF COURSE, IT WOULD BE PERFECT WITH A BURNS NIGHT HAGGIS.

EASY ~ SERVES 4 ~ PREP 10 MINS ~ COOK 1½ HRS

2 medium swedes, peeled and cut into 1cm cubes
100g unsalted butter
2g fresh thyme leaves
2g sea salt
200ml white chicken stock (see page 155)
3 tbsp clear honey

1 Preheat the oven to 170°C/325°F/Gas 3.

2 Heat a pan on medium, then add 50g of the butter. When it has melted, add the swede, thyme and salt. Sweat for a couple of minutes, then cover with a lid and continue cooking gently for 10 minutes.

3 Add the chicken stock, and cook for a further 10 minutes. Add the honey and cook until the swede is soft, about another 5–10 minutes.

4 Mash the swede with the remaining butter, then place into an ovenproof dish and bake in the preheated oven for 1 hour.

THIS CAN BE SERVED WITH ANY BRAISED MEATS SUCH AS BEEF OR VENISON.

EASY ~ SERVES 4 ~ PREP 25 MINS ~ COOK 25 MINS

500g celeriac, peeled and chopped
35g unsalted butter
4g salt
4–6 turns freshly milled black pepper
2g fresh thyme leaves
20ml lemon juice

1 Place a medium pan on a medium heat and add the butter. When it has just melted, add the celeriac, salt, pepper and thyme. Put a lid on the pan and cook slowly for 15–20 minutes, adding the lemon juice halfway through cooking.

2 Remove the lid, and cook for a further 5 minutes. Mash with a masher.

CELERIAC AND APPLE SOUP

CELERIAC AND TRUFFLE GRATIN

A GREAT WINTER SOUP. SERVE IT WITH LITTLE SQUARES OF TOASTED BREAD, WITH SOME CHEESE ON TOP, GRILLED.

THIS CAN BE SERVED WITH ANY SUNDAY ROAST, AND WITH GAME WHEN IT IS IN SEASON.

EASY ~ SERVES 4 ~ PREP 20 MINS ~ COOK 25 MINS

EASY ~ SERVES 4 ~ PREP 20 MINS PLUS INFUSING TIME ~ COOK 35–45 MINS

500g celeriac, peeled and cut into 1cm pieces
50g unsalted butter
11g salt
400g Cox's apples
25ml fresh lemon juice
15g caster sugar
1 litre white chicken stock (see page 155)
120ml double cream

1 large celeriac
500ml double cream
3 garlic cloves, peeled and sliced
6g fresh thyme leaves
2 large white potatoes
4 small Périgord black truffles, thinly sliced
sea salt and black pepper
25g Gruyère cheese, grated

1 Melt the butter in a pan over a low heat then add the celeriac and salt. Cover with a lid and cook slowly for 10 minutes, stirring the celeriac now and again so it doesn't brown or colour.

2 Core the apples using an apple corer, and chop them into 1cm pieces. Add these to the pan with the lemon juice and sugar. Cook slowly on the same temperature for a further 5 minutes with the lid on, stirring now and again so nothing colours.

3 Add the stock and cream, turn the temperature up to full, and bring to a slow boil. Then turn the heat down to a simmer again, and cook for 5 minutes.

4 Then turn the heat off and ladle the soup into the blender jug to half full, and purée for 2–3 minutes until very fine. Pass through a fine sieve into another pan. Do the same with the remainder of the soup. Heat gently to serve.

1 Preheat the oven to 180°C/350°F/Gas 4.

2 Place the cream, garlic and thyme in a pan, bring to a simmer, then remove from the heat and leave to infuse for 10 minutes. Pass through a sieve.

3 Meanwhile, peel the celeriac and potatoes, and slice on a mandolin about 1–2mm thick. In an earthenware dish or flat tray about 2.5cm, start with a layer of cream then place alternative layers of vegetables and truffles in the dish, topping each layer with a little cream, salt and pepper. Once built up, the gratin should be 1.5cm deep. Sprinkle the Gruyère over the top of the gratin.

4 Bake in the preheated oven for about 35–45 minutes. To check to see if it's done, plunge a knife into the gratin: it should go through without resistance.

CHOUCROUTE

THIS CAN BE USED IN A LOT OF DISHES, BUT MAINLY WITH BOILED MEATS AND POT AU FEU OF LAMB OR DUCK. IT WOULD BE GREAT AS WELL WITH VENISON FILLET.

EASY ~ SERVES 4 ~ PREP 25 MINS ~ COOK 1½ HRS

1 medium white cabbage
2 onions, peeled
250g duck fat
a small bunch of fresh thyme, leaves picked
12 juniper berries
20 black peppercorns

1 x 200g piece smoked back bacon with skin, cut into thick chunks
1 saucisse morteau (smoked sausage), left whole
2g sea salt
1 bottle dry white wine

1 Slice the cabbage and onions very thinly. Heat a large pan on a medium heat, then add the duck fat. When it has melted, add the onion, thyme, juniper, peppercorns, bacon and sausage. Cook this for 4–5 minutes without colouring.

2 Plunge the shredded cabbage into boiling water and drain straight away. Add this to the soft onions along with the salt. Cook together for a couple of minutes, then add the wine and stir well.

3 Place a sheet of greaseproof paper over the top, and cook slowly on top of the stove for about 1½ hours, stirring now and again. You could also cook it in the oven at 170°C/325°F/Gas 3, with a lid on, for 1½–2 hours.

4 Slice the bacon and sausage about 5mm thick, and mix through the cabbage to serve.

COURGETTE BEIGNETS WITH A HERB MAYONNAISE

THESE FRITTERS CAN BE EATEN AS A STARTER OR MAIN COURSE. YOU COULD SERVE THE BEIGNETS (OR ANY OF THE OTHER BEIGNETS, SEE PAGES 27 AND 32) WITH SALAD LEAVES. THE BASIC MAYO CAN BE USED IN MANY OTHER CONTEXTS.

MEDIUM ~ SERVES 4 ~ PREP 30 MINS ~ COOK 20 MINS

1 large courgette
1 large round courgette
4 baby courgettes
4 courgette flowers
vegetable oil for deep-frying
1 tsp paprika
10g flour, for dusting
1 recipe beignet batter (see page 32)
a little lemon juice

Herb mayonnaise
2 egg yolks
2g sea salt
5 turns freshly milled black pepper
1 tsp white wine vinegar
300ml vegetable oil
a little water if necessary
15g mixed chopped fresh herbs (chervil, chives, tarragon, dill, parsley, basil)
a little lemon juice

1 For the mayonnaise, whisk the egg yolks, salt, pepper and vinegar together until they are emulsified, about 2–3 minutes, then slowly whisk in the oil. If it starts to get too thick, add a little water. Then add all the herbs to the mayonnaise, taste and add a little lemon juice if needed. Leave in the fridge until ready to serve.

2 Slice all the courgettes, large and small, very thinly. Cut the courgette flowers in half.

3 Heat the deep-frying oil to 180°C/350°F.

4 Dust the courgette slices with paprika and then flour. Dip them one by one into the batter and then deep-fry until slightly golden. Reserve on kitchen paper. Do the same with the courgette flowers. Fry the slices and flowers for a second time until golden and crisp, then drain well on kitchen paper.

5 Season with salt and a squeeze of lemon juice. Divide the beignets between individual bowls and dust with paprika. Use the herb mayonnaise as a dip.

WHITE ONION AND THYME SOUP

WHOLE BRAISED ROSCOFF ONIONS

USE ENGLISH ONIONS FOR THIS, NOT SPANISH, AS THE LATTER ARE FULL OF WATER. THE SOUP CAN BE USED AS A SAUCE AS WELL AND IS GOOD WITH FISH.

ROSCOFF ONIONS ARE SMALLER THAN NORMAL ONIONS, BUT HAVE A BETTER TASTE. IF YOU CAN'T GET THEM, USE ENGLISH. GREAT WITH A ROAST JOINT OR BRAISED MEAT AS THEY'RE SO SWEET.

EASY ~ SERVES 4 ~ PREP 20 MINS ~ COOK 25 MINS

EASY ~ SERVES 4 ~ PREP 10 MINS ~ COOK 40 MINS

500g white onions, peeled and sliced
80g unsalted butter
6g fresh thyme leaves
3g chopped garlic
15g salt
20g caster sugar
1 litre white chicken stock (see page 155)
200g mascarpone cheese

8 Roscoff onions, or 8 small English onions
a little vegetable oil
25g unsalted butter
sea salt and black pepper
a small sprig of fresh thyme
2g caster sugar
350ml brown chicken stock (see page 155)

1 Heat a pan on a low heat, then add the butter. When it has melted, add the onion, thyme, garlic, salt and sugar, cover with a lid, and sweat the onion for 15 minutes on a low heat without colouring.

2 When the onions are soft, add the stock and mascarpone, then bring to the boil. Turn the heat down to a simmer, and cook for a further 10 minutes.

3 Turn the heat off and ladle the soup into the blender jug to half full, and purée for 2–3 minutes until very fine. Pass through a fine sieve into another pan. Do the same with the remainder of the soup. Heat gently to serve.

1 Peel the onions. Trim the root end, taking the knife as close to the root as possible, so the onions will remain whole when they are cooking. Then slice off about a quarter of the way down from the top, so you can see all the layers in the onion.

2 Place a pan on a medium heat and add the oil. When hot, add the onions cut-side down, plus the butter, and cook slowly until the onions become golden, about 10 minutes. Season the onions, then add the thyme and sugar, and cook for a further 5 minutes.

3 Add the stock, cover with a lid, and cook slowly on top of the stove for a further 15–20 minutes, until soft. Then reduce the liquid so the onions become glazed and sticky. Alternatively, cook in the oven with a lid on at 170°C/325F/Gas 3 for 20 minutes.

ONION AND BLACK OLIVE TART

YOU COULD VARY THIS TART BY USING LEEKS (ABOUT 800G) AND SORREL (ABOUT 300G) INSTEAD OF THE ONIONS AND OLIVES.

EASY ~ SERVES 4 ~ PREP 50 MINS PLUS RESTING TIME ~ COOK 1¼–1½ HRS

1 recipe shortcrust pastry (see page 23)
150g unsalted butter
800g large onions, peeled and sliced
3g salt
2g chopped fresh thyme leaves
a large pinch each of dried thyme and rosemary

1g freshly milled black pepper
3 large eggs plus 2 large egg yolks
400ml double cream
2g chopped fresh parsley
4g chopped fresh chives
40g stoned black olives, chopped

1 Preheat the oven to 180°C/350°F/Gas 4, and grease and flour a 30cm quiche tin. Line the tin with pastry and bake blind as described on page 23. Remove the pastry from the oven and reduce the heat to 170°C/325°F/Gas 3.

2 Heat a pan on a medium heat, and add the butter. When it has melted add the sliced onion, a third of the salt, the fresh and dried herbs, and half the pepper. Cover with a lid and cook for 10 minutes without colouring until soft.

3 Remove the lid, turn the heat up slightly, and slowly caramelise the onion, stirring all the time, about 15 minutes. Remove the onion from the pan and leave to cool.

4 Beat the eggs and egg yolks with the cream and remaining pepper, and pass through a sieve. Add the fresh parsley and chives, the olives and cooled onion.

5 Place this mixture in the baked pastry case and bake in the preheated oven for 30 minutes.

ARTICHOKE SOUP WITH SAUTERNES

A COMBINATION OF BOTH TYPES OF ARTICHOKE, WITH AN INTENSE FLAVOUR. THE SOUP WOULD ALSO BE GOOD AS A SAUCE FOR FISH.

MEDIUM ~ SERVES 4 ~ PREP 30 MINS ~ COOK 30 MINS

600g Jerusalem artichokes

8 baby globe artichokes, peeled (see page 57)

juice of 3 lemons

50g unsalted butter

4g caster sugar

sea salt

2g fresh thyme leaves

400ml Sauternes white wine

500ml white chicken stock (see page 155)

400ml double cream

100g buckler sorrel (baby sorrel leaves)

Artichoke pickling liquor

100g shallots, peeled and sliced

50g caster sugar

8 black peppercorns

1 small tsp coriander seeds

a sprig each of fresh thyme and tarragon

400ml water

150ml olive oil

100ml each of white wine vinegar and white wine

1 Fill a bowl with 1 litre cold water and add the juice of one lemon. Peel the Jerusalem artichokes. Cut 100g of them into 5mm dice. Put all the artichoke into the acidulated water to prevent the flesh browning. Put the baby globe artichokes into the acidulated water for a moment, then remove and slice them very thinly.

2 Place the pickling liquor ingredients into a large pan with 2g sea salt, bring to a simmer, and simmer for 10 minutes. Pass through a sieve.

3 Place the baby artichoke slices into the strained pickling liquor along with the Jerusalem artichoke dice. Cook for about 6–8 minutes so everything remains a little crisp, then leave the artichokes to cool in the liquor.

4 Chop the rest of the Jerusalem artichokes very finely. Heat a pan on a medium heat, melt the butter, then sweat the chopped artichoke for 3–4 minutes. Add the sugar, 2g sea salt, the thyme and remaining lemon juice. Cook for a further 2 minutes, then add the Sauternes. Reduce by half, then add the cream. Reduce by half, then add the stock. Bring back to the boil, then simmer for 5 minutes.

5 Pour the soup into a blender and purée until fine. Pass through a fine sieve, pushing through with a ladle. Heat through.

6 Strain the sliced baby artichokes and Jerusalem artichoke dice from the pickling liquor. Pour in a small pan and heat through in a little of the soup. Divide between four bowls, then pour in the hot soup. Top with the sorrel.

ARTICHOKE, MOZZARELLA AND OLIVE TART

HERE IS ANOTHER SAVOURY TART, USING AN EGG AND MASCARPONE BASE.

MEDIUM ~ SERVES 4 ~ PREP 1 HR ~ COOK 1¾ HRS

3 large globe artichokes
I recipe artichoke pickling liquor (see page 54)
1 recipe shortcrust pastry (see page 23)
300g red onions, peeled and quartered
150ml olive oil
4–6 turns freshly milled black pepper
25g soft brown sugar
a pinch each of dried thyme and rosemary

2g salt
300g mascarpone cheese
2 eggs plus 4 egg yolks
40g stoned black olives
120g fresh rocket
1 tbsp chopped fresh basil
200g mozzarella cheese, sliced

1 Preheat the oven to 180°C/350°F/Gas 4, and grease and flour a 23cm quiche tin. Line the tin with pastry and bake blind as described on page 23.

2 Put all the pickling liquor ingredients in a pan and bring to a simmer. Peel away all the outer leaves of the globe artichokes until you reach the base and snap off the stalk close to the base. With a sharp knife, remove all the remaining dark green bits by slowly turning the artichoke, taking away all the green so you have a smooth, round surface. Using a serrated knife, cut straight across the artichoke to remove the hairy choke. Use a spoon to scrape out the rest of the choke in the base. Place the artichokes into the pickling liquor and cover with a sheet of greaseproof paper. Bring to a simmer, then cook for 15 minutes and leave to cool in the liquor.

3 Place the onion quarters on a baking tray and add the olive oil, pepper, sugar, thyme, rosemary and salt and bake in the preheated oven for 25 minutes. When they are cooked, place in a bowl, cover with clingfilm and leave to cool. Drain them well before using.

4 Drain the artichokes and discard the liquid. Slice the artichokes in half. Cut them into 5mm-thick semi-circular slices.

5 Mix the mascarpone with the eggs and egg yolk, then add the artichoke slices and cooled onions, olives, rocket and basil. Pour this mixture into the baked pastry case and cover with the sliced mozzarella. Bake in the preheated oven for 25–30 minutes.

ROAST BABY ARTICHOKES WITH THYME

THESE ARE GREAT SERVED AS AN ALTERNATIVE VEGETABLE WITH A SUNDAY ROAST.

MEDIUM ~ SERVES 4 ~ PREP 20 MINS ~ COOK 20 MINS

16 baby artichokes
150ml olive oil
a sprinkle of sea salt
1 sprig fresh thyme
1 small sprig fresh rosemary
250ml white chicken stock (see page 155)

1   Take the outer leaves off the baby artichokes. Peel the
    leaf bases with a peeler until they are smooth and no
    dark green bits are left. Cut the top off, so you have
    only the stalk and heart left, leaving 10cm of stalk
    attached. Peel the stalks until they are nice and white,
    then carefully cut all the artichokes in half.

2   Heat a frying pan on a low heat, add the olive oil then
    lay in the artichokes, top to end, so they fit in tightly.

3   Season with the sea salt, add the herbs, and cook
    slowly for about 10 minutes on each side.

4   Add the chicken stock and reduce this until thick
    and the artichokes are glazed, about another
    10 minutes maximum.

ARTICHOKE AND SALSIFY SALAD

THIS WOULD MAKE A GOOD AND LIGHT WINTER SALAD STARTER. IT'S NICE WITH GRILLED SCALLOPS AS WELL.

CHALLENGING ~ SERVES 4 ~ PREP 1½ HRS PLUS COOLING TIME ~ COOK 1 HR

2 large globe artichokes (see page 56)

5 baby artichokes, peeled (see page 57)

1 recipe artichoke pickling liquor (see page 54)

4 salsify sticks

2 Pink Fir Apple potatoes

2 Charlotte or Ratte potatoes

50ml double cream

200g small mixed salad leaves

Truffle dressing

1 medium fresh black truffle, finely grated

1 egg yolk

a squeeze of lemon juice

200ml olive oil

1 Simmer the artichoke pickling liquor (see page 54), then pass through a sieve. Bring back to a simmer.

2 Meanwhile, peel the globe artichokes as on page 56, and leave them whole. Peel the baby artichokes as on page 57. Cut 3 of the baby artichokes into thin slices and leave 2 of them whole.

3 Simmer the baby artichoke slices in the pickling liquor for 3 minutes. Remove with a slotted spoon. Add the globe artichokes to the pickling liquor, and simmer for 20 minutes. Add the whole baby artichokes for the last 10–12 minutes. Leave them to cool in the liquor and then remove with a slotted spoon.

4 Wash the salsify sticks (they are usually covered in dirt), then peel to remove the dark brown skin. Wash again. Either using a vegetable peeler or a mandolin, slice lengthways into very fine strips 15cm long. Add to the pickling liquor for 3 minutes; remove with a slotted spoon.

5 Put all the blanched vegetables back into the liquor and leave to cool.

6 Leaving the skin on the potatoes, slice them all 1mm thick on a mandolin. Cook them in boiling water – they will take less than a minute – then refresh them in iced water to stop the cooking.

7 Take one of the pickled large globe artichokes, chop it roughly, then mix it with 200ml of the cooking liquor and the cream. Bring to a simmer and cook for 2–3 minutes, then purée. Take the other globe artichoke, halve it, and cut each half into four. Halve the whole baby artichokes.

8 For the dressing, put the truffle into a bowl with the egg yolk, lemon juice and seasoning to taste, then whisk in the olive oil. If it is too thick, thin with a little water.

9 Put all the artichoke pieces into a bowl with the salsify. Add a little dressing, and season. Smear the artichoke purée on four plates, and drizzle on a little dressing. Place on all the artichoke and salsify. Put the potato slices into the same bowl, mix with a little more dressing, season, and add them to the plates. Do the same with the salad leaves.

THICK TOMATO SAUCE

THIS CAN BE USED AS A PASTA SAUCE OR AS THE BASIS FOR A MOUSSE (SEE PAGE 62).

EASY ~ SERVES 4 ~ PREP 10 MINS ~ COOK 40 MINS

1kg good tomatoes, chopped
100ml olive oil
400g onions, peeled and diced
20g peeled and chopped garlic
16g sea salt
4g fresh thyme leaves
300ml white wine
35g caster sugar
80g tomato purée

1 Place a pan on a medium heat, then add the olive oil, onion, garlic, salt and thyme. Cook without colouring for about 5 minutes, then add the white wine and reduce until it has virtually evaporated.

2 Add the tomatoes and sugar, bring this up to a simmer, then cook for 25 minutes, stirring it now and again. Add the tomato purée, and cook for a further 5 minutes.

3 Place into a blender and purée, then pass through a fine sieve.

TOMATO CONFIT

THESE OVEN-DRIED PIECES OF TOMATO ARE SLIGHTLY CHEWY AND QUITE JAMMY IN FLAVOUR. THEY CAN BE USED IN SALADS OR ON THEIR OWN, JUST WITH SOME BASIL, OR IN SOUPS.

EASY ~ SERVES 4 ~ PREP 10 MINS ~ COOK 2½ HRS

1kg plum tomatoes (preferably San Marzano)
12g peeled and thinly sliced garlic
2g fresh thyme leaves
200ml olive oil
8g sea salt
2–3 turns freshly milled black pepper
20g icing sugar

1 Preheat the oven to 100°C/212°F/the very lowest gas, and line a baking tray with a piece of greaseproof paper.

2 Cut the tomatoes in half then place in a bowl along with the rest of the ingredients. Mix well.

3 Place the tomato halves on the baking tray in rows, then bake in the very low oven for about 2½ hours.

Note
You could also use cherry tomatoes in this recipe. They would take a little less time in the oven.

TOMATO CONSOMME WITH TOMATO CONFIT AND BASIL JELLY

THIS TOMATO CONSOMME IS GREAT SERVED ON THOSE RARE SUMMER DAYS WHEN WE ACTUALLY GET SOME SUNSHINE.

CHALLENGING ~ SERVES 4 ~ PREP 20 MINS PLUS DRIPPING AND SETTING TIME ~ COOK 2½ HRS

12 pieces tomato confit (see page 60)
2 punnets basil cress or small basil leaves
100ml olive oil
sea salt

Basil jelly
1 large bunch fresh basil
4 gelatine leaves, soaked in cold water

Tomato consommé (makes about 800ml)
2kg cherry tomatoes
1 bunch fresh basil
1 bunch fresh coriander
80g icing sugar

1 For the tomato consommé, pick the leaves off the basil and coriander and place in a bowl along with the sugar, 8g salt and the cherry tomatoes. Crush them all together and then place in a blender and purée to a pulp. The texture must still be quite coarse.

2 Place this mixture into a piece of muslin and tie up with string. Suspend above a bowl so it will drip into the bowl. A clear liquid will take about 6 hours to drip through. Squeeze the muslin a little now and again to get the remaining juice out of the bag. Once all the juice has dripped out, leave it to settle, then pour into a clean container, leaving the sediment in the bowl. Chill this tomato consommé in the fridge.

3 For the basil jelly, pick the leaves from the basil, reserving a few for the garnish. Place a pan of water on to boil, add a little salt then add the basil leaves, and cook for 2–3 minutes until soft. Place in a blender

with about 150ml of the cooking liquor. Add the drained and squeezed gelatine and pass through a fine sieve into a bowl over ice. Leave to cool and set for 30 minutes.

4 Cut the reserved basil leaves into fine julienne strips, and place in the bottom of the serving bowls with the confit tomato. Spoon in the set basil jelly, then pour the tomato consommé on top.

5 Mix the basil cress in a bowl with half the olive oil. Sprinkle this over the consommé, followed by the remaining oil.

TOMATO AND BASIL JELLY WITH TOMATO MOUSSE

THIS IS A GREAT SUMMER DISH, FANTASTIC SERVED AS A STARTER JUST BEFORE YOU ENJOY YOUR BARBECUED FISH OR MEAT.

CHALLENGING ~ SERVES 4 ~ PREP 30 MINS PLUS SETTING TIME ~ COOK 2½ HRS

Tomato mousse

200g thick tomato sauce (see page 60)

3 gelatine leaves, soaked in cold water

4 fresh basil leaves, cut into fine julienne strips

150ml double cream, semi-whipped

4 pieces tomato confit (see page 60), finely diced

sea salt and black pepper

Tomato jelly

600ml tomato consommé (see page 61)

2 gelatine leaves, soaked in cold water

4 fresh basil leaves, cut into fine julienne strips

8 pieces tomato confit (see page 60), finely diced

1 For the tomato mousse, warm a tablespoon of the tomato sauce, then add the drained and squeezed gelatine leaves. Stir over a gentle heat until the gelatine has melted completely. Place in a bowl along with the rest of the tomato sauce and set this over iced water. Keep stirring now and again until it has almost set, then add the basil. Fold in the semi-whipped cream and the tomato confit. You may need to add a little more salt and pepper to this. Pipe this mousse mixture into four tall glasses and leave to chill in the fridge.

2 For the tomato jelly, warm a tbsp of tomato consommé, then add the drained and squeezed gelatine. Stir until it has melted, then add the rest of the consommé and pass through a fine sieve into a bowl set over ice. This needs to be stirred now and again until it has almost set. Then add the basil and tomato confit; they should be suspended in the jelly.

3 At this point, spoon the jelly on top of the mousse in the glasses. You should have one-third mousse and two-thirds jelly. Chill for about 15 minutes, until completely set.

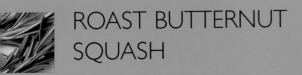

ROAST BUTTERNUT SQUASH

PUMPKIN, HONEY AND SAGE SOUP

YOU COULD DO THIS WITH PUMPKIN AS WELL. A GOOD ACCOMPANIMENT TO MEAT DISHES.

EASY ~ SERVES 4 ~ PREP 10 MINS ~ COOK 40 MINS

2 whole butternut squash
25g unsalted butter
2g coarse sea salt
4–6 turns freshly milled black pepper
100g clear honey
1g chopped fresh rosemary
juice of 1 lemon

1　Preheat the oven to 180°C/350°F/Gas 4.

2　Chop the squash in half lengthways and then scoop out and discard the seeds. Place the squash halves into a roasting tray, smear with butter and season with salt and pepper. Pour on the honey.

3　Roast in the preheated oven for about 40 minutes, sprinkling with the rosemary and lemon juice in the last 10 minutes.

4　When ready, serve the pieces as they are, and eat the flesh out of the skin.

YOU COULD MAKE THIS WITH SQUASH TOO. 'HARD' HERBS LIKE SAGE, ROSEMARY AND THYME GO WELL, AS THEY EMPHASISE THE SWEETNESS OF THE VEGETABLE.

EASY ~ SERVES 4 ~ PREP 20 MINS ~ COOK 25 MINS

1kg pumpkin, peeled and cut into 1cm cubes
80g unsalted butter
6g fresh sage leaves, finely chopped
15g sea salt
85g clear honey
1 tbsp lemon juice
1 litre white chicken stock (see page 155)
130ml double cream

1　Heat a pan on a low heat, melt the butter, and add the pumpkin along with the sage, sea salt, honey and lemon juice. Cover with a lid so the vegetables sweat, and cook for 10 minutes on a low heat. Stir the vegetables now and again so they don't catch or brown.

2　Add the stock and cream, and bring the soup up to a slow boil. Turn the heat down to a simmer for 5 minutes.

3　Turn the heat off and ladle the soup into the blender jug to half full, and purée for 2–3 minutes until very fine. Pass through a fine sieve into another pan. Do the same with the remainder of the soup. Heat gently to serve.

SHALLOT CHUTNEY

AS WITH ALL CHUTNEY RECIPES, THIS ONE IS BEST IF LEFT FOR 2–3 MONTHS BEFORE USING, AS THE FLAVOUR IMPROVES WITH AGE. THIS WOULD BE GREAT WITH THE DUCK LIVER PARFAIT ON PAGE 156.

EASY ~ MAKES ABOUT 1.5KG ~ PREP 10 MINS PLUS WAITING TIME ~ COOK 2½ HRS

1kg shallots, peeled and sliced

600g pears, cored, peeled and diced

100g raisins

4g powdered cinnamon

20g mustard seeds

2g mustard powder

2g powdered ginger

25g bottled stem ginger, diced

500ml cider vinegar

300g dark brown sugar

1 Place all the ingredients in a pan and bring to a slow boil, stirring every now and again. Turn the heat down to a simmer, then cook for 2 hours with a lid on.

2 Remove the lid and continue to cook for another 30 minutes, stirring occasionally, until the mixture has thickened up.

3 Put into sterilised bottles while still hot. Then do not use for at least a couple of weeks, if not months.

CARROT VINAIGRETTE

THIS RECIPE NEEDS TO BE MADE THE DAY BEFORE TO IMPROVE THE FLAVOUR. IT IS DELICIOUS WITH THE PICKLED CARROT SALAD ON PAGE 28 AND IS GOOD WITH COLD ROAST CHICKEN WITH ORANGE SEGMENTS AND FRESH HERBS.

MEDIUM ~ SERVES 4 ~ PREP 15 MINS ~ COOK 25 MINS

150g small organic carrots, peeled and finely diced

250ml olive oil

a sprig each of fresh thyme and tarragon

2g sea salt

4g caster sugar

100ml white wine vinegar

200ml Sauternes white wine

300ml carrot juice

1 Heat 100ml of the oil in a saucepan, add the carrots and lightly cook until pale golden in colour, about 4–5 minutes.

2 Add the thyme, tarragon, salt, sugar and vinegar, and boil gently to reduce by half. Add the Sauternes and boil to reduce by two-thirds, then add the carrot juice and boil to reduce by two-thirds again. Finally add the remaining olive oil, and simmer for 5 minutes.

3 Leave to cool, then store in the fridge for a day so the flavour will improve. This will keep in the fridge for up to a week.

MASHED POTATO

Robuchon in Paris was famous for its purée de pommes de terre or mashed potato. When I was working there, I was fortunate enough not to have to prepare it, as it was one of the hardest jobs in that kitchen, taking about 2 hours from start to finish. We used Ratte potatoes – a good waxy potato. They would first be scrubbed and slowly cooked, still in the skins to protect them from the water. After about 30–35 minutes they would be drained and kept over simmering water, so they remained warm while being peeled. They were then put into a mouli with a lot of butter, then placed in another pan with even more butter, and then it was all brought together with hot milk. It was then passed through a very fine sieve (so fine you couldn't actually see through the mesh). This would take another 30 minutes, and it was so hard the chefs would be exhausted by the end. When the time came to use the potato, it was placed in a copper pan and warmed, then more butter was whisked in to make it light and fluffy. This would take another 45–60 minutes! There was more butter than potato, and it was so rich you could only eat a small amount.

I do mine a little differently, and a little more simply! I bake the potatoes instead of boiling them in water as this makes the purée a little less starchy. You can also flavour the mash, and use it in a number of different ways.

Preheat the oven to 200°C/400°F/Gas 6. Wash and prick 5 large red Desirée potatoes with a fork, place on a tray with some coarse sea salt, and bake in the oven for about 1¾ hours. Do not overcook the potatoes or they will turn into a starchy mess.

When cooked, cut the potatoes in half and scoop the flesh into a mouli. Add 125g butter and purée. Place the purée into a pan and mix in another 125g butter with a wooden spoon. When the butter has been added, add 250ml warm milk, mixing with a spatula until it has all been incorporated. Pass through a fine sieve, season with at least 2g salt and freshly ground black pepper, and it is ready for use.

BLACK OLIVE MASH

This is good with fillet of lamb (see page 136). Simply add 50g stoned and chopped black olives to the mashed potato.

HERB GNOCCHI

Herb gnocchi are good with meat or fish. Weigh out 400g mashed potato, without added butter or milk, into a bowl. Add 1 egg yolk, 2–3g chopped fresh herb (such as rosemary, basil or dill), 15g freshly grated Parmesan (omit this from the dill gnocchi), and 80g Italian 00 plain flour. If it needs more flour, add 20g or so. Mix well and season.

Divide into four, then roll each piece in extra flour into a long sausage shape 3–4mm in diameter. Use enough flour so they do not stick, then cut them into 3–4mm lengths so they are like little barrels. Place on a tray.

To cook, put a pan of water on to simmer with a little salt and olive oil, then add the gnocchi. Once they float, remove from the heat and place in iced water to cool. Remove from the water, drain and place on a tray with a little olive oil before proceeding as in the individual recipes.

BLACK OLIVE GNOCCHI

Good with fish, especially red mullet. Weigh out 400g mashed potato, without added butter or milk, into a bowl. Add 1 egg yolk, 2g chopped fresh basil, 15g freshly grated Parmesan, 50g stoned and chopped black olives, and 80g Italian 00 plain flour. If it needs more flour, add 20g or so. Mix well and season. Make, shape and cook as above.

POTATO AND TRUFFLE SALAD

I USE TWO TYPES OF POTATO HERE. WHEN THEY ARE SLICED, YOU CAN SEE THE SHAPE OF EACH, WHICH GIVES A NICE VISUAL EFFECT.

MEDIUM ~ SERVES 4 ~ PREP 30 MINS ~ COOK 40 MINS

Truffle vinaigrette
100ml olive oil

200g shallot, peeled and finely chopped

200g black truffle, chopped (fresh or frozen)

1g fresh thyme leaves

125ml Madeira

75ml balsamic vinegar

100ml sunflower oil

100ml truffle oil

8 Ratte or Charlotte potatoes

4 Pink Fir Apple potatoes

sea salt and black pepper

200g mixed salad leaves

50g Parmesan shavings

1 For the vinaigrette, place a pan on a medium heat. Add the olive oil, shallot and some salt and pepper, and sweat without colouring the shallot for about 3–4 minutes. Add the chopped truffle and the thyme, then cook for a further 5 minutes. Add the Madeira, then reduce to almost nothing. Add the balsamic vinegar and reduce by two-thirds. Add the remaining oils, bring to a slow simmer and cook for 2–3 minutes. Season again with salt and pepper, and cool.

2 Place the Ratte potatoes into a pan of cold water with a little salt, and bring to a slow simmer. Cook for about 15–20 minutes, then drain the potatoes and peel them. Slice them into discs about 5mm thick, place on a plate, then season with salt and pepper. Smear in a little of the truffle vinaigrette to marinate.

3 Slice the Pink Fir Apple potatoes, unpeeled, very thinly on a mandolin lengthways and then cook in boiling salted water for about a minute, until aldenté. Place in iced water, then drain well and put in a bowl. Add a little seasoning and some truffle vinaigrette.

4 Lay the slices of Pink Fir Apple on the plates diagonally across the Ratte potatoes. Dress the salad leaves with some more of the truffle vinaigrette and seasoning, and place on top, with the Parmesan shavings. Then drizzle more vinaigrette around.

DRESSINGS AND SALAD LEAVES

There is only one man in this world that I will trust to grow my salad leaves. Richard Vine is a messiah of the salad world, and I have known him for about 15 years now. I met him whilst I was working at the Argyll on the Kings Road. He was bringing vegetables into London back then, and they were amazing and beautiful.

This man will not rest or stop until he has achieved the impossible, for he is essentially a creator, and the utter master of his field. Only very rarely does someone come along who is so in love with what they are doing, and who takes things to such extremes in terms of achieving the ultimate. It must be a magical thing to be so involved, literally to make something from nothing. Watching this man work and hearing him talk about his salads sends a shiver down my spine.

He grows just about everything I might like to use in my kitchen: healthy, bright leaves of everything, all of them delicious: from baby cresses and leaves, baby mâche and chard, crisp little beet tops, and baby cos and little gems. He picks all these by hand with little tweezers or scissors. Working the hours that he does is unbelievable. I know that my hours are long, but when you have done a full day's work outdoors, and then you have to drive from Hampshire to London and back again to deliver the produce is just total madness. But I have to thank Richard from the bottom of my heart, for without him and his salads, I could not create the things I do.

Some of the vegetable starters have salad leaves in them. I know you may not be able to get some of the salads I might use (that's mostly why I haven't specified them in individual recipes), but always try to get the best you can. So what I have done here is give you a few recipes for dressings to use with and on your salads. All these dressings can be made in minutes.

SHALLOT AND CAPER DRESSING

This could be served with roast skate wing or with a duck salad. It would go well with sautéed duck livers because of the acidity in the capers and shallots.

300ml sunflower oil
150g shallots, peeled and finely chopped
4g peeled and crushed garlic
3g sea salt
4–6 turns freshly milled black pepper
100ml white wine vinegar
100g baby capers, drained and rinsed

Place a pan on a low heat then add the oil, shallots, garlic, salt and pepper. Cook for 5 minutes until soft without colouring. Remove from the heat, then add the vinegar and capers.

BEETROOT DRESSING

This can be used in all sorts of salads and with pickled fish.

200g diced beetroot (from 2 baked beetroots, see page 38)
400ml beetroot juice (see page 38)
300ml olive oil
200g shallots, peeled and diced
2g fresh thyme leaves
2g sea salt
100ml balsamic vinegar

Place half the oil in a pan, place on a low heat then add the shallot. Cook for 2–3 minutes, then add the diced beetroot and beetroot juice. Boil to reduce by two-thirds.

Add the rest of the ingredients, including the remaining oil. Bring up to a very low simmer, and cook for 2 minutes. Then remove from the heat and chill.

FRENCH DRESSING

This is the one for all your green or mixed salads.

80g Dijon mustard
150ml white wine vinegar
4g sea salt
1g freshly milled black pepper
600ml sunflower oil

Whisk the mustard, vinegar, salt and pepper together. Slowly pour in the oil, whisking, until emulsified.

LEMON DRESSING

Good with seafood, Dover sole and crab.

300ml fresh lemon juice (from about 6 lemons)
10g finely grated lemon zest
60g caster sugar
100ml white wine vinegar
300ml sunflower oil
100ml water

Reduce the juice, zest and sugar in a pan to 100ml. Place in a blender with the vinegar, or whisk by hand, and slowly whisk in the oil. Add the water halfway through if it gets too thick, and whisk until emulsified.

ORANGE DRESSING

Use this with scallops or fish such as halibut.

500ml fresh orange juice (from about 5 oranges)
10g finely grated orange zest
30g caster sugar
100ml white wine vinegar
400ml sunflower oil
100ml water

Reduce the juice, zest and sugar in a pan to 200ml. Place in a blender with the vinegar, or whisk by hand, and slowly whisk in the oil. Add the water halfway through if it gets too thick, and whisk until emulsified.

WALNUT DRESSING

Good with grilled fish, and with salads incorporating fish or cold meat.

100ml sunflower oil
200ml walnut oil
150g shallots, peeled and finely chopped
4g peeled and chopped garlic
4g sea salt
4-6 turns freshly milled black pepper
100g shelled walnuts, chopped
100ml white wine vinegar

Place a pan on a medium heat then add the oils, shallots, garlic, salt and pepper. Cook for about 5 minutes until soft without colouring. Remove from the heat, then add the walnuts and vinegar.

HONEY AND MUSTARD DRESSING

This can be used with cold meats such as pork belly or gammon.

80g grain mustard
100ml white wine vinegar
40g clear honey
4g sea salt
2g freshly milled black pepper
600ml sunflower oil
2 tsp water (optional)

Place the mustard, vinegar, honey, salt and pepper in a bowl and whisk lightly. Slowly pour in the oil in a steady stream, whisking all the time, until it gets thick. If you need to thin it down, add the water.

SUPPLIES OF MOST OF THE FISH THAT WE ENJOY IN THIS COUNTRY ARE RAPIDLY RUNNING OUT DUE TO POLLUTION AND OVER-FISHING.

This shortage can also be put down to the fact that more people are now eating fish, because it's a healthier option to meat and because it contains essential oils, vitamins and minerals.

But good fresh and wild fish are hard to find. Many fish are now farmed, including sea bass, salmon and brill, but try to avoid these and go for the truly wild instead. Line-caught fish are the best option, but for these you pay a premium price, as you would for the best diver-caught scallops. It's an impossible situation: the demand for fish is there, the fishermen need to earn a living, but we are taking too much from our seas.

FISH

COD · CRAB · JOHN DORY · LOBSTER · PRAWNS · RED MULLET ·
SCALLOPS · SALMON · SEA BASS · SEA TROUT · SOLE · TUNA

WHAT TO BUY

COD

Cod used to be widely available, but now, because of overfishing, it is one of the most expensive fish to buy. I just hope that we never run out of it for fish and chips.

JOHN DORY

This is a curious-looking fish, long and deep-bodied, with two spots on either side, said to be made by the thumbprints of St Peter (thus the fish is known as St Pierre and San Pedro in France and Spain). The John Dory is popular in Mediterranean cuisines, but we can get it along our shorelines as well. It has a nice sweet flesh.

LOBSTER, PRAWN AND CRAB

I get my crabs from Dorset, my lobsters from Scotland, and my prawns from Madagascar.

RED MULLET

Red mullet come less frequently now from the Mediterranean, and are available in spring and summer from the UK coast. The best are those caught from what are called day-boats, rather than trawled.

SALMON AND SEA TROUT

Salmon used to be the most expensive fish to buy, but now it is one of the cheapest as it is mostly all farmed. For the dishes in this chapter, you should try to find wild salmon, which are in season for about 6 weeks from the end of May. Freshwater trout are farmed, and can be of good quality, but a real sea trout, or salmon trout, is a rare treat. Don't touch anything that is not line-caught or from a fishmonger.

SCALLOPS

The best scallops are diver-caught, many of them from Scotland, because they are generally alive. I like to use the biggest scallops I can find, as they are meatier.

SEA BASS

This is a fine fish, which you can find both wild and farmed. The farmed fish are generally smaller, around 500g, so it's better if you try to go for a line-caught fish of around or over 1kg.

SOLE

I would always use Dover sole, as it is firmer and tastier than lemon sole. Dover sole is quite expensive, but I think it is worth every penny.

TUNA

Tuna is a fabulous fish, which should always be eaten rare. If cooked to well done, it can get rather dry.

TURBOT

Turbot is the king of the flat fish, both in size and in flavour. It is very meaty, and yet very sweet tasting flavour.

SALT COD BRANDADE

THIS IS A VERY SIMPLE RECIPE, ALTHOUGH IT DOES TAKE A FEW DAYS TO PREPARE.
IT CAN BE USED FOR MANY THINGS, FROM CANAPES TO AN APPETISER OR STARTER.
YOU CAN SERVE IT ON TOAST OR PASTRY AS A CANAPE WITH CAVIAR, FOR INSTANCE,
OR WITH A SIMPLE SALAD.

MEDIUM ~ SERVES 4 ~ PREP 30 MINS PLUS SOAKING AND SETTING TIME ~ COOK 8 MINS

Poaching stock
25g unsalted butter
1 onion, peeled and thinly sliced
3 garlic cloves, peeled and sliced
2 bay leaves
1 sprig fresh thyme
250ml milk

300g fresh cod
500g coarse sea salt
6 gelatine leaves, soaked in cold water
250ml double cream, semi-whipped
sea salt and black pepper

1   Cut the cod into 2.5cm cubes, and put in a glass or
    ceramic dish. Cover with the sea salt and leave for
    2–3 days in the fridge. Rinse in cold water and then
    leave for 6 hours soaking in some more cold water.

2   To start the poaching stock, put the butter, onion,
    garlic and bay leaves in a large pan, and sweat for
    about 5 minutes, without colouring anything. Add
    the thyme, milk and salted cod and cook gently for
    a couple of minutes.

3   Add the drained and squeezed gelatine to melt.

4   Remove the bay leaves and thyme, and place
    everything into a blender for 2–3 minutes until you
    get a fine purée. Pass this through a sieve into a bowl
    set over ice. Stir with a plastic spatula until nearly set,
    then fold in the semi-whipped cream and some salt
    and pepper to taste. Leave to set for 1 hour.

BAKED COD, PAPRIKA PORK BELLY, BABY SQUID AND CHICKPEAS

THIS DISH IS SPANISH INFLUENCED, WITH ITS COMBINATION OF FISH AND MEAT, PAPRIKA AND CHICKPEAS. YOU COULD COOK SKATE, ANOTHER MEATY FISH, IN A SIMILAR WAY.

CHALLENGING ~ SERVES 4 ~ PREP 40 MINS PLUS SOAKING AND SETTING TIME ~ COOK 3 HRS

1 x 400g piece of cod fillet, halved

500ml milk

2 bay leaves

3 garlic cloves, peeled and halved

1 sprig fresh thyme

10 black peppercorns

50ml olive oil

paprika

300ml double cream

sea salt and black pepper

30g chorizo sausage

20g unsalted butter

1 tsp chopped fresh rosemary

juice of 1 lemon

Pork belly and squid

300g baby squid

150ml olive oil

8 slices braised pork belly (see page 112)

100ml vegetable oil

100ml balsamic vinegar

Chickpeas

150g dried baby chickpeas, soaked in cold water for a day

1 carrot, peeled and halved

1 onion, peeled and quartered

1 sprig fresh thyme

3 garlic cloves, peeled and halved

30g chorizo sausage

1   Drain the chickpeas, place in a pan of fresh cold water and bring up to a boil. Drain again, and place in a clean pan with water to cover. Add all the other chickpea-cooking ingredients, and bring to a slow simmer. Cover and cook gently until the chickpeas are tender, about 2 hours.

2   Place the milk over a very low heat, then add the bay leaves, garlic, thyme and black peppercorns. Leave to infuse for about 15–20 minutes.

3   Bring the milk up to just below simmering point. Place the cod into the milk and poach for about 8–10 minutes until the cod just starts to flake. Remove the pieces of fish from the milk and place on a tray. Flake

into large chunks. Place these chunks on two sheets of greaseproof paper greased lightly with olive oil and dusted with paprika.

4   To prepare the squid, remove the outer skin and then the heads from the bodies. Squeeze out the insides of the main bodies, then remove the mouth parts from the tentacles. Wash the bodies and tentacles, and dry. Cut the body into rings; leave the tentacles whole.

5   Place a third of the cooked chickpeas (discard the other ingredients) into a pan with two-thirds of their liquid, half the cream and a level teaspoon of paprika. Bring this to a simmer, and add salt to taste. Place in a blender and purée, then pass through a fine

sieve. This will be used as a froth to go around the finished dish.

6 Cut the uncooked chorizo into 4mm dice. Cook in 50ml of the olive oil in a pan on a medium heat for a couple of minutes until the oil turns red. Add the drained whole chickpeas, and cover them with some of their cooking stock. Cook to reduce this by two-thirds, then add the remaining cream. Reduce until sticky, then add the butter and rosemary, a large pinch of paprika, salt to taste and a squeeze of lemon juice.

7 Preheat the oven to 180°C/350°F/Gas 4.

8 Heat a pan, add the remaining olive oil and when very hot fry the squid pieces for about 30 seconds. Drain, then add a little lemon juice and seasoning.

9 Pan-fry the pork belly in a non-stick frying pan in the vegetable oil for 2–3 minutes on each side. When golden, remove the pork from the pan and season it. Remove the oil from the pan, and pour in the vinegar. Boil to deglaze the pan, and reduce until sticky.

10 Place the cod in the preheated oven for 5 minutes only, just to reheat.

11 To serve, place some of the whole chickpeas on each plate with two pieces of pork belly and some cod. Put the little pieces of squid around. Froth the chickpea sauce over and around. Dust with paprika.

ROAST JOHN DORY WITH CAULIFLOWER GAZPACHO AND PICKLED GRAPES

THIS CAULIFLOWER GAZPACHO COULD BE SERVED HOT AS WELL AS COLD. START PREPARING THE PICKLED GRAPES AT LEAST A COUPLE OF DAYS BEFORE YOU WANT TO SERVE THE DISH.

CHALLENGING ~ SERVES 4 ~ PREP 20 MINS PLUS MARINATING TIME ~ COOK 30 MINS PLUS DRYING TIME

4 x 80g pieces of John Dory fillet
1 medium cauliflower
1 recipe cauliflower pickling liquor (see page 26)
400ml milk
400ml double cream
6g chopped fresh dill
100ml olive oil
juice of 1 lemon

Pickled grapes
½ bunch white seedless grapes
6 star anise
300ml water
80ml lemon juice
3 tsp Pernod
a sprig each of fresh thyme and tarragon
60g caster sugar

1 Preheat the oven to 90°C/195°F/the lowest gas.

2 Place all the ingredients for the grape pickling liquor in a large pan, and bring up to a simmer. Add the grapes, bring back to a simmer, then remove from the heat to cool. If you can, leave the grapes in the liquor for at least a day. Remove the grapes from the pickling liquor. Place the grapes on a small-mesh wire tray, and dry out in the very low oven for 4–6 hours until they are like raisins.

3 Cut half of the cauliflower into small florets and then pickle them in the cauliflower pickling liquor as described on page 26. Drain.

4 Chop all the remaining cauliflower, and place in a pan with the milk and cream. Bring to a slow simmer and cook until the cauliflower is just tender, about 8–10 minutes. Place in a blender and purée until fine, then pass through a fine sieve. Cool, mix in the chopped dill, lemon juice and half the olive oil, then chill in the fridge.

5 Place the pickled grapes in with the cauliflower florets, and then warm up on a low heat with a little of the pickling liquor.

6 To cook the fish, season the fillets, then heat up a non-stick frying pan on a medium heat. Add the remaining olive oil and cook the seasoned fillets for 2–3 minutes on each side. Add a squeeze of lemon juice.

7 Place the cold cauliflower soup in four bowls, then put the pickled grapes and cauliflower florets around. Top with the fish.

JOHN DORY FILLETS WITH CABBAGE, CELERIAC AND HORSERADISH

THIS IS QUITE A REFRESHING DISH BECAUSE OF THE ACIDITY OF THE HORSERADISH, WHICH GIVES THE DISH A BIT OF A KICK.

MEDIUM ~ SERVES 4 ~ PREP 35 MINS ~ COOK 25 MINS

4 x 90g pieces of John Dory fillet
1 small celeriac
35g unsalted butter
sea salt and black pepper
1 sprig fresh thyme
juice of 1 lemon

400ml milk
300ml double cream
1 tbsp horseradish sauce
1 small stick fresh horseradish
1 small Savoy cabbage
100ml olive oil

1 Cut off the outer skin of the celeriac, and then cut a third of the flesh into 4mm dice. Chop the rest of the celeriac into rough 1cm dice.

2 Heat up a pan on a low to medium heat, then add 30g of the butter. When it has melted, add the 1cm celeriac dice, 2g salt, the thyme and 2 teaspoons of the lemon juice. Cook this on a low heat with a lid on for 10 minutes until soft. Remove half into a clean pan for the sauce. Mash the remaining celeriac with a fork, leaving it a little chunky.

3 Add the milk and cream to the celeriac in the clean pan, along with the horseradish sauce, then bring to a slow simmer. Cook for just 5 minutes, then grate about 6g fresh horseradish into this. Place into a blender and purée until smooth, then pass through a fine sieve and cool. Add a little lemon juice.

4 Take the outer leaves off the cabbage and cut the remainder into 4mm dice. Place a pan of salted water on to boil, and cook the raw celeriac dice for 2 minutes, then remove and refresh in iced water. Add the diced cabbage to the boiling salted water and cook for 1 minute. Refresh in iced water to cool. Mix the blanched cabbage with the blanched celeriac dice.

5 To cook the fish, first season the fillets with salt and pepper. Heat a non-stick frying pan on a high heat. Add the olive oil, and cook the seasoned fillets for about 3 minutes, then turn the fish over and the heat down and cook for a further 3 minutes, adding the remaining 5g butter at the end. Then squeeze a little lemon juice over it.

6 Place 100ml sauce into a pan and bring to a simmer. When the fish is cooking, add the cabbage and celeriac to the sauce to reheat. Warm through the celeriac mash at the same time, grating in a little more of the fresh horseradish.

7 Place the celeriac mash in the middle of each bowl, with the fish on top. Scatter the cabbage and celeriac dice around, then froth the horseradish sauce with a hand blender until aerated. Spoon this sauce over the fish and serve.

BAKED SEA BASS WITH AVOCADO AND SESAME

THE SYRUP COULD ALSO BE USED AS A DIPPING SAUCE OR WITH ROAST PORK BELLY.

MEDIUM ~ SERVES 4 ~ PREP 35 MINS ~ COOK 20–30 MINS

4 x 110g pieces of sea bass fillet

2 avocados

olive oil

3 limes

sea salt and black pepper

2 tbsp sesame seeds, toasted

25g caster sugar

50ml sesame oil

a large bunch of fresh coriander

50g Greek yoghurt

1 medium cucumber

Sweet and sour syrup

1 garlic clove, peeled and halved

1 tbsp sesame oil

2 tbsp light soy sauce

2 tbsp dark soy sauce

75g caster sugar

3 tbsp rice wine vinegar

juice and finely grated zest of 1 lime

1 Preheat the oven to 180°C/350°F/Gas 4. Place a baking tray in the oven, upturned, to cook the fish on.

2 Peel the avocados. Slice off eight slices with a mandolin, place on a plate with a little olive oil, and squeeze the juice of one lime over. Finely grate the zest of the lime, and sprinkle this, plus a little salt and a few toasted sesame seeds over the avocado slices. Put the remaining avocado into a blender and blend to a fine purée, adding a little salt, sugar, 1 teaspoon of lime juice and a tablespoon of sesame oil.

3 For the syrup, gently fry the garlic in sesame oil. Add the soy sauces, sugar, vinegar, lime juice and zest. Bring the mixture to the boil and reduce until it starts to gets syrupy, then leave to cool and infuse. Pass through a fine sieve just before serving.

4 Pick off and reserve a small handful of coriander leaves, then chop the rest finely, stopping when you reach the stalks. Put the chopped coriander into boiling salted water and cook for 2 minutes or until soft,

then drain. Reserve a couple of tablespoons of the cooking liquid. Place this and the cooked leaves into a blender and purée. Pass through a fine sieve and cool.

5 Mix the yoghurt with the puréed coriander, adding a little sugar and salt to taste. Chop the reserved raw coriander leaves and add half of them to the yoghurt.

6 Peel and de-seed the cucumber and slice it very thinly lengthways with a mandolin. Sprinkle with half the toasted sesame seeds, a little sesame oil, the remaining chopped coriander, and some sugar, salt and lime juice to taste.

7 Sprinkle a little sesame oil onto the sea bass with a little lime zest, juice and ½ teaspoon of toasted sesame seeds per fillet. Season, then place on baking paper on the tray in the preheated oven for 5–7 minutes.

8 To serve, put a little cucumber on each plate with the fish. Arrange the avocado slices with the syrup, yoghurt sauce and avocado purée around.

ROAST SEA BASS WITH BASIL AND CUCUMBER SAUCE VIERGE

THIS IS A GOOD DISH FOR SUMMER, USING BASIL, CUCUMBER AND PLUM TOMATOES. IT'S SLIGHTLY PROVENÇAL IN INFLUENCE.

MEDIUM ~ SERVES 4 ~ PREP 25 MINS ~ COOK 30 MINS

4 x 90g pieces of sea bass fillet
2 bunches fresh basil
sea salt and black pepper
10 plum tomatoes (preferably San Marzano)
3 courgettes
210ml olive oil

1 small cucumber
100ml fish stock (see page 101)
juice of 1 lemon
10g unsalted butter
8 tomato confit pieces (see page 60)
1 punnet basil cress (or small basil leaves)

1 Pick all the basil leaves from the stalks, and wash. Keep 10 leaves to one side. Place a small pan of water on to boil, add a little salt, then place three-quarters of the leaves into the water and cook until soft, about 2 minutes. Drain well, reserving a little of the cooking water. Blend to a fine purée with the reserved water, then pass through a fine sieve and cool straight away.

2 Blanch the tomatoes in boiling water for 5 seconds and then plunge them into iced water. Peel off the skins, then cut into quarters. Remove the seeds and cut the flesh into small dice.

3 Cut two of the courgettes into 5mm dice, then sauté in 50ml of the olive oil until just cooked, with no colour. Season with salt and pepper, then cool. Slice the remaining courgette lengthways on a mandolin very thinly. Peel the cucumber and then slice 5mm thick on a mandolin. Cut these cucumber slices into small dice.

4 Meanwhile, heat a frying pan on medium heat, then add 50ml olive oil. Season the fish with salt and pepper, then cook for around 3–4 minutes. Add the butter to the fish pan, and turn the heat down a little. Turn the fish over and cook for a further 2–3 minutes.

5 Put the fish stock on to heat, with 100ml olive oil and most of the lemon juice. When simmering, add the diced tomato, cucumber and courgette, and cook for 1 minute. Put a little water on to heat with a drop of olive oil and salt in it, add the courgette slices, cook for 1–2 minutes and drain. Cut the remaining basil into fine julienne strips, and add to the fish stock sauce.

6 Divide the tomato, cucumber and courgette sauce between four shallow bowls, then place a piece of fish on top, with some tomato confit, the courgette slices and the basil cress dressed with the remaining olive oil and lemon juice and some salt.

SEA BASS WITH LIME AND LEMONGRASS

THIS IS VERY QUICK AND EASY, AND A GOOD FAT-FREE WAY OF COOKING, USING THE OVEN INSTEAD OF THE FRYING PAN. I USE AN UPTURNED BAKING TRAY SIMPLY BECAUSE IT'S EASIER TO SLIDE THE FISH OFF ONCE COOKED!

MEDIUM ~ SERVES 4 ~ PREP 1¼ HRS ~ COOK 35 MINS

2 medium sea bass fillets, about 1kg in total, cut into 12 thin slices or escalopes
50ml olive oil
8 limes
6g each of fresh chervil, dill and tarragon
50g caster sugar
3 Braeburn or Granny Smith apples
sea salt and black pepper

Lemongrass sauce
500ml fish stock (see page 101)
500ml double cream
6 lemongrass stalks, bashed and finely chopped
juice of 2 lemons

1 Preheat the oven to 200°C/400°F/Gas 6. Place a baking tray in the oven, upturned, to cook the fish on.

2 Cut four pieces of greaseproof paper and rub them with olive oil. Using a microplane, grate a little lime zest on to each of the sheets. Chop half the mixed herbs, and divide this between the pieces of paper. Put three pieces of fish on top of each.

3 For the lime syrup, finely grate the zest of five of the limes into a small pan, and squeeze in their juice. Add 100ml water and 40g of the sugar, bring to the boil and cook to reduce by two-thirds, to a thick syrup. Leave to cool.

4 For the apple and lime purée, peel the apples, then core and chop into 1cm cubes. Place in a pan and add the juice and finely grated zest of the three remaining limes, plus the remaining sugar. Cook on a low heat, covered, for 8–10 minutes until soft. Purée in a blender and pass through a fine sieve.

5 For the lemongrass sauce, place the fish stock on to reduce by half. Then add the double cream and four of the lemongrass stalks, and reduce by two-thirds. Place in a blender and add the remaining lemongrass and purée. Pass this through a fine sieve into a small pan. Add a little lemon juice for some sharpness and season.

6 Season the fish and lift the pieces of paper with the bass on them onto the preheated tray in the oven. The fish will take about 2 minutes to cook.

7 Place a smear of apple purée on each plate and then the lime syrup next to it. When the fish is cooked, lift it off the paper and place it next to the purée. Froth the lemongrass sauce up and then spoon this around. Sprinkle over the remaining whole herbs.

ROAST TURBOT WITH CELERIAC FONDANT, BRAISED CHICKEN AND THYME SAUCE

IT MAY SEEM UNUSUAL TO SERVE FISH AND CHICKEN TOGETHER, BUT THE COMBINATION WORKS WELL AS THEY BOTH HAVE A SWEET TASTE.

CHALLENGING ~ SERVES 4 ~ PREP 50 MINS ~ COOK 1½ HRS

4 x 90g pieces of turbot fillet

8 x 3-joint chicken wings

100ml vegetable oil

45g unsalted butter

1 carrot, peeled and chopped into 1cm dice

1 onion, peeled and chopped into 1cm dice

2 garlic cloves, peeled and chopped

2 sprigs fresh thyme

100ml Madeira

50ml olive oil

sea salt and black pepper

juice of 1 lemon

Celeriac fondant and purée

1 celeriac, peeled

20g unsalted butter

juice of ½ lemon

300ml white chicken stock (see page 155)

1 sprig fresh thyme

600ml milk

250ml double cream

1 Peel the tough skin off the celeriac, and then cut down through the celeriac lengthways into four slices, 1cm thick. Using a round cutter 5cm in diameter, cut these slices into four discs (keep the trimmings for the next step). Place these into a flat pan with the butter, a little lemon juice, half the stock, thyme and some salt and pepper. Simmer over a medium heat for 10–12 minutes until tender. When nearing serving time, reduce this liquid down with the discs so that it coats them.

2 To make the celeriac purée, chop all the celeriac trimmings, and place in a pan with the milk, cream and a little salt. Bring to a slow simmer, then cook for 15–20 minutes until tender. Drain the liquid through a fine sieve, and place this into a small pan for later. Purée all the celeriac in a blender with the juice of half a lemon (it can remain coarse).

3 Chop the ends and tips off the chicken wings, so that you are left with the middle pieces. Heat the vegetable oil in a large casserole. When hot, add 20g of the butter and all the chicken pieces, including the ends and tips. Lightly caramelise for 3–5 minutes, then add the carrot, and continue cooking for 5 minutes. Add the onion, garlic and thyme, and cook for a further 5 minutes until well caramelised. Then add the Madeira, cover with the remaining stock, and bring to a slow simmer. Skim, then cook gently for 30 minutes, uncovered. Remove the middle pieces of wing from the stock, and place on a tray to cool a little. Remove the middle bone, then leave to cool completely.

4 Cook this chicken stock for a further 10 minutes, then pass through a fine sieve. Return to the heat and skim. Reduce the stock to 200ml, then add half the remaining butter. Reheat the wings in this when serving.

5 Heat a frying pan on a medium heat, and add the olive oil. Season the fish with salt and pepper, then place in the pan and cook for around 3–4 minutes. Add the remaining butter to the fish pan, turn the heat down a little, turn the fish over and cook for a further 2 minutes. Add a squeeze of lemon juice.

6 While cooking the fish, heat up the celeriac purée and fondant, and warm the celeriac milk and the chicken wings in their stock.

7 Put a celeriac fondant on each plate, and top with the fish. Put a spoonful of celeriac purée at the side with the chicken wing on top. Froth the celeriac-flavoured milk with a hand blender, and spoon the froth around, along with the reduced chicken stock.

COOKING IS A FUN, LOVING AND LIGHT-HEARTED THING TO DO. THERE IS NO NEED TO GET STRESSED WHEN IT COMES TO PREPARING A MEAL.

SALMON SASHIMI

THIS JAPANESE-INSPIRED SALMON DISH USES THE FISH RAW, SO YOU SHOULD TRY TO GET HOLD OF WILD SALMON.

EASY ~ SERVES 4 ~ PREP 15 MINS ~ MARINATE 12 HRS

1 x 250g piece wild salmon

yoghurt and coriander sauce
(see below)

1 punnet coriander cress (or picked coriander leaves)

Marinade

4 tbsp sweet mirin

4 tbsp soy sauce

2 tbsp sesame oil

1 tbsp chopped bottled stem ginger

1 tbsp chopped fresh red chilli

1 tbsp chopped fresh coriander

1 Mix all the marinade ingredients together. Cut the salmon into small batons, then place in the marinade and leave for 12 hours.

2 Place the batons on wooden skewers, and serve with the sauce and coriander cress.

Note
The ideal accompaniment to this is the yoghurt and coriander sauce used in the sea bass recipe on page 78. Mix 50g Greek yoghurt with some puréed coriander, with a little sugar and salt to taste, then add some chopped raw coriander.

MARINATED SALMON WITH PICKLED BEETROOT, ORANGE DRESSING

MARINATING FISH IS EASY, TAKING NO EFFORT, JUST TIME. THE SCANDINAVIANS HAVE BEEN COMBINING FISH AND BEETROOT FOR YEARS, AND I THINK THEY ARE GREAT TOGETHER. THE ORANGE FLAVOURS LIGHTEN THE WHOLE DISH.

EASY ~ SERVES 4 ~ PREP 20 MINS ~ MARINATING TIME 6–8 HRS

1 side fresh wild salmon, about 1.5kg, skin on and scaled

2 avocados, peeled, halved and stoned

olive oil

sea salt

juice of 1 lemon

200g mixed salad leaves

200ml orange dressing (see page 69)

1 recipe pickled beetroot (see page 41)

1 recipe beetroot dressing (see page 68)

Marinade

1 bunch fresh dill, finely chopped

200g sea salt

100g caster sugar

50g black peppercorns, crushed

finely grated zest of 4 lemons

finely grated zest of 6 oranges

1 Your fishmonger can scale the salmon and take all the bones out for you (you may need to order this in advance). If not, use a small pair of pliers or tweezers. Wash the salmon in cold water and then pat dry on a cloth.

2 For the marinade, mix all the ingredients together. Place half of this on a tray, then lay the salmon on top and cover with the rest of the mix. Cover with clingfilm and place in the fridge with a small weight on top to press the salmon. Leave for 6–8 hours, depending on the size of the fillet.

3 When ready, remove the marinade and then slice the marinated salmon very thinly. Lay the slices on a clean tray and place in the fridge.

4 Slice the avocado thinly on a mandolin and place on greaseproof paper. Sprinkle on a little olive oil, salt and lemon juice. Purée the trimmings in a blender until fine, adding salt and lemon juice to taste.

5 Dress the salad leaves with some of the orange dressing.

6 Smear some puréed avocado down the centre of each plate, and then drizzle with a little of the orange dressing. Lay the salmon down next, with the slices of avocado and some pickled beetroot. Then add some salad leaves with the rest of the beets and salad on top. Drizzle the beetroot dressing around and over the dish.

BAKED SEA TROUT WITH DILL GNOCCHI AND SUMMER VEGETABLES

SEA TROUT IS A LARGER, SEA-GOING VERSION OF THE BROWN TROUT, AND IS
A FAVOURITE OF MINE.

CHALLENGING ~ SERVES 4 ~ PREP 30 MINS ~ COOK 2 HRS

500g sea trout fillet, very thinly sliced

olive oil

1 lemon

14g mixed picked herb leaves (tarragon, chervil, dill
and chives), kept separate

250ml white wine

200ml fish stock (see page 101)

200ml double cream

1 recipe herb gnocchi made with dill (see page 66)

20g unsalted butter

sea salt and black pepper

Summer vegetables

200g podded peas

500g podded broad beans

1 round lettuce, broken down into little leaves

2 punnets pea shoots

edible flowers

1 Take four sheets of greaseproof paper, and lightly
grease them with olive oil. Finely grate on the lemon
zest using a microplane (or very fine grater), and
then scatter with half of each of the herbs. Lay the
sea trout slices on the greased paper and then chill
in the fridge.

2 For the summer vegetables, bring a large pan
of salted water to the boil, and boil the peas for
2–3 minutes then cook until tender, about 5 minutes.
Remove from the water with a slotted spoon, and
refresh in iced water. Next, blanch the broad beans
in the water for 30 seconds, and then refresh in iced
water. Leave to cool for a couple of minutes and then
remove the bright green beans from their grey shells.
Discard the shells.

3 For the sauce, put the white wine into a medium
pan and boil to reduce by half. Add the fish stock
and again boil to reduce by half. Add the cream and
once more reduce by half.

4 Preheat the oven to 200°C/400°F/Gas 6. Place an
upturned tray into the oven to heat up.

5 Place the sauce on to heat gently in two small pans.
Divide the remaining dill between them, then add the
peas and broad beans to one pan and the gnocchi
to the other. Place 100ml water on to heat with the
butter in another small pan, and bring to a simmer.
Add a little salt.

6 As you place the fish into the oven on the tray for
2–3 minutes, place the lettuce into the water and
butter, and cook for 2 minutes.

7 Invert the fish on to each plate so that the herbs are
on top. Pour the peas and broad beans over the fish,
and put the lettuce leaves and gnocchi to the side.

8 Dress the pea shoots and edible flowers with a little
olive oil, lemon juice and salt, and sprinkle these over
everything, along with the remaining herbs.

TUNA TARTARE WITH PICKLED CAULIFLOWER AND AVOCADO

IN THIS RECIPE THE TUNA IS NOT COOKED AT ALL, SO YOU CAN APPRECIATE THE FULL FLAVOUR OF THE FISH.

MEDIUM ~ SERVES 4 ~ PREP 30 MINS PLUS COOLING TIME ~ COOK 20 MINS

1 x 300g piece of tuna fillet
1 recipe cauliflower pickling liquor (see page 26)
1 small cauliflower
sea salt and black pepper
200ml double cream
200ml milk

1 large bunch fresh coriander, leaves picked, half of them chopped
3 avocados
200ml sesame oil
juice of 1 lemon
1 tsp sesame seeds, toasted

1 Bring the cauliflower pickling liquor to a simmer. Cut the cauliflower into small florets, keeping all the trimmings, and cook the florets in the liquor for 8–10 minutes. Leave to cool in the liquor.

2 Chop all the cauliflower trimmings, and put in a small pan with a little salt, the cream and milk. Bring to a slow simmer, and cook for 8–10 minutes until soft, then season. Add the chopped coriander and purée in a blender. Pass through a fine sieve, then cool over ice.

3 Peel the avocados, and then slice 12 thin slices on a mandolin. Place these slices on a sheet of greaseproof paper topped with a little sesame oil, lemon juice, salt and pepper.

4 Place the avocado trimmings into the blender and purée. Add some seasoning and about 50ml sesame oil, then pass through a fine sieve.

5 Chop the tuna into neat small dice, place in a bowl and add the remaining sesame oil, half of the remaining coriander and the toasted sesame seeds. Add a little avocado purée to this to bind it together

6 Arrange the fish on each plate in three piles, and put a slice of avocado over each pile. Using a dessertspoon, put two quenelles, or mounds, of the cauliflower purée and the pickled florets around. Then sprinkle the rest of the coriander over and around.

MARINATED TUNA ROLL

THE LEFTOVER TRIMMINGS COULD BE FINELY DICED, MIXED WITH A LITTLE OF THE MARINADE AND EATEN SEPARATELY, OR PLACED UNDER THE TUNA ROLL SLICES.

EASY ~ SERVES 4 ~ PREP 25 MINS PLUS MARINATING TIME ~ COOK 5 MINS

Marinade
2 tbsp sesame oil

2 tsp chopped bottled stem ginger in syrup

1 tbsp ginger syrup from the bottle

4 tbsp soy sauce

2 tbsp sweet mirin

3cm piece of fresh root ginger, peeled and chopped

2 tbsp fresh lime juice

3 kaffir lime leaves, chopped

3 lemongrass stalks, bashed and chopped

1 x 250g piece of tuna fillet, trimmed into a tube shape

sea salt

100ml olive oil

50g sesame seeds, toasted

1 tbsp sesame oil

30g chopped fresh coriander

30g shizo cress

30g mizuna

1 Season the tuna lightly with salt. Heat a frying pan on a high heat, add the olive oil and then sear the tuna on all sides, about 2 minutes altogether. Remove from the pan and place in a small tray.

2 Mix all the marinade ingredients, pour over the tuna and leave for 6 hours. Turn occasionally.

3 Remove the tuna from the marinade. Put the sesame seeds on a flat tray, and roll the tuna in them to coat all sides. Roll the tuna tightly in clingfilm so that it takes on a round tube shape. Leave this in the fridge for a few hours to firm up. When ready to serve, slice thinly.

4 Take a couple of tablespoons of the marinade and mix with the sesame oil and coriander. Dress the cress and mizuna leaves with half of this. Divide the tuna slices between four plates, with the leaves over the tuna, and sprinkle the remaining dressing around.

RED MULLET WITH COURGETTE PUREE, PISTACHIO RISOTTO AND 'CRUMBS'

IF YOU CAN'T GET HOLD OF PISTACHIO OIL, BLEND 100G GREEN PISTACHIOS WITH 200ML OLIVE OIL, AND PASS THROUGH A FINE SIEVE.

MEDIUM ~ SERVES 4 ~ PREP 30 MINS ~ COOK 30 MINS

4 x 170g red mullet, scaled, cleaned, filleted and pin-boned

3 large courgettes

6 baby courgettes

35g unsalted butter

sea salt and black pepper

100ml olive oil

2 punnets basil cress

100ml pistachio oil (or see above)

a little lemon juice

1 tbsp black olive oil (see page 34)

50g shelled pistachio nuts, very finely chopped

Pistachio risotto

500ml white chicken stock (see page 155)

50ml olive oil

15g unsalted butter

2 banana or round shallots, peeled and finely diced

120g risotto rice

250ml white wine

2 tbsp crème fraîche

40g Parmesan cheese, freshly grated

50g shelled pistachio nuts, very finely chopped

1 Preheat the oven to 90°C/195°F/the lowest gas.

2 Chop the large courgettes finely. Heat a pan on a medium heat, melt 25g of the butter, then add the chopped courgette and salt and pepper. Cover with a lid and cook gently for 8–10 minutes until soft. Put in the blender and purée until fine, then pass through a fine sieve. Leave to cool. Slice the small courgettes very thinly on a mandolin.

3 For the risotto, heat the chicken stock to a simmer. Heat a medium pan on a low heat, add the olive oil, 10g of the butter and the shallots. Sauté gently for about 2–3 minutes, without colouring. Add the rice, and cook for 2 minutes, stirring, then add the wine. Stir well, and when this has all been absorbed by the rice, add the hot stock slowly, stirring continuously. Keep adding the stock to the rice in 150ml quantities, waiting for the last lot to be absorbed before adding the next. The risotto will take about 12 minutes to be

completely cooked. To finish, stir in the crème fraîche, Parmesan, chopped pistachios and remaining butter. Season.

4 To cook the fish, heat a non-stick frying pan on a high heat, add the olive oil and cook the fillets, skin-side down, for about 2 minutes on each side.

5 Meanwhile, cook the courgette slices in a little water and the remaining butter to reduce and emulsify the liquid, adding a little salt and lemon juice. Cook for 1 minute altogether. Warm through the courgette purée.

6 Dress the basil cress with half the pistachio oil and season. Place the courgette purée on the plates and the risotto on top. Top with slices of courgette and the fish. Add a squeeze of lemon and drizzle on the remaining pistachio oil and black olive oil. Sprinkle the cress over, followed by the pistachio 'crumbs'.

MARINATED AND ROAST RED MULLET WITH AUBERGINE

MULLET CAN BE MARINATED IN MUCH THE SAME WAY AS SALMON, AND YOU CAN USE THE SAME MARINADE (SEE PAGE 87). HALF THE MULLET FILLETS ARE MARINATED HERE, AND THEN YOU SERVE THEM WITH PAN-ROASTED MULLET.

CHALLENGING ~ SERVES 4 ~ PREP 45 MINS ~ COOK 30 MINS PLUS MARINATING TIME

10 x 175–225g red mullet, scaled, boned and filleted

1 recipe marinade (see page 87)

3 medium aubergines

400ml olive oil

6 banana shallots, peeled and finely diced

2g thyme leaves, chopped

sea salt and black pepper

8 pieces tomato confit (see page 60), finely chopped

4g fresh coriander leaves, finely chopped

2g fresh basil leaves, finely chopped

juice of 1 lemon

1 Marinate half of the mullet fillets in the marinade for 6 hours, weighted down as for the salmon, in the fridge. When ready, wash in cold water, dry well and chill.

2 Cut the skin off the aubergines and cut three-quarters of the flesh into rough dice. Sauté the aubergine dice in a hot frying pan with half the olive oil and colour slightly. After 5 minutes, add four of the chopped shallots and half the thyme, season and cook for another 5 minutes. Purée this aubergine mixture in a blender until fine, then leave to cool.

3 Cut the remaining aubergine flesh into neat 5mm dice, and sauté in a pan with 50ml olive oil, the remaining chopped shallot and thyme and some seasoning. Lightly colour for a few minutes, then leave to cool.

4 Chop the marinated mullet finely, and mix with the aubergine dice and chopped tomato confit. Mix in half the chopped fresh herbs. Mix in a couple of tablespoons of the aubergine purée to bind it

together, season if need be, and add a little lemon juice. While you cook the remaining mullet fillets, shape this marinated mullet mixture between two tablespoons, and place two quenelles (or mounds) of it on each plate. Place a quenelle of the aubergine purée on each plate as well.

5 Heat up a non-stick frying pan, add another 50ml olive oil and then when it is hot, season the remaining mullet fillets, cut into three pieces and pan-fry, skin-side down, for 2 minutes until they start to go golden at the edges. Then turn the mullet over and cook for 30 seconds. Add a squeeze of lemon juice.

6 Remove the fish from the pan, and place next to the aubergine on the plate. Place the remaining herbs in a bowl, add the rest of the olive oil and some seasoning, and sprinkle over the dish.

Note
If banana shallots are not available, replace with round shallots (you may need to increase the quantity slightly as they are smaller).

PAN-FRIED RED MULLET WITH TOMATO CONFIT TARTE FINE, AVOCADO AND TOMATO DRESSING

A NICE SUMMERY DISH, WITH A CLEAN TASTE BECAUSE OF THE SWEETNESS OF THE TOMATOES.

CHALLENGING ~ SERVES 4 ~ PREP 40 MINS ~ COOK 2½ HRS

4 x 175g red mullet, scaled, cleaned, filleted and pin-boned

3 sheets filo pastry

25g unsalted butter, melted

1 tsp chopped fresh rosemary leaves

1 tsp fresh thyme leaves

sea salt and black pepper

1 avocado

4g fresh coriander leaves

1 recipe tomato confit (see page 60)

10 large fresh basil leaves

50ml olive oil

juice of 1 lemon

2 punnets basil cress

Tomato dressing

150ml olive oil

100ml thick tomato sauce (see page 60)

2g fresh thyme leaves

1 Preheat the oven to 180°C/350°F/Gas 4.

2 To make the tarte fine base, take one sheet of filo and brush with a third of the melted butter. Sprinkle with a third of the rosemary and thyme, then do the same with the remaining two sheets of filo. Put them on top of each other, season the top layer, and cut into four large round discs about 10cm in diameter. Place on a non-stick baking sheet with a sheet of greaseproof paper on top, and then a weighted tray on top. Bake in the oven for about 12 minutes until golden brown.

3 For the tomato dressing, mix the olive oil and the tomato sauce together with the thyme leaves.

4 Peel and stone the avocado. Purée the flesh in a blender with the coriander leaves, but not too finely, it should still be a little coarse.

5 Spread the avocado purée onto the filo discs, and then top with the tomato confit. Chop the basil and sprinkle this over the tomato.

6 To cook the fish, heat a non-stick frying pan on a high heat, add the olive oil, and cook the seasoned fillets, skin-side down, for about 2 minutes on each side. Drain and squeeze on a little lemon juice.

7 Place two fillets of fish on top of each tart. Dress the basil cress with a little of the tomato dressing, and sprinkle over the fish. Finish with the remaining tomato dressing around the dish.

RED MULLET DARNES, BLACK OLIVE GNOCCHI, BORLOTTI BEANS AND PESTO

CUTTING THE FISH INTO SMALL DARNES – WHICH ARE WIDTHWAYS SLICES THROUGH THE BACKBONE – IS SLIGHTLY EASIER TO DO THAN FILLETING. YOU SHOULD GET ABOUT 3–4 DARNES FROM EACH FISH.

CHALLENGING ~ SERVES 4 ~ PREP 30 MINS ~ COOK 2 HRS

4 x 225g red mullet, scaled, cleaned, and cut into 1cm thick darnes

100ml olive oil

juice of ½ lemon

40 cherry tomato confit halves (see page 60)

1 recipe borlotti bean casserole with pesto (see page 37)

1 punnet basil cress (or small basil leaves)

sea salt

Gnocchi

250ml white chicken stock (see page 155)

100g crème fraîche

1 recipe black olive gnocchi (see page 66)

4g fresh basil leaves, finely sliced

1 For the gnocchi, place the stock on to boil and reduce by half then add the crème fraiche. Add the gnocchi to this, and warm through for about 2 minutes. Add the basil at the very last minute.

2 During this time, cook the fish. Heat up a non-stick frying pan on a high heat, add 50ml of the olive oil, and cook the darnes, skin-side down, for about 1 minute per side. Add a squeeze of the lemon, then remove from the pan.

3 Place the gnocchi and some of their sauce on each plate, the tomato halves around, and the fish on top. Put some of the borlotti beans alongside. Dress the basil cress with a little lemon juice, the remaining olive oil and a little salt, and sprinkle around.

SOLE WITH ROAST SHALLOTS

THIS IS A GREAT DISH AS THE SOLE, SHALLOTS AND THYME GO SO WELL TOGETHER.

MEDIUM ~ SERVES 4 ~ PREP 25 MINS ~ COOK 45 MINS

8 sole fillets, cut from 2 fish, each weighing 450–500g
500ml milk
2 garlic cloves, peeled and halved
2 bay leaves
5 sprigs fresh thyme
8 long banana or round shallots

30g unsalted butter
caster sugar
sea salt and black pepper
450ml brown chicken stock (see page 155)
olive oil

1 Place the milk in a saucepan with the halved garlic, bay leaves and a couple of sprigs of thyme. Heat gently to a little more than blood heat (test the temperature by dipping your finger in it), then leave to stand for an hour.

2 Preheat the oven to 180°C/350°F/Gas 4.

3 Peel four of the shallots, leaving the root intact so they stay together. Melt 12g of the butter in a frying pan on a medium heat, and add four of the thyme sprigs, a pinch of sugar, some salt and the peeled shallots. Colour slowly until golden, which will take about 10–12 minutes. Add 200ml of the stock and cook for a further 5–10 minutes until the shallots are soft, and the stock has become sticky.

4 Peel the remaining four shallots, and dice them finely. Place in a pan with another 12g butter, plus a sprig of thyme and some sugar and salt. Cook gently until soft, without colouring, for about 5 minutes. Leave to cool.

5 Lay out the sole fillets on the work surface, and spread them with the diced shallot. Roll each fillet up, securing with a wooden cocktail stick. They will look like roll-mop herrings.

6 For the sauce, boil the remaining stock over a medium heat until it has reduced to the consistency of oil, about 5 minutes, adding the remaining butter at the end.

7 Heat a frying pan, and season each sole roll. Add a little olive oil to the pan, put in the fillets and colour, turning every minute until they are golden brown, about 4–5 minutes. Then give them 3–4 minutes in the preheated oven.

8 Put the four whole roasted shallots and their juices into the reduced stock and reheat.

9 Strain the garlic-infused milk to remove the thyme and garlic, and froth the milk with a hand blender. Lay two sole fillets side by side on each plate and surround with the sauce and a whole shallot. Spoon a little of the milk foam around the edge of the plate. If you wish, garnish with the thyme cooked with the shallots.

ROAST SCALLOPS WITH PORK BELLY

THIS DISH IS A FAVOURITE OF MINE. IT IS SO SIMPLE YET WORKS SO WELL AS THE PORK FAT COMPLEMENTS THE CLEAN, SWEET TASTE OF THE SCALLOPS. THE PORK BELLY SHOULD BE COOKED THE DAY BEFORE.

MEDIUM ~ SERVES 4 ~ PREP 20 MINS ~ COOK 20 MINS

8 large scallops, cut in half horizontally
4 slices braised pork belly (see page 112)
60g unsalted butter
3 large onions, peeled and sliced
1 sprig fresh thyme
10g caster sugar

2g sea salt
4 banana shallots (or round shallots), peeled and finely diced
300ml balsamic vinegar
250ml brown chicken stock (see page 155)
100ml olive oil

1 For the onion purée, melt 50g of the butter in a saucepan on a medium heat. Add the sliced onions with the thyme, sugar and salt. Cook this with a lid on for 10 minutes without colouring, then remove the lid and slowly start to colour the onion. When it has caramelised nicely, purée the onion in the blender. When fine, pass it through a sieve.

2 For the shallot sauce, melt half the remaining butter in a small pan on a low heat. Add the shallots and cook without colouring for 3–4 minutes. Add three-quarters of the vinegar and boil to reduce to nothing, then add the brown chicken stock, and boil to reduce by two-thirds. Add the remaining butter.

3 Heat a frying pan on a medium heat, then add the oil. Sauté the scallops and the pork belly together for 2 minutes. Turn the scallops and the belly over, and cook for a further minute. Deglaze the pan with the remaining balsamic vinegar.

4 Warm up the onion purée, and put a line of it to the side of each plate. Place a slice of pork belly next to it, with the scallops on top and overlapping. Pour the shallot sauce and balsamic vinegar over and around.

ROASTED SCALLOPS WITH BALSAMIC CARROTS

FISH STOCK

CARROTS GO WELL WITH SCALLOPS, AND THERE IS A NICE COMBINATION OF SHARPNESS AND SWEETNESS HERE.

MEDIUM ~ SERVES 4 ~ PREP 15 MINS ~ COOK 25 MINS

8 large scallops
1 recipe balsamic glazed carrots (see page 31)
1 recipe carrot purée with star anise (see page 30)
50ml olive oil
10g unsalted butter

1 When both the carrot dishes are ready, then you can cook the scallops. Place a non-stick frying pan on to a high heat, then add a little olive oil.

2 When the oil is hot, add the scallops. Cook them on the first side for 2–3 minutes, then add a little butter. Turn them over after a few seconds, and continue to cook for another minute.

3 Meanwhile, heat the purée and the carrots through. Place the purée in a line along each plate and then the scallops by the side and the glazed carrots on top. Use the glazing syrup to pour around the dish.

USE THIS IN SAUCES FOR FISH DISHES, AND FOR FISH SOUPS. IT CAN BE FROZEN.

EASY ~ MAKES 700ML ~ PREP 10 MINS ~ COOK 45 MINS

2 fennel bulbs, thinly sliced
100ml olive oil
500g white fish bones (sole, sea bass, turbot), chopped
300ml white wine
1 litre water
6g sea salt
1 tsp black peppercorns
½ bunch fresh chervil

1 Sweat the fennel in the olive oil for about 2–3 minutes, not allowing it to colour. Add the fish bones, wine and water, and bring to a slow simmer. Skim.

2 Add the salt, peppercorns and chervil, and simmer for 40 minutes, skimming occasionally. Pass through a fine sieve into a clean container.

3 It is now ready for use. If you are not using the stock straight away, place in the fridge for no longer than 2 days.

ROAST SCALLOPS WITH HAM AND LEEK

SCALLOPS HAVE A NUTTY FLAVOUR WHEN ROASTED, SO THIS IS INTENSIFIED BY ADDING SOME GRATED FRESH HAZELNUTS AND SOME HAZELNUT OIL.

CHALLENGING ~ SERVES 4 ~ PREP 30 MINS PLUS SETTING TIME ~ COOK 20 MINS

8 extra-large scallops
8 large leeks
sea salt and black pepper
100g shelled hazelnuts, toasted
about 3 tbsp toasted hazelnut oil
1 bunch fresh chervil
2g caster sugar

juice of 1 lemon
10 gelatine leaves
about 20g Parmesan shavings
olive oil
4 slices Jabugo or Parma ham
200g mixed salad leaves

1 Strip the first couple of layers of leaves from all the leeks. Chop these finely, then wash well along with the whole leeks. Place the whole leeks into boiling salted water and cook for 10–12 minutes until tender. Plunge into iced water for a few minutes to stop the cooking.

2 Remove and discard a couple of layers of the cooked leeks, and then dry the leeks. Place six of them on a tray, close together, then grate over 20g of the nuts using a microplane, add a drizzle of hazelnut oil, a tablespoon of chopped chervil and seasoning.

3 Place the chopped raw leek layers into a pan with 600ml water and a few sprigs of chervil. Bring this to the boil, turn off the heat and leave to stand for a couple of minutes then pass through a sieve discarding the chopped leek and reserving the liquid. Add the sugar and a squeeze of lemon juice to taste. Put 400ml of this warm liquid in a bowl with eight of the gelatine leaves. Stir to dissolve, then place into a bowl over ice to set. Stir with a ladle now and again.

4 When the leek liquid is nearly set, pour it over the six leeks on the tray. Move them around a little so that they are well coated, then lift these leeks with their jelly onto a sheet of clingfilm. Roll tightly into a neat tube so

the clingfilm overlaps several times; some of the jelly will come out at the end, which is fine. Seal with string at each end, then chill in the fridge for at least 2 hours. Add a teaspoon of chopped chervil and the remaining gelatine to the rest of the leek liquid, and place in the fridge to set as well.

5 Preheat the grill.

6 Cut the two remaining leeks in half lengthways, and scatter each half with a few Parmesan shavings, a little hazelnut oil and some grated hazelnut, then season lightly. Grill until golden.

7 Cut the scallops in half horizontally, and season. Heat a little olive oil in a frying pan and, when hot, add the scallops. Turn them over after about 2 minutes, when you see a golden colour around the edges, then cook for a further 30 seconds. Add a little lemon juice and take out of the pan.

8 Slice the leek boudin in 5mm thick slices and place on four plates with the ham, scallops and grilled leeks. Spoon around the set jelly, and add the leaves dressed with hazelnut oil, lemon juice and grated hazelnuts.

CRAB AND LEMONGRASS SOUP

THE LEMONGRASS GOES VERY WELL WITH CRAB, MAKING THIS A VERY LIGHT AND
REFRESHING SOUP TO EAT.

CHALLENGING ~ SERVES 4 ~ PREP 35 MINS ~ COOK 1¼ HRS

1 x live 2.5kg cock crab

300ml olive oil

1 large fennel bulb, finely sliced

6 star anise

1 level tbsp fennel seeds

1 tsp pink peppercorns

2g sea salt

500ml white wine

a small bunch of fresh tarragon

700ml double cream

6 lemongrass stalks, bashed and chopped

juice and finely grated zest of 2 lemons

1 tsp caster sugar

1g each of chopped fresh dill, chervil and tarragon

1 Place a large pan of water on to boil. There is a flap on the crab's underside, which you lift up. Stick a sharp knife through this into the body. The crab will die straight away. Cook the crab in the boiling water for 8–10 minutes, then remove and leave to cool for about 15 minutes. Remove all the claws and open up the head. Do not keep any of the brown crabmeat. The central part of the body can be cut into eight pieces and then all the meat picked out with a skewer.

2 Crack all the claws open and remove the meat as well. The smaller claws need to be pulled apart at the joints, so you have less shell to pick through. Once you have picked out all the meat, then you need to go through it with your fingers on a tray to check that there are no sharp pieces of shell left. Break all the shells into small pieces.

3 Heat 200ml of the olive oil in a large pan over a medium heat, then add the crab shells. Lightly cook these for 3–4 minutes, then add the fennel and cook for a further 3–4 minutes. Add all the spices and the salt, then pour in the white wine. Simmer to reduce this by two-thirds.

4 Pour in approximately 1 litre water, bring to a slow simmer, then skim off all the scum. Add the tarragon, and simmer for 20 minutes. Add 500ml of the cream, bring back up to a simmer, and add two of the lemongrass stalks. Cook for another 10 minutes, then pass all this through a fine sieve.

5 Place the soup into a clean pan and add three more lemongrass stalks and the rest of the cream. Bring to a simmer, cook for 10 minutes, then add most of the lemon juice. Place in a blender with the last lemongrass stalk and the sugar, and purée. Pass through a fine sieve into a clean pan.

6 Mix the crabmeat with the chopped herbs, remaining olive oil, a little lemon juice and the lemon zest. Place this into four bowls. Froth the soup with a hand blender and spoon this into each bowl.

PRAWN AND CHILLI SOUP WITH PRAWN DUMPLINGS

TRY TO GET LARGE PRAWNS (I USE ONES FROM MADAGASCAR) OR TIGER PRAWNS, AND USE THEIR SHELLS FOR THE SOUP STOCK.

MEDIUM ~ SERVES 4 ~ PREP 30 MINS ~ COOK 35 MINS

450g large prawns

100ml olive oil

700ml white chicken stock (see page 155)

2 lemongrass stalks, bashed and finely chopped

2 sweet red peppers, seeded

1 small bunch fresh coriander

1 x 80g nugget fresh root ginger, peeled and finely chopped

4 Kaffir lime leaves, crushed and sliced

3 whole red chillies, sliced

6 Thai shallots (these are very small), peeled and finely diced (or use 4 round shallots)

2 tbsp rice vinegar

1 tbsp soy sauce

juice and finely grated zest of 1 lime

sea salt and black pepper

1 Peel the shells from the prawns. Place a pan on to heat, add the oil and then the shells, and cook for 3–4 minutes, then add the chicken stock and lemongrass. Chop the red peppers into rough 1cm dice and add these to the soup, along with half the coriander, chopped leaves and stalks, two-thirds of the chopped ginger, the lime leaves and 2 of the red chillies. Bring this to a slow simmer, then skim and cook for 30 minutes.

2 Whilst this is cooking keep four whole prawns aside, and chop the rest finely, almost to a purée. Add to this the diced shallots, the remaining red chilli, diced, the rice vinegar, soy sauce, lime juice and zest. Add the remaining ginger to the mixture. Chop half of the remaining coriander, and mix into the prawn mixture. Season.

3 Roll the prawn mixture into small 1cm balls.

4 After the stock has been cooking for 30 minutes, pass it through a fine sieve into a clean pan. Poach the prawn balls in the stock for 3–4 minutes, along with the whole prawns. When they are almost cooked, add the remaining chopped coriander and ladle into bowls.

NATIVE LOBSTER WITH LOBSTER MAYONNAISE AND SALADE MACHE

START MAKING THIS ABOUT A DAY IN ADVANCE, AS THE LONGER THE OIL IS ALLOWED TO INFUSE, THE BETTER THE FLAVOUR WILL BE.

CHALLENGING ~ SERVES 4 ~ PREP 45 MINS PLUS MARINATING TIME ~ COOK 30 MINS

2 x 675g native lobsters
2 carrots, peeled
1 small fennel bulb
2 banana shallots (or round shallots), peeled
700ml olive oil
3 garlic cloves, peeled and split
sea salt and black pepper
1 sprig each of fresh thyme and rosemary

6 star anise
12 black peppercorns
1 tsp fennel seeds
1 tbsp tomato paste
a small bunch each of fresh chervil and tarragon
2 egg yolks
juice of 1 lemon
500g mâche salad leaves

1 Kill the lobsters by piercing their heads with a sharp knife. Remove the claws and head. Blanch the lobster tail in boiling water for 30 seconds and the claws for 4 minutes. Refresh in iced water to stop the cooking.

2 Remove the insides from the head and discard. If there is any coral there, or eggs on the tail, keep this for the lobster oil. Cut the head into 1cm pieces with scissors. Take the meat out of the claws: tap a knife blade on the side of the claw to pierce it, then twist the knife to open the shell. Keep all the shells and cut them up as well. Cut the lobster tail in half lengthways and remove the intestinal tract. Place the tail halves on a cloth with the meat from the claws to dry briefly, then chill.

3 Cut the carrots, fennel and shallots into 5mm pieces. Keep them separate from each other.

4 For the lobster oil, heat up a pan on a medium heat then add 200ml of the olive oil. When hot, add all the lobster shells and sauté for 3–4 minutes. Add the carrot and cook for 3–4 minutes, then add the shallot, garlic and fennel, and cook for a further 4 minutes. Add 3g salt, the thyme, rosemary, anise, peppercorns and fennel seeds. If there were any eggs or coral, add

them now, as they will improve the flavour and the coral will turn the oil pinker. Cook for a further 3 minutes, then add the tomato paste. Add 400ml more olive oil 3 minutes after that. Bring to a simmer, then cook for 5 minutes. Pick the herb leaves off the stalks. Place the stalks into the oil, then put it all in a bowl and chill. Leave for 12 hours to marinate to improve the flavour.

5 To make the mayonnaise, pass the lobster oil through a fine sieve. Place the egg yolks in a bowl with half the lemon juice and a little salt and pepper, and whisk well. Add the lobster oil in a slow stream, saving 100ml for cooking the lobster. If the mayonnaise gets too thick, add a little water. Add the remaining chopped herbs, season again, then chill.

6 Season the lobster and claws. Heat a large sauté pan on a medium heat. Add the remaining 100ml lobster oil and tail pieces. Cook in the shell for 3–4 minutes, then add the claws and cook for a further 2 minutes.

7 Dress the salad leaves with a little mayonnaise, then place on the plates, with pieces of the lobster tail and claws by the side. Sprinkle a little lemon over the lobster, then spoon the pan oil and juices over the lobster.

ORGANIC MEAT IS NOW VIEWED AS THE BEST, GIVING BETTER FLAVOUR, AND IT IS REARED AND BRED MORE SUSTAINABLY. IF YOU CAN, ALWAYS TRY TO BUY ORGANIC PRODUCE.

One major tip I can give you is that any meat, whether beef, veal, pork, lamb or poultry, will cook better if it is left at room temperature for some time before cooking, particularly roasting. Leave any meat out of the fridge for at least an hour before roasting. This will allow the meat to cook more evenly because the whole piece will be at the same temperature, inside and out. As the meat will have warmed up before it starts to cook, it will also be more relaxed which means it should be much more tender once it has been rested after cooking.

It is also better to cook it at a lower temperature than you might think; this again will help to keep the meat tender. And if you don't rest your roasted meat after cooking and before carving it, the meat will be less juicy; if you carve it too soon you'll notice that your chopping board will be swimming in liquid – juices that should be retained in the meat.

MEAT

BEEF · CHICKEN · DUCK · HARE · LAMB · OXTAIL · PHEASANT · PORK · QUAIL · VEAL · VENISON

WHAT TO BUY

BEEF AND VEAL

Beef and veal are second to none in this country, but sadly a lot of our home-reared veal is exported. I struggle to buy English veal, and most of what I see is re-imported from France, Italy and Holland, which is madness and which I will not touch. They say the veal market here is non-existent, but I know we eat a lot of it. If we demanded more British veal, rather than imported, we would be supporting our farmers more. If possible, get your beef from a reputable butcher, rather than ready-wrapped and sitting in a plastic tray: the taste and cooking qualities will be vastly different from meat stored in an open tray. And never buy that horrible bright red meat, which is too fresh and probably won't have been hung properly.

CHICKEN

When you buy your chicken, please do not get those pre-packed, clingfilmed chickens. I don't believe they should be sold, as they have been pumped full of water, look so flabby, and taste of nothing. Those ready-to-roast birds are really a false imitation of what a chicken should look and taste like. The birds will have probably been kept inside in battery conditions, and are reared from egg to chicken in about 45 days. A proper organic chicken will have lived for 65 days' minimum. It's not difficult to guess which will be tastier.

DUCK

Duck is a very versatile bird in the kitchen, as you can use virtually every part of it – the legs, breast, the liver (as foie gras), and even the eggs. I buy foie gras ducks from France to cook, which supply me with everything I need. They also have a lot of fat: I cut this off, mince it and render it for my own duck fat, which is great.

GAME

Game, furred and feathered, is obviously very seasonal produce, and the season goes from the 12th August for grouse through to March for the last of the hares. Venison is available all year round now, but I only like to use it in the winter months, when it's best eaten anyway: you don't really want to see it on a menu in the middle of summer.

LAMB

The lamb that we use in the restaurant is organic and from Daylesford whom I know well. You should always try to buy lamb from an open counter as opposed to pre-packed meat. The lambing season here starts in about January or February, which means we have nice baby lambs after about 4 months. These have a pale flesh, which is slightly sweet. But most British lambs are slaughtered when slightly older, at about 9–12 months. These have a better, more mature flavour. If you want mutton, it will come from a lamb which is at least 2 years old. It has a very strong taste, and is mostly braised, as most of the animal will be quite tough.

PORK

For the restaurant I buy half pigs, mainly Gloucester Old Spot and Tamworth, which are organic, and we butcher them ourselves. These breeds have a better quality of fat, the flesh is more flavourful as a result, and the crackling is out of this world! They are also great for slow cooking, as the fat is rendered down and goes through the meat.

SLOW-ROASTED PORK SHOULDER

YOU'LL HAVE TO ALLOW QUITE A LONG TIME TO COOK THIS – SOME 20 HOURS!
WHEN YOU ARE COOKING SUCH LARGE PIECES OF MEAT, SLOW-ROASTING REALLY
IS THE BEST WAY OF COOKING.

EASY ~ SERVES 6–8 ~ PREP 10 MINS ~ COOK 20 HRS

1 shoulder of pork, boned out and tied
250ml olive oil
30g sea salt
400ml white wine
300ml white chicken stock (see page 155)
100ml double cream
1 tbsp Pommery mustard (moutarde de Meaux)

1 Preheat the oven to 200°C/400°F/Gas 6.

2 Rub the shoulder all over with the olive oil and then
the salt; place this in a roasting pan, then put into the
preheated oven for 20 minutes to crisp the skin. The
oven will be quite smoky, as all the fat will come out
at this high temperature. Then turn the oven down
to 90°C/195°F/the lowest gas, and cook for a further
20 hours. This will turn into the most delicious piece of
meat that you could eat, as it is basically self-basting
in its own juices. You can make it even better by
basting it with the fat every hour or so.

3 When the meat is cooked, remove it from the oven
and the pan. Place the pan on the heat, add the
white wine, and boil to reduce this by two-thirds. Add
the chicken stock and reduce by a third, then add
the cream and mustard. Bring this back to a simmer,
then reduce by a third again.

4 Slice the meat — it will virtually fall apart — and serve
with the sauce.

Note
The temperature is so low that the meat relaxes during
cooking rather than tensing up, thus all the fat melts
and it releases its juices slowly. You can serve this with
some choucroûte or braised onions and carrots (see
pages 49, 52 and 30).

BRAISED PORK BELLY WITH BABY SQUID

THIS IS A COMBINATION I HAVE USED ELSEWHERE AS AN ACCOMPANIMENT TO FISH (SEE PAGE 74), AND IT'S SUCCESSFUL BECAUSE THE RICHNESS OF THE PORK CONTRASTS WELL WITH THE CLEANNESS OF THE SQUID.

MEDIUM ~ SERVES 4 ~ PREP 20 MINS PLUS SETTING TIME ~ COOK 2½–3 HRS

1 x 1kg piece pork belly
4 large carrots, peeled and split in half
1 garlic bulb, split in half
4 celery sticks, cut in half
3 onions, peeled and quartered
5 banana (or round) shallots, peeled and halved
sea salt
12 black peppercorns
1 small bunch fresh thyme

3 bay leaves
500g baby squid
300ml brown chicken stock (see page 155)
1 sprig fresh rosemary, leaves picked and chopped
5g unsalted butter
150ml vegetable oil
100ml olive oil
100ml balsamic vinegar

1 Place the belly in a large pan of cold water to cover, and bring to the boil. Pour out this water, refresh the pork in cold water, then place the pork into a clean pan with some more clean cold water to cover. You have to do this because of all the impurities that come out of the pork; there will be quite a bit of scum in the water.

2 Then add all of the vegetables, 20g salt, the peppercorns, thyme and bay leaves, and bring to a slow simmer. Skim off any scum that comes to the surface. Put a weight on the pork to keep it submerged and cook at a gentle simmer for 2–2½ hours.

3 Prepare a tray big enough for the belly to lie flat in. Clingfilm the tray and then lift the belly out of the water and place it skin-side down on the tray. Make sure that there are no vegetables or peppercorns sticking to the skin, as these will make an indentation in the belly,

which is not what you want. Then clingfilm over the pork and tray, put a light weight on top to compress the pork belly, then place in the fridge. Leave this for at least 5 hours until the pork has set firm.

4 When it has set, take a sharp serrated knife, and cut the belly widthways into 1cm thick slices. You should get 2–3 nice slices per person.

5 Prepare the baby squid by separating the head from the body, the mouth parts from the tentacles, and removing the outer skin. Take out and discard the cartilage and insides from the body. Wash well in cold water. Dry the pieces well on a cloth and slice the body tubes into rings, and leave the tentacles whole.

6 Place the chicken stock on to heat with the rosemary, and boil to reduce by half. Stir in the butter and leave for later, warming up at the last minute.

7 Put a non-stick frying pan on a medium heat then
add the vegetable oil. When almost smoking, add
the pork belly slices. Be very careful, as they will spit
a little. Season them with salt and cook on each side
until golden brown, about 2 minutes on each side.

8 Remove the fat from the pork belly pan, and deglaze
with the balsamic vinegar. Boil until it reduces and
becomes sticky.

9 At the same time, place another frying pan on
to heat, add the olive oil and when smoking hot,
add the squid pieces. Cook for 30 seconds only.
Drain well.

10 Divide the pork belly slices between four plates, and
place the squid on top. Pour over the hot reduced
chicken stock.

Note

Pork belly is a very versatile and cheap cut of meat,
and for me is one of the most flavoursome because of
the fat to meat content. Start preparing the pork the
day before, as it has to cool and 'set' before you can
take it to the next stage.

PORK LOIN WITH ROAST APPLES AND CIDER

THIS IS MY TAKE ON THE TRADITIONAL COMBINATION OF PORK AND APPLES.

MEDIUM ~ SERVES 4 ~ PREP 20 MINS ~ COOK 1 HR

1 x 4-bone piece of pork loin, cleaned, about 1.2kg
150ml vegetable oil
sea salt and black pepper
3 large onions, peeled
3 sprigs fresh rosemary
60g unsalted butter

1 sprig fresh thyme
8 Granny Smith apples
15g caster sugar
juice of 1 lemon
250ml dry cider
300ml brown chicken stock (see page 155)

1 Make sure all the bones on the pork are scraped clean. Score the fat. Tie the piece of meat up with string and then leave to stand at room temperature for 30 minutes. Meanwhile, preheat the oven to 180°C/350°F/Gas 4.

2 Heat a large casserole dish or sauté pan on a medium heat, and add the oil. Season the pork all over, then sear it on all sides. Turn the heat down and cook the pork on the fat side so it renders down a bit.

3 Chop two of the onions roughly and place around the pork with two sprigs of the rosemary. When the pork skin starts to go crisp after about 15 minutes, place the dish into the oven for about 40 minutes. Stir the onions around in the oven now and again.

4 Meanwhile, slice the remaining onion very finely, and cook in a small pan on a medium heat with 15g of the butter and the thyme. Add seasoning to taste, and cook gently for 10–15 minutes until caramelised.

5 Meanwhile, prepare the apples. Cut five into quarters, removing the pips, cores and skin. Using a small knife, turn each of these quarters into barrel shapes.

6 Peel and core the rest of the apples then chop them plus all the peeled trimmings from the other apples.

Heat a pan on a medium heat, then add 20g of the butter, the chopped apple, half the sugar and a sprig of rosemary. Cover with a lid and sweat for 5–10 minutes, then add the lemon juice. Gently reduce the apple until thick, discard the rosemary, then place the apples in a blender to purée. Pass this through a fine sieve and leave to cool.

7 To roast the apple barrels, place a small ovenproof pan on a medium heat and add the last of the butter. Add the apples when it has melted and move them around the pan with the remaining rosemary to roast on all sides. Add the rest of the sugar and caramelise, then place the pan in the oven for the last 10 minutes of the pork's cooking. Move the apples around from time to time.

8 Place the cooked pork on a tray to rest. Pour the cider into the pan and boil to reduce by two-thirds. Add the stock and reduce again by half. Pass this through a fine sieve and add 1 tablespoon of apple purée to thicken it.

9 Heat the caramelised onion and apple purée separately. Place some onion on each plate with a dollop of purée on top. Put the roast apples in the middle of the plate. Slice the pork into four, and place a cutlet on each plate. Pour the sauce over.

PORK PATE

ONCE COOKED, THIS PATE WILL LAST OVER A WEEK IF WRAPPED AND CHILLED. IT IS VERY SIMPLE TO MAKE. SERVE WITH SOME HOME-MADE CHUTNEY — SUCH AS THE SHALLOT CHUTNEY ON PAGE 65 — AND SOME SOURDOUGH TOAST AND A LIGHTLY DRESSED SALAD.

EASY ~ SERVES 10–12 ~ PREP 10 MINS PLUS SETTING TIME ~ COOK 1½ HRS

500g pork belly
500g pork liver
400g thin smoked bacon rashers
vegetable oil for greasing
12g peeled and chopped garlic
250g shallots, peeled and finely chopped
250g onions, peeled and finely chopped
120g fresh white breadcrumbs
6 eggs, beaten
250g unsalted butter, melted

250ml Cognac
250ml port
8g fresh parsley leaves, chopped
8g fresh thyme leaves, chopped
1g freshly ground nutmeg
1g dried sage
250ml double cream
20g sea salt
2g freshly milled black pepper

1 Preheat the oven to 140°C/275°F/Gas 1. Lightly grease a 32 x 11 x 8cm terrine mould. Then take a roll of clingfilm and roll it out flat on the table, a little longer than the terrine. Cut it and then do this twice more so that you have 3 layers in all. Place this clingfilm inside the oiled terrine, smoothing over all the corners and sides so there are no air bubbles. Then line just the sides with the bacon, overlapping it slightly in the middle, allowing the rashers to overhang the long sides of the mould.

2 Mince the pork belly and the liver together, medium coarsely, then mix well with all the remaining ingredients.

3 Pack the mixture carefully into the bacon-lined mould, and fold over the overhanging bacon. Cover the top with foil and then place into a bain-marie, or a roasting tray half-filled with hot water. Bake in the preheated oven for about 1½ hours.

4 Remove the terrine from the oven and then take the terrine out of the tray. Place a flat piece of clingfilmed cardboard or wood, the same shape, on top of the terrine with a weight on top of that, to keep it flat whilst it is cooling. Leave in the fridge for 24 hours to firm up.

5 Cut into slices, and serve as suggested above.

PORK KNUCKLE WITH BRAISED VEGETABLES

THIS IS ONE OF THE SIMPLEST AND EASIEST WAYS OF COOKING YOUR MEAT ALONG WITH VEGETABLES, AND ALL IN ONE POT. IT'S ONE OF THOSE DISHES THAT YOU CAN LEAVE ALONE WITHOUT HAVING TO WATCH OVER IT, AND YOUR KITCHEN WILL FILL WITH THE MOST WONDERFUL SMELL OF BRAISED MEAT AND VEGETABLES.

EASY ~ SERVES 4 ~ PREP 15 MINS PLUS SOAKING TIME ~ COOK 2–2½ HRS

2 pork knuckles (or 1 knuckle if large)

6g sea salt

1 small bunch fresh thyme

14 black peppercorns

2 bay leaves

1 small bunch fresh parsley, leaves picked, and chopped (keep the stalks)

50g unsalted butter

60g plain flour

200ml double cream

Braised vegetables

1 small Savoy cabbage

600ml pork stock

1 saucisse morteau (smoked sausage)

4 medium carrots, peeled

4 medium onions, peeled close to the root

4 medium turnips, peeled

4 medium leeks, trimmed and washed

4 celery sticks, trimmed and cut in half

1 Soak the pork in cold water to cover for a day; this will clean it.

2 Place the pork into a clean pan of cold water and bring this up to a simmer. Tip out the water, and run the pork under the cold tap to cool. Place the pork into a clean pan of fresh cold water and bring to a simmer. Skim off any of the scum that comes to the surface, then add the salt, thyme, black peppercorns, bay leaves and parsley stalks. Keep this on a low simmer, as this stock will take about 2–2½ hours to cook.

3 To braise the vegetables, trim the outer leaves off the cabbage. Cut it into quarters, leaving as much of the stalk on as possible. Place the vegetables and sausage into the stock in a sensible order, as obviously they all take different times to cook. The sausage will take about 45 minutes, the cabbage about

40 minutes (be careful with the latter, as there is nothing worse than overcooked cabbage). The hard vegetables — the carrots, onions, turnips — will take about 30 minutes; the leeks and celery about 20 minutes. All the vegetables must be cooked to just soft and then removed. If you are not sure then stick a knife through the middle of the vegetable; if it's ready it will drop off the knife.

4 As the vegetables are cooked, remove them from the stock, and place on a tray (you will be reheating them later in the stock when everything is ready). Slice the carrots into lozenge shapes at an angle, about 5mm thick. Quarter the turnips, and cut the leeks in half. Peel the outer skin off the sausage, and slice it into 5mm rounds. Then arrange all the vegetables nicely in a roasting tray and pour some of the stock over them. When the meat is almost cooked, reheat them in a low oven or on top of the stove.

5 Put a medium pan on a low heat and melt the butter. Add the flour and stir in well using a wooden spoon. Cook for a couple of minutes, then start to add the hot stock slowly, stirring all the time. It will be very thick at first, but as you keep adding the stock, it will thin out. Bring it up to a slow simmer once it gets thinner, then add the cream and parsley and heat through.

6 Serve the pork in pieces, with a portion of the braised vegetables and some of the sauce. Boiled parsley potatoes would go well.

PIGS' CHEEKS WITH SHALLOT SAUCE

THE CHEEKS ARE PROBABLY THE TENDEREST PARTS OF THE PIG'S HEAD, ONCE THEY HAVE BEEN BRAISED. THE SPICES GIVE THEM LOTS OF FLAVOUR, AND THEY ARE SERVED WITH THEIR BRAISING LIQUOR. SERVE WITH BRAISED ONIONS AND MASHED POTATO (SEE PAGES 52 AND 66).

EASY ~ SERVES 4 ~ PREP 15 MINS PLUS SOAKING TIME ~ COOK 2½ HRS

8 pigs' cheeks, soaked in cold water for a day

2 carrots, peeled

2 celery sticks

1 large onion, peeled

2 banana (or round) shallots, peeled

100ml vegetable oil

45g unsalted butter

1 sprig fresh rosemary

2 sprigs fresh thyme

5 garlic cloves, peeled and split

2g sea salt

14 juniper berries

1 tsp fennel seeds

½ tsp cumin seeds

14 black peppercorns

6 star anise

2 bay leaves

1 tsp coriander seeds

1 x 25g piece fresh root ginger

4 whole plum tomatoes, roughly chopped

1 large tbsp tomato paste

600ml white chicken stock (see page 155)

100g shallots, peeled

1 Preheat the oven to 170°C/325°F/Gas 3.

2 Chop the carrots, celery, onion and banana shallots into 5mm cubes, and keep in separate piles.

3 Heat the vegetable oil and 30g of the butter together in a large casserole on a medium heat. When the butter has melted, add the carrots first and slowly caramelise. Add a sprig each of thyme and rosemary, and after 4–5 minutes, add the chopped celery. Carry on cooking, then after 3–4 minutes, add the onion, shallot, garlic and salt, and cook for a further 8 minutes. Add all the spices, the rosemary and half the thyme. Cook this for a further 2–3 minutes, then add the tomatoes and tomato paste. Cook this for another 2–3 minutes, then add the chicken stock.

4 Bring the casserole up to a simmer. Add the pigs' cheeks, and top up with water if need be. Check the seasoning. Cover the top with greaseproof paper, then place a lid on the casserole and bake in the preheated oven for 2–2½ hours, checking every now and again.

5 Take the pigs' cheeks from the oven, remove from the stock and keep warm. Pass the cooking liquor through a fine sieve into a pan, bring to a slow simmer, and reduce to about 400ml. Skim.

6 Cook the chopped shallot slowly in the remaining butter with the remaining sprig of thyme, but do not let it colour. Then add the reduced braising stock, replace the cheeks, and heat through briefly. Serve.

PORK RILLETTES

THIS TERRINE IS VERY TASTY AND, USING CHEAPER CUTS OF MEAT, MAKES A GREAT FILLING SNACK FOR AN INEXPENSIVE, EASY MEAL. IT WILL LAST FOR OVER A WEEK IF WRAPPED AND CHILLED IN THE FRIDGE. SERVE WITH TOASTED SOURDOUGH BREAD, AND A DRESSED MIXED LEAF SALAD.

EASY ~ SERVES 10 ~ PREP 25 MINS PLUS SETTING TIME ~ COOK 3½–4 HRS

800g pork belly
400g pork fat
400ml white wine
2g juniper berries, chopped
40g sea salt
4g freshly milled black pepper
2g dried thyme

1g ground ginger
1g freshly ground nutmeg
1g ground allspice
1g ground cloves
6 garlic cloves, peeled and split in half
12g fresh thyme leaves
3 bay leaves

1 Preheat the oven to 120°C/250°C/Gas ½.

2 Cut the meat and fat into short strips or 2–3cm cubes, and place in a large casserole with the rest of the ingredients. Mix really well. Cover with a lid, and cook in the low oven for about 3½–4 hours. By then the pork will be soft and surrounded by liquid fat.

3 Tip the contents of the casserole into a colander with a bowl underneath to catch all the fat. Pass the fat and liquid through a sieve into a deep bowl. Place this in the fridge for 20 minutes, so that the fat sets on top, and you can separate fat and liquid.

4 Mix the liquid into the pork meat, and shred the meat with a fork. Check the seasoning, then pack into a 32 x 11 x 8cm terrine mould. Melt the pork fat gently, and pour this on top of the meat. Leave to set for a day in the fridge.

5 Scoop the rillettes out on to plates, and serve with dressed salad and toast.

BEEF AND GINGER SALAD

THIS IS A THAI-INFLUENCED SALAD. IT HAS A LOT OF INGREDIENTS, BUT THE PREPARATION AND COOKING ARE VERY SIMPLE, AND IT CAN BE PUT TOGETHER IN MINUTES. THE TASTE IS GREAT, FRESH AND LIGHT.

EASY ~ SERVES 4 ~ PREP 10 MINS ~ COOK 5 MINS

4 x 225g sirloin steaks
50ml olive oil
sea salt and black pepper
1 red onion, peeled and thinly sliced
100g mixed salad leaves

Sauce
2 tbsp chopped bottled stem ginger and syrup
6g piece fresh root ginger, peeled and finely chopped
2 fresh red chillies, finely chopped
2 garlic cloves, peeled and very thinly sliced
1 small bunch fresh mint, leaves picked
1 small bunch fresh Thai basil (or regular basil)
2 tbsp soy sauce
1 tbsp oyster sauce
2½ tbsp lime juice
1 tbsp sesame seeds, toasted
1 tsp caster sugar
50ml sesame oil

1 Preheat the overhead grill or a stove-top ridged cast-iron grill.

2 For the sauce, grind together the gingers, the chilli, garlic and half the mint and basil. Mix in all the remaining sauce ingredients, including the rest of the whole herb leaves.

3 Brush the steaks with the olive oil and season with salt and pepper. Place under or on to the grill, and cook to medium rare, about 2 minutes on each side.

4 Remove the beef from the grill and put on a cutting board. Put the red onion on the grill while you are slicing the steak into thin slices.

5 Mix the meat, onion, salad leaves and sauce together in a large bowl and eat straight away.

BEEF STEW WITH LENTILS AND SHALLOTS

THIS BASIC BEEF STEW COULD BE ADAPTED, IF YOU DELETED THE LENTILS. FOR BOEUF BOURGUIGNON, ADD 8G PEELED AND SLICED GARLIC AND 160G SLICED BUTTON MUSHROOMS AT STAGE 5, ALONG WITH THE BACON, AND COOK FOR A LITTLE LONGER. SERVE THIS WITH SOME MASHED POTATO OR PARSNIP PUREE (SEE PAGES 46 AND 66).

EASY ~ SERVES 4 ~ PREP 15 MINS ~ COOK 2½ HRS

400g chuck steak, diced
1g sea salt
4–6 turns freshly milled black pepper
20g plain flour
200ml vegetable oil
25g unsalted butter

300g small round shallots, peeled
50g smoked bacon, cut into 1cm lardons
8g fresh thyme leaves
250ml red wine
350ml white chicken stock (see page 155)
30g Puy or black lentils, washed

1 Preheat the oven to 170°C/325°F/Gas 3.

2 Put the beef into a bowl, season with the salt and pepper, and then rub in the flour. Reserve any excess flour.

3 Heat a large casserole on a medium heat, add the oil, and when it's hot, add a proportion of the beef. Don't add it all at once as it could splash and burn. Seal the meat until golden brown all over, about 5 minutes. As you cook, remove the meat from the pan using a slotted spoon, and place on a clean plate or tray. Continue until all the meat is sealed.

4 Using the same casserole, turn the heat to low, then add the butter. When melted add the shallots, and cook for 2–3 minutes until golden brown. Remove from the pan and place with the beef, but don't mix them, keep them separate.

5 Add the bacon and thyme to the pan and brown for 2–3 minutes.

6 Place the beef back into the pan along with any remaining flour, and cook for a minute before adding the red wine. Boil to reduce the wine by half, then add the stock and turn the heat to full. Bring to a slow simmer for 3 minutes, and skim off any scum.

7 Cover the casserole, and cook in the preheated oven for 1 hour. Add the shallots to the beef, and cook for a further 15 minutes, then add the lentils and cook for a further 45 minutes.

8 Remove from the oven and enjoy. Serve with some roast vegetables.

MINCED BEEF AND ONION PIE

THE MINCED BEEF MIX MAKES 950G, MORE THAN YOU NEED FOR THE PIE, SO YOU COULD SAVE SOME FOR ANOTHER DISH. YOU CAN TURN THIS BASIC MEAT MIXTURE INTO SEVERAL THINGS: A PASTRY PIE AS HERE, OR PUT MASHED POTATO ON TOP FOR A COTTAGE PIE, OR SERVE AS IT IS AS A PASTA SAUCE (LIKE A TRADITIONAL BOLOGNESE).

EASY ~ SERVES 4 ~ PREP 20 MINS ~ COOK 30 MINS

500g minced beef
30g unsalted butter
250g onions, peeled and diced
a large pinch of dried thyme
2g caster sugar
4g salt

2g freshly milled black pepper
4 tbsp vegetable oil
8g plain flour
400ml white chicken stock (see page 155)
300g ready-made puff pastry
2 egg yolks, beaten with 1 tbsp water

1 Preheat the oven to 200°C/400°F/Gas 6. Have ready a 20cm pie tin.

2 Place a pan on a medium heat, add the butter, and when it has melted, add the diced onion, thyme, sugar, and half the salt and pepper. Cook on a medium heat for 12 minutes until the onion is golden brown and caramelised. Stir the onion well, as it can catch and burn on the pan.

3 While the onion is cooking you can start to cook the mince. Place a non-stick frying pan on a high heat and add the oil. When this is hot, slowly add the mince; don't add it all at once as it could splash. Don't move the mince at first, as it will cool the pan down. Wait for 2 minutes before you do. Add the rest of the salt and pepper and cook, stirring, until the mince is golden brown, about 4–5 minutes.

4 Pour the meat into a colander with a bowl underneath to catch any excess oil. Put the pan back on a low heat, and add the cooked onion

to deglaze the pan of all the meat flavour. Stir for a couple of minutes, then return the meat and mix them well together. Add the flour and cook for 1 minute, then add the stock a little at a time, stirring well. Once all the stock has been incorporated turn the heat up to full so the mince comes to a slow boil. Reduce the heat and simmer for 10–12 minutes. The meat is ready. For the pie you will need 500g of the beef filling.

5 Take the pastry and divide roughly in half (you need 160g for the base and 140g for the lid). Dust your work surface with flour, and roll out the two pieces — the base piece to 5mm thickness, and the lid a little thinner. Let these rest for about 30 minutes.

6 Put the base piece of pastry into the tin. Pour in the meat filling. Egg-wash the edges of the pastry, and then place the lid on top. Crimp to seal, and make a couple of little holes in the middle. Egg-wash the top of the pie, and then bake in the preheated oven for 30 minutes.

COTE DE BOEUF WITH SHALLOT AND THYME SAUCE

THESE RIBS OF BEEF ARE COOKED AT A LOWER TEMPERATURE THAN YOU MIGHT EXPECT. THE REASON FOR THIS IS THAT THE MEAT IS MORE RELAXED WHILST COOKING AND DOES NOT TENSE UP AS IT MIGHT IF BLASTED BY A HOT HEAT. SERVE WITH TRADITIONAL ACCOMPANIMENTS, BUT I PARTICULARLY LIKE IT WITH THE BIG CHIPS ON PAGE 158.

MEDIUM ~ SERVES 8 ~ PREP 5–10 MINS PLUS RESTING TIME ~ COOK ABOUT 2 HRS

1 x 4-bone beef rib, trimmed and tied
50ml vegetable oil
sea salt and black pepper

To serve
1 recipe red wine shallots and sauce (see page 158)
1 small bunch fresh thyme
1 recipe big chips (optional, see page 158)

1 Preheat the oven to 200°C/400°F/Gas 6.

2 Smear the beef in oil and then season it very well all over with sea salt and pepper. Place in a large roasting tray with a wire cooling rack in the bottom. This will help the meat cook more evenly in the oven, preventing the bottom of the beef being in direct contact with the metal tray and overcooking.

3 Place the beef into the preheated oven for 15 minutes. This seals and sears the meat on a high temperature. The oven may get quite smoky due to the fat dripping off the meat. Turn the oven down to 160°C/325°F/Gas 3, and cook the beef for around 1½–1¾ hours. The reason we cook at this low temperature is because the meat will be more relaxed.

4 Alternatively, you could seal the meat on the stove in a hot pan with oil which would be the less smoky option (which is sometimes preferred amongst chefs, as you are sealing the juices in straight away). Then, when you cook the beef in the oven, do so at a lower temperature (150°C/300°F/Gas 2), which will take approximately 1¾–2 hours.

5 A meat thermometer is a useful tool. If you want the beef medium-rare, it should be cooked to around 40–45°C/104–113°F, which is just above your own body temperature. (You could stick a needle or a carving fork into the middle of the joint and place it on your lower lip: it should be just a little warmer than your lip.) For medium, the meat should be around 60–65°C/140–149°F. Well-done should be above 90°C/194°F. You can turn the beef over halfway through cooking and then it will need to rest on the wire rack for at least 20 minutes before carving.

6 During the time the meat is cooking, braise the shallots (and make the chips if using). Add half the thyme when cooking the chopped shallot, the remainder when braising the whole shallots.

7 After passing the sauce through a sieve, bring the shallots up to a simmer in the sauce and reduce slightly until the sauce thickens. If using, place the chips in a tower on the plate. Carve the beef through the bone and place on to the shallots, then pour the sauce over.

BEEF FILLET WITH POLENTA, GRILLED FIELD MUSHROOMS

POLENTA IS A GREAT ACCOMPANIMENT TO FILLET STEAK, AS IT'S A GOOD SUBSTITUTE FOR A STARCH, AND IS PERFECT FOR MOPPING UP THE SAUCE. YOU COULD VARY THE POLENTA, ADDING CHOPPED FRESH ROSEMARY, USING WATER INSTEAD OF STOCK, OR ADDING LESS BUTTER. YOU COULD ALSO MAKE POLENTA STICKS (SEE PAGE 133).

EASY ~ SERVES 4 ~ PREP 10 MINS PLUS SETTING ~ COOK ABOUT 25 MINS

800g beef fillet, cut into 4 pieces
sea salt and black pepper
8 slices Parma ham
50ml vegetable oil
20g unsalted butter
4 large field mushrooms, brushed clean
100ml balsamic vinegar

Basic polenta
200ml white chicken stock (see page 155)
60g unsalted butter
100g fast-cook polenta
freshly grated nutmeg

1 Preheat the oven to 170°C/325°F/Gas 3.

2 To make the polenta, place the chicken stock on to simmer, with 1g sea salt and 5g of the butter. Add the polenta in a steady stream, stirring constantly with a wooden spoon; it will only take about 2 minutes to cook. Add the remaining butter and a little nutmeg, and tip the wet polenta out onto an oiled metal tray. Spread out with dampened fingers to a nice and flat thickness of about 2cm. Leave to cool for at least 30 minutes, then cut into 5–6cm squares.

3 Season the fillet steaks with 2g salt and 3–4 turns of freshly milled black pepper, then wrap the Parma ham around them and tie with string.

4 Place a grilling or frying pan on a medium heat with half the oil, add the steaks and cook them for 10–12 minutes, on all four sides, about 2–3 minutes on each side. Remove the steaks from the pan and keep warm in the low oven (120°C/250°F/Gas ½) while you cook the mushrooms and do the reduction.

5 Add the butter, the mushrooms and 1g sea salt to the pan, and cook until the mushrooms are golden, about 3–4 minutes. Then add the balsamic vinegar and reduce by half.

6 Meanwhile, heat the remaining oil in a small frying pan and fry the polenta until golden on each side (or you could grill it).

7 Place a square of polenta on each plate, then the beef on top and finally the mushrooms with the reduced vinegar.

BRAISED OXTAIL WITH CEPS, SALSIFY AND BEEF MARROWBONE

THIS IS A GREAT WINTER DISH, USING OXTAIL, WHICH PERHAPS CARRIES THE GREATEST BEEF FLAVOUR. IF YOU CAN'T GET HOLD OF SALSIFY, USE PARSNIPS INSTEAD, AND DRIED CEPS INSTEAD OF FRESH. REDUCE THE SAUCE WITH THE OXTAIL IN IT UNTIL STICKY, SO THE OXTAIL IS WELL COATED.

MEDIUM ~ SERVES 4 ~ PREP 15 MINS ~ COOK 2 HRS

4 large pieces oxtail
4 pieces beef marrowbone, 5cm long
sea salt and black pepper
plain flour
150ml vegetable oil
60g unsalted butter
30 button onions, peeled

100g smoked bacon, cut into lardons
500g fresh cep mushrooms, sliced lengthways
1 small bunch fresh thyme
1 bottle red wine
1 litre white chicken stock (see page 155)
10 salsify sticks

1 Preheat the oven to 170°C/325°F/Gas 3.

2 Season the oxtail and then lightly dust with flour. Place a large casserole on a medium heat, add the oil and then the pieces of oxtail. Turn the oxtail pieces on to all sides until they are golden brown all over. This should take no more than 10 minutes. Remove them from the pan and place on a tray.

3 Add 25g butter to the oil in the casserole, then add the peeled button onions and bacon lardons. Cook these for 4–5 minutes on a low to medium heat until nicely golden. Remove these onto the tray as well.

4 Add another 10g butter then, when the butter is almost golden, add the ceps, and turn the heat up a little so that they colour well. Season them a little then, when they are evenly coloured all over, return the onions and bacon to the pan. Stir, then add three-quarters of the thyme and 1 tablespoon of flour. Cook for a couple of minutes more, stirring, then pour in the red wine and 750ml of the chicken stock.

5 Place the oxtail back in the pan and bring up to a simmer, skimming off any scum. Cover, place into the preheated oven and braise for 2 hours.

6 Wash and peel the salsify, and then wash again. Cut it into 4–5cm batons. Place a sauté pan on a medium heat and add the rest of the butter. When this has melted, add the salsify, the remaining thyme and a little seasoning. Move this around the pan and after 10 minutes the batons should be golden brown. Add the rest of the chicken stock and carry on cooking on a medium heat for about 10 minutes. The stock will reduce slowly and glaze the salsify at the same time.

7 Place the marrowbones, sprinkled with a little sea salt, into the oven alongside the oxtail for the last 20 minutes of cooking.

8 Put a piece of oxtail at the front of each plate, with the sauce and bacon over it, and the glazed salsify on top. Put the bone marrow behind and eat out of the bone with a teaspoon.

BRAISED VEAL SHIN RAGOUT WITH PASTA AND CHERVIL

YOU WILL FIND THE RECIPE FOR FRESH HOME-MADE PASTA ON PAGE 132, BUT YOU COULD, OF COURSE, USE BOUGHT VERMICELLI. OR, IF YOU WANTED, YOU COULD JUST SERVE THE RAGOUT WITH SOME BABY GLAZED BUTTON ONIONS AND PARSNIP PUREE (SEE PAGE 46). YOU COULD EVEN SERVE THE RAGOUT IN A RAVIOLI (SEE PAGE 132).

CHALLENGING ~ SERVES 4 ~ PREP 30–45 MINS ~ COOK 2½ HRS

Veal shin ragoût

1 whole veal shin on the bone

sea salt and black pepper

4 carrots, peeled

3 onions, peeled

200ml vegetable oil

40g unsalted butter

1 garlic bulb, cut in half

a small bunch of fresh thyme

12 black peppercorns, crushed

4 plum tomatoes, quartered

2 tbsp tomato paste

1 litre white chicken stock (see page 155)

To serve

250g fresh pasta (see page 132)

olive oil

300ml chicken stock (see page 155)

100ml double cream

3 bunches fresh chervil, leaves picked

a squeeze of lemon

25g unsalted butter

1 Preheat the oven to 170°C/325°F/Gas 3.

2 To start the ragoût, season the veal with salt and pepper. Slice the carrots at an angle across the carrot into 1cm thick slices. Cut the onions in half, cutting down the onion as opposed to across. Cut each half into three pieces and then into four, so the onion pieces are more or less the same size as the carrot.

3 Heat a large casserole on a medium heat, then add the oil and 25g of the butter. When it has caramelised, add the seasoned veal shin and slowly colour all over until golden brown. Remove the meat from the casserole.

4 Add the carrots, garlic and thyme to the casserole and cook for 5–8 minutes until they start to colour. Add the onions, 6g salt and the peppercorns, and cook for a further 5–8 minutes so they are all caramelised. Add the tomatoes and cook for 3–4 minutes, then add the tomato paste and cook for 2 minutes. Add the stock and the veal shin, bring to a simmer, cover with a lid or foil, and cook in the preheated oven for 2 hours.

5 Once the veal shin is cooked, remove all the meat from the bone and flake the meat into small pieces. Pass the veal stock through a fine sieve, place in a pan and bring this up to a simmer. Skim and pass through a fine sieve into a clean pan. Simmer to reduce by two-thirds until it thickens.

6 Roll out your pasta until it is very thin (using the number 1 setting on a pasta machine), and then cut into 35cm-long pieces. Using the vermicelli cutter on the machine, put them through to get thin vermicelli.

7 Have a pan of boiling salted water ready with a little olive oil added, then place all the pasta into the water. Gently stir with a roasting fork so the pasta strands are nicely separated. Cook for just 1 minute and then drain and refresh in cold running water. Drizzle a little olive oil over the pasta and then cover with clingfilm until ready to heat through and serve.

8 Place the chicken stock on to boil with the cream. Chop three-quarters of the chervil, keeping the remainder for the garnish. Keep a tablespoon of the chopped chervil back for the pasta, and then drop the rest into the stock. Bring back to the boil and cook for just 30 seconds, then place into a blender and purée for 30 seconds. Pass this through a very fine sieve into a bowl set over ice. Leave to cool.

9 Reheat the pieces of veal in the veal sauce. Put 150ml water on to heat with the lemon juice and the butter. Bring this to a simmer then add the cooked pasta. Move this around the pan so that it reheats, then toss the pasta with the reserved chopped chervil, and season with salt and pepper. Reheat the chervil sauce, and add the remaining chervil leaves.

10 Place a portion of pasta in each bowl, and then the veal-pieces on top. Pour some of the thickened veal jus over, and then pour the chervil sauce around the pasta.

BLANQUETTE OF VEAL

THIS IS A VERY TRADITIONAL BLANQUETTE, VERY SIMPLE BUT VERY TASTY. IT IS EASY TO PUT TOGETHER, AND REQUIRES ONLY A SMALL AMOUNT OF WORK. SERVE WITH SOME BRAISED ROSCOFF ONIONS AND MASHED POTATO (SEE PAGES 52 AND 66).

EASY ~ SERVES 4 ~ PREP 20 MINS ~ COOK 1½ HRS

800g veal rump, trimmed

12 black peppercorns

a small bunch of fresh thyme

5 bay leaves

2g sea salt and black pepper

500ml white chicken stock (see page 155)

25g unsalted butter

2 onions, peeled and finely diced

30g plain flour

300ml white wine

300ml double cream

400g Paris or button mushrooms

24 button onions, peeled

4g fresh parsley, finely chopped

1 Preheat the oven to 180°C/325°F/Gas 3.

2 Cut the veal into 2.5–3cm cubes, giving roughly four pieces per portion. Place these into a pan of cold water and give them a light wash. Drain, then top up the pan with clean water. Add the peppercorns, half the thyme, 3 of the bay leaves and a little salt. Bring this to a simmer and then refresh in cold water. Then drain into a colander.

3 Put the stock on to heat in a medium pan. Place another medium pan on to heat, then add the butter. When it has just melted, add the diced onion and the rest of the thyme tied into a small bunch. Add a little salt, cover with the lid, and cook without colouring for 4–5 minutes.

4 Start to add the flour, stirring so that it does not stick, then start pouring in the white wine, little by little, stirring all the time, until all the wine has been added. Cook for 2 minutes.

5 Add the hot stock little by little, then add the cream and the remaining bay leaves, and bring to a slow simmer. Place a sheet of greaseproof paper over the casserole and a tight-fitting lid, then place in the preheated oven for 1½ hours. After 45 minutes of the cooking time, add the onions; after 1 hour add the mushrooms.

6 Add the chopped parsley just before serving.

BRAISED VEAL SHIN RAVIOLI WITH CARAMELISED ONION

THIS IS A VERY SIMPLE RAVIOLI, BUT VERY TASTY. YOU ONLY NEED TO USE A PROPORTION OF THE PASTA DOUGH I GIVE YOU HERE. KEEP THE REST IN THE FRIDGE FOR A DAY OR TWO, OR FREEZE.

CHALLENGING ~ SERVES 4 ~ PREP 30–45 MINS ~ COOK 2½ HRS

1 recipe veal shin ragout (see page 128), prepared to the end of stage 4
10g unsalted butter
a large pinch of chopped fresh rosemary leaves
olive oil
sea salt and pepper
4 braised Roscoff onions (see page 52)

Fresh pasta (makes 1.2kg)
50ml olive oil
9 eggs
1kg Italian 00 plain flour

1 To make the pasta, mix the oil and eggs together. Put the flour in a mixer bowl, turn on the power, then slowly pour on the egg and oil mix until the texture is like fine breadcrumbs. Add a couple of tablespoons of water at the end which, if you continue beating on a medium speed, will make it all come together to a dough.

2 Take the pasta out of the machine, and knead for 5 minutes. Roll into a ball, cut this into eight pieces, and individually wrap these in clingfilm. Leave to rest for about half an hour.

3 Taking one piece at a time, knead the pasta, and put through the pasta machine, rolling and folding, taking it from thick to thin. Roll and fold up, wrap in clingfilm again, and leave to rest before using.

4 When the veal shin is ready, remove it from the pot and place it on a tray. Take it off the bone and then it should naturally come apart along the muscle and sinew line into nice big pieces – you need four. Once this is done trim them up a little, removing any fat or cartilage, then place in the fridge to set.

5 Pass all the cooking liquor through a fine sieve and into a clean pan, bring to a slow simmer and skim off all the scum. Reduce this by two-thirds until it thickens up into a sauce. Then add the butter and rosemary.

6 For the ravioli here, you only need 100g of the pasta dough. Bring a large pan of simmering water to the boil with a little olive oil and some salt added. Roll your 100g pasta dough out to a thickness of 3mm, then cut into 10cm strips. From these cut 8 x 10cm squares.

7 Put four of the pasta squares on your work surface, and put a piece of meat on top. Flour your hands, and take the piece of pasta and meat in one hand, and place another square of pasta on top. Squeeze together, then pinch around the edges of the pasta to seal. Do this with all four ravioli, before placing each one into the simmering water for 2 minutes. Drain well.

8 Reheat the onions briefly in a little of the sauce. Put the onion at the top of the plate, the ravioli below, and then the sauce around.

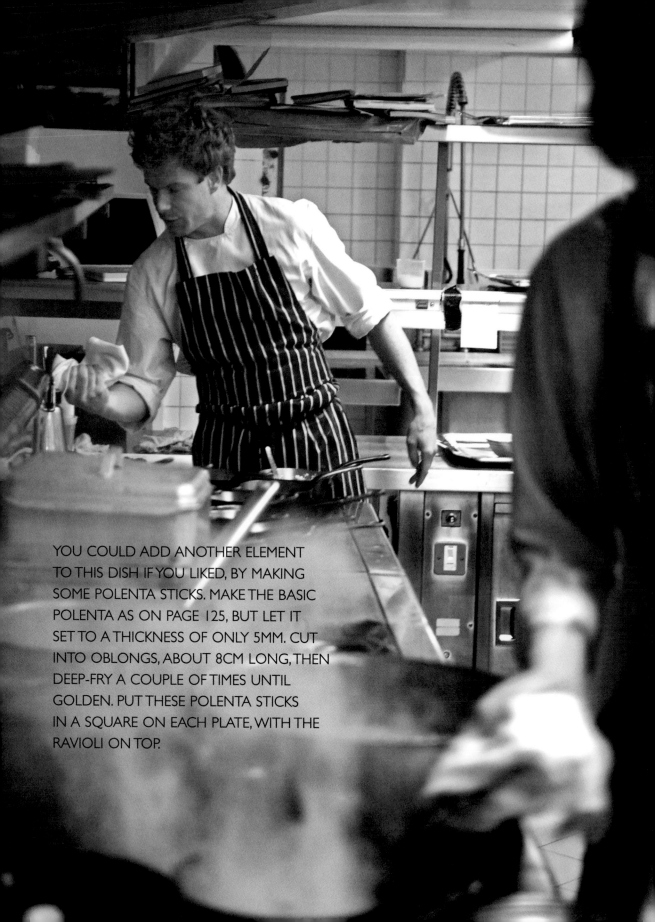

YOU COULD ADD ANOTHER ELEMENT
TO THIS DISH IF YOU LIKED, BY MAKING
SOME POLENTA STICKS. MAKE THE BASIC
POLENTA AS ON PAGE 125, BUT LET IT
SET TO A THICKNESS OF ONLY 5MM. CUT
INTO OBLONGS, ABOUT 8CM LONG, THEN
DEEP-FRY A COUPLE OF TIMES UNTIL
GOLDEN. PUT THESE POLENTA STICKS
IN A SQUARE ON EACH PLATE, WITH THE
RAVIOLI ON TOP.

RACK OF LAMB WITH FENNEL RISOTTO AND ROAST GARLIC

THIS DISH FOR SPRING OR SUMMER IS QUITE LIGHT, DESPITE INCLUDING A RISOTTO, BECAUSE THE RISOTTO IS MADE WITH A FENNEL STOCK AND FINISHED WITH CREME FRAICHE. FENNEL AND GARLIC ARE BOTH VERY GOOD FLAVOURS WITH LAMB.

CHALLENGING ~ SERVES 4 ~ PREP 25 MINS ~ COOK ABOUT 1 HR

2 x 6-bone racks of lamb, tied and trimmed

2 large fennel bulbs

45g unsalted butter

sea salt and black pepper

juice of ½ lemon

a pinch of caster sugar

100ml double cream

1 small bunch fresh tarragon

8 baby fennel bulbs with green tops

3 star anise

100ml olive oil

2 garlic bulbs, cut in half and roasted (see page 137), but without the honey

100g bronze fennel

Fennel risotto

fennel stock (see method)

50ml olive oil

2 shallots, peeled and finely diced

160g arborio risotto rice

200ml white wine

2 tbsp crème fraîche

35g Parmesan cheese, freshly grated

juice of ½ lemon

1 Preheat the oven to 170°C/325°F/Gas 3.

2 To make the fennel purée, chop the green tops off the large fennel bulbs, and put to one side. Chop the fennel finely, and put into a small pan over a low heat with 25g of the butter. Add a little salt, cover with a lid, and cook slowly without colouring for 5 minutes. Add the lemon juice, sugar and cream, and cook for a further 5 minutes with the lid on. Remove the lid, and slowly reduce for about 2–3 minutes. When it is nice and soft, add about half the tarragon, and purée in a blender until smooth. Cool straight away.

3 For the fennel stock for the risotto, chop just the green tops from the baby fennel, and place these tops into a pan with the large green fennel tops. Add most of

the remaining tarragon and the anise to the pan, and cover with 500ml water. Place this over a high heat and bring to a quick boil. Remove the anise, then purée in a blender and pass this through a fine sieve into a clean pan.

4 Cook the baby fennel itself in boiling salted water for 3–4 minutes, and then refresh in iced water.

5 Heat a sauté pan on a medium heat, and add the olive oil and remaining butter. When the butter has melted, put in the seasoned lamb racks. Slowly colour the lamb, fat-side down, for 6–8 minutes, then turn over and seal the rest of the meat. At the same time, add the baby fennel and cook to a golden colour on each side, then place onto a tray.

6 Place the lamb into the preheated oven for about 10–12 minutes. When it is cooked, leave to rest for 3–5 minutes before you reheat it.

7 During this time make the risotto. Heat the fennel stock. Place a pan over a medium heat, add the olive oil, then the finely chopped shallots. Cook these slowly without colouring for 2–3 minutes then add the rice. Cook, stirring with a wooden spoon, for 2 minutes, then add the white wine. Simmer to reduce this down until it has completely evaporated, and then start to add the hot fennel stock. Do this slowly, and little by little, stirring all the time, and not adding any more stock until the last addition has been absorbed by the rice. The risotto will take around 12 minutes to cook.

8 At the end of cooking, reheat the lamb, half garlic bulbs and baby fennel in the low oven. Gently heat the fennel purée in a small saucepan.

9 When the risotto is ready, add the crème fraîche and Parmesan, along with some salt, pepper, lemon juice and the remaining chopped tarragon.

10 Place a line of fennel purée on each plate, then a portion of risotto alongside. Cut the lamb through the cutlets, and place three cutlets onto each plate, with a half garlic bulb and two baby fennel bulbs. Sprinkle the bronze fennel on top.

FILLET OF LAMB WITH TOMATO CONFIT AND GOAT'S CHEESE TARTE FINE

GOAT'S CHEESE HAS AN ACIDITY THAT BALANCES WITH THE SWEETNESS OF THE TOMATO CONFIT AND THE TENDER LAMB. IT CUTS THE RICHNESS AS WELL.

MEDIUM ~ SERVES 4 ~ PREP 15 MINS AND 2½ HOURS FOR THE CONFIT ~ COOK ABOUT 1 HR

2 lamb fillets

3 sheets filo pastry

50g butter

4g thyme leaves

sea salt and black pepper

2 red onions, peeled and thinly sliced

100ml balsamic vinegar

200ml olive oil

100ml white chicken stock (see page 151)

juice of 1 lemon

6 plum tomatoes, skinned, seeded and finely diced

caster sugar

100g hard goat's cheese (such as Ossau Iraty), cut into big thin slices

10 leaves fresh basil, red is better, cut into fine julienne strips

150g fresh goat's curd or soft goat's cheese (such as Bouton d'Oc)

12 pieces tomato confit (see page 60), halved

1 Preheat the oven to 180°C/350°F/Gas 4.

2 Lay one of the sheets of filo on a sheet of baking paper on a baking sheet. Melt 10g of the butter, and have ready 2g of the thyme. Brush this first filo sheet with butter, and sprinkle with a few of the thyme leaves. Lay the second and third sheets of filo on top, buttering and sprinkling with thyme in the same way. Season the top layer with salt and pepper, and then put another piece of greaseproof and a baking sheet on top. Bake in the preheated oven for 10 minutes until golden brown. Remove from the oven, but keep on the baking sheet. Cut into four pieces. Reduce the oven temperature to 170°C/325°F/Gas 3.

3 Place a small pan on a medium heat and melt 20g of the butter. Add the sliced onions, a little salt and the remaining thyme. Cook this for about 10 minutes until it is just starting to colour and go soft. Add the balsamic vinegar, and simmer gently to reduce this down until it has evaporated. Leave to cool.

4 Heat a sauté pan on a medium heat, and add 100ml of the olive oil and the remaining butter. Season the lamb, add to the sauté pan, and cook for 3–4 minutes on each side until sealed. Place into the preheated oven for another 3–4 minutes, then remove from the oven and leave to rest for 2 minutes on a wire rack.

5 Meanwhile, make the tomato sauce. Place the remaining oil in a pan with the stock, lemon juice, tomato dice, a large pinch of sugar and a little salt. Bring to a simmer, and cook for a couple of minutes.

6 Now spread the red onion onto the filo pieces plus half the tomato confit. Put the sliced hard goat's cheese on top and place in the oven for 2–3 minutes.

7 Reheat the lamb in the low oven. Add the basil to the tomato sauce and place a spoonful in the middle of each plate, with the remaining tomato confit. Spoon the goat's curd in little pieces on to the tomato sauce, and arrange the tart to the side. Slice the lamb fillets lengthways, and place on each portion of sauce.

BRAISED LAMB SHANKS WITH PEARL BARLEY AND HONEY-ROAST GARLIC

EVERYTHING IN THIS DISH IS COOKED IN THE SAME POT, AND THE PEARL BARLEY TAKES ON THE FLAVOUR FROM THE MEAT BRAISING JUICES. SERVE WITH ROAST VEGETABLES AND MASHED POTATO. THE ROAST GARLIC HERE CAN BE SERVED WITH MANY OTHER DISHES,

MEDIUM ~ SERVES 4 ~ PREP 20 MINS ~ COOK 3 HRS

4 lamb shanks
sea salt and black pepper
150ml vegetable oil
6 large carrots, peeled
5 banana shallots, peeled
4 onions, peeled
25g unsalted butter
8 garlic cloves, peeled and split in half
2g fresh thyme leaves
20g tomato paste
20g plain flour

1 litre white chicken stock (see page 155)
6 plum tomatoes, quartered
60g pearl barley

Honey roast garlic

3 whole garlic bulbs, split in half
100ml olive oil
20g unsalted butter
1 small sprig fresh thyme
40g clear honey

1 Preheat the oven to 170°C/325°F/Gas 3.

2 Season the lamb with salt and pepper. Place a large casserole on a medium heat, add the vegetable oil and then the lamb. Colour the lamb all over until golden brown, about 8–10 minutes. Remove from the casserole.

3 During this time cut the carrots, shallots and onions into 2.5cm pieces, but keep them separate. Add 25g of the butter to the oil in the casserole, and when it melts, add the carrot. Start to colour this up, then after 5 minutes add the split garlic cloves and thyme. Keep colouring these and then after a few more minutes add the onion, shallot, 4g sea salt and 4–6 turns of freshly milled black pepper.

4 After another 5–8 minutes, when they are all coloured, turn the heat down and add the tomato paste. Cook

for a further 2 minutes, then add the flour, and cook for 2 more minutes. Add the stock and chopped tomato, bring this to a simmer, then skim off the scum.

5 Add the pearl barley and lamb to the casserole. Cover with a lid and cook in the oven for 2½ hours.

6 While this is cooking you can then make your honey roast garlic. Place a small sauté pan on a very low heat. Add the olive oil and butter and when the butter has just melted, add the garlic, cut-side down, with the thyme. Add a little salt and then cook very slowly until the garlic starts to colour. After 15 minutes, add the honey, then continue cooking until the garlic is soft, about another 15–20 minutes.

7 When the lamb is cooked, serve a shank on each plate, with some of the pearl barley and vegetables, and a half garlic bulb.

SLOW-ROAST SHOULDER OF LAMB WITH ONIONS AND THYME, BALSAMIC VINEGAR

THIS IS ONE OF THOSE DISHES THAT DOES NOT NEED ANY ATTENTION AT ALL, SO YOU CAN FORGET ABOUT IT WHILE YOU ATTEND TO SOMETHING ELSE.

EASY ~ SERVES 8 ~ PREP 24 HRS IF MARINATING THE LAMB ~ COOK 6–7 HRS

1 shoulder of lamb, about 2.5kg in weight

150ml olive oil

1 bunch fresh thyme

2 garlic bulbs, peeled, plus extra sliced cloves if marinating

sea salt and black pepper

8 medium onions, peeled

250ml balsamic vinegar

1 If you like, you can marinate the lamb for a day in the olive oil with 6–8 sprigs thyme and some extra thinly sliced garlic. Turn it occasionally. Before you cook the lamb leave it out of the fridge for a good hour or two, so that the meat is at room temperature.

2 Preheat the oven to 180°C/350°F/Gas 4.

3 If you have marinated the lamb, remove the thyme and garlic, then season with 2g salt and 4–6 turns of freshly milled black pepper. If not, rub the olive oil into the meat, and then season with the salt and pepper. Place the meat in a large casserole with the whole peeled onions; the latter can be drizzled with olive oil and seasoned as well. Place a little olive oil in the bottom of the pan, then place the casserole into the preheated oven for 15–20 minutes until the lamb and onions have coloured.

4 Remove the casserole from the oven, then add about 8 sprigs thyme along with the garlic cloves. Reduce the oven temperature to 110°C/225°F/Gas ¼, and return the meat to the oven. Cook for 5 hours with the lid on.

5 Add the balsamic vinegar, remove the lid, and continue to cook for a further 1 hour.

6 Place the casserole on to a low heat to reduce any excess liquid. Baste the lamb with this during the reducing, along with the onions. Just be careful that they don't stick or burn.

7 Serve the soft meat cut in pieces with the onions, some of the jus, a few cloves of garlic, and some mashed potato (see page 66).

Note

Depending on when you are going to be eating this dish, whether at lunch or dinner, you want to put it into the oven a 'meal' before: so for lunch, you want to put it into the oven at 8am, and for the evening you would put it in at around 2pm. It will take between 6 and 7 hours to cook.

ROAST LEG OF LAMB STUDDED WITH GARLIC AND ROSEMARY

THIS IS A GREAT SUNDAY ROAST AND IS DELICIOUS WITH ALL THE USUAL TRIMMINGS, AND ROAST ROOT VEGETABLES (PARSNIPS, CARROTS, SWEDE). THE MEAT WILL TAKE ON THE FLAVOUR OF THE GARLIC AND ROSEMARY. IF YOU LIKE, YOU CAN PLACE THESE INTO THE MEAT THE DAY BEFORE, AS THEY WILL GIVE THE MEAT A LOT MORE FLAVOUR.

EASY ~ SERVES 8 ~ PREP 30 MINS ~ COOK 3 HRS

1 leg of lamb, about 3kg in weight, bone in
2 garlic bulbs, peeled
1 small bunch fresh rosemary
200ml olive oil
sea salt and black pepper

5 medium carrots, peeled
3 medium onions, peeled
500ml white chicken stock (see page 155)
1 tsp cornflour

1 Using a sharp knife, make about 15–20 small incisions all over the leg of lamb. Cut about 10 of the garlic cloves in half and insert these slivers into the small holes in the leg. Break the rosemary into little pieces to go into the same holes as the garlic. Then cover the lamb with half the olive oil and sprinkle with 2g salt. Place on a wire rack over a roasting tray, then leave at room temperature for about an hour before roasting.

2 Preheat the oven to 180°C/350°F/Gas 4.

3 Cut the carrots in half lengthways and then into 2.5cm pieces. Cut the onions in half, and each half into six pieces. Place these in the bottom of the roasting tray with the rest of the olive oil, garlic and rosemary leaves.

4 Place the lamb leg into the preheated oven for 10–15 minutes to brown the meat, then turn the oven down to 170°C/325°F/Gas 3. This will also help to keep the meat tender, as you are not roasting it so fiercely. Roast for about 1½ hours, turning the vegetables around occasionally so that they colour evenly.

5 The best way to tell whether the meat is cooked is by inserting a roasting fork (or a needle) into the centre of the meat, and then lightly placing it on your upper lip. It should be a bit hotter than your own body temperature – 37°C – so for medium rare, cook the lamb to 55°C. Medium would be around 65°C. If you want to cook the lamb all the way through until it's well done, it will need about 2½ hours.

6 When the meat is ready, remove from the oven, and leave the lamb to rest on a plate for 10–15 minutes, while you make the gravy and prepare and cook your other vegetables.

7 Place the roasting tray on top of the stove, add the stock, bring to a simmer and season with salt and pepper. Place the cornflour into a little bowl, mix in a tablespoon of cold water, then whisk this into the gravy. Simmer for a few minutes, then pass this through a fine sieve into a clean pan. Press the vegetables through really well for maximum flavour. If there is any juice from the lamb, add it to the sauce. Reheat to serve.

8 Carve the lamb, and serve with the sauce and your chosen vegetables.

LAMB MINCE PIE WITH ROOT VEGETABLES

THE LAMB MINCE MIX WILL MAKE 1KG, SO YOU COULD MAKE TWO PIES FROM THIS AND FREEZE ONE TO BE USED AT A LATER DATE. YOU COULD FREEZE HALF THE MINCE, AND USE THE REMAINDER WITH MASH ON TOP TO MAKE A TRADITIONAL SHEPHERD'S PIE OR IT WOULD BE GOOD AS A PASTY FILLING.

EASY ~ SERVES 4 ~ PREP 20 MINS ~ COOK 30 MINS

300g shortcrust pastry (see page 23)
2 egg yolks, mixed with 1 tbsp cold water

Filling
500g minced lamb
4 tbsp vegetable oil
sea salt and black pepper
a good pinch of dried thyme

100g each of potatoes, carrots, swede and parsnips, peeled and diced
20g unsalted butter
200g onion, peeled and finely diced
4g peeled and chopped garlic
8g plain flour
600ml brown chicken stock (see page 155)

1 Place a large non-stick frying pan on a high heat, and add the oil. When hot, slowly add the mince, but not all at once as it could splash. Add 3g salt, the dried thyme and 2g freshly milled black pepper, and cook until golden brown, about 4–5 minutes. The mince will spit, so be careful. Don't move the mince at first, as it will cool the pan down. Wait for 2 minutes before you do. Stir to brown on all sides. Turn the heat off and pour the meat into a colander with a bowl underneath to catch any excess oil.

2 Return the oil to the frying pan, then turn the heat up to medium. Add the diced potato, and cook for 3 minutes, then add the rest of the vegetables, apart from the onion, along with some more salt and pepper. Cook for 5 minutes until nearly golden. Stir the vegetables now and again so they don't burn or catch on the pan. Turn the heat off and drain the vegetables in the colander as above. Mix with the mince.

3 Turn the heat up to medium, and return any oil to the pan along with the butter. When it has melted, add the onion and cook slowly for 3–4 minutes, then add the garlic. At this point you stir in the mince and vegetables.

4 Add the flour and cook for a minute, then add the stock a little at a time, stirring. Turn the heat up, bring to a boil then simmer for 10 minutes, stirring now and again, then chill.

5 Meanwhile, preheat the oven to 200°C/400°F/Gas 6. Grease and flour a 20cm pie tin.

6 Roll out the pastry and line the tin, fill with the filling and top with the pastry lid. Bake the pie as described on page 122.

BRAISED MIDDLE NECK OF LAMB

IF YOU FANCY A WARMING WINTER'S STEW, THIS RECIPE IS PERFECT. MIDDLE NECK OF LAMB IS SUCH A LOVELY PIECE OF MEAT, WHICH IS SO MOIST AND TENDER AFTER IT HAS BEEN BRAISED. IT IS BEST COOKED ON THE BONE AND THEN SERVED EITHER ON OR OFF THE BONE.

EASY ~ SERVES 4 ~ PREP 15 MINS ~ COOK 2 HRS

4 lamb neck fillets off the bone or 2 whole middle necks of lamb on the bone

150ml vegetable oil

sea salt and black pepper

25g unsalted butter

6 carrots, peeled and cut into 2cm dice

2 garlic bulbs, split in half

1 small bunch fresh thyme

3 onions, peeled and cut into 2cm dice

25g tomato paste

8 plum tomatoes, skinned, seeded and diced

1 litre white chicken stock (see page 155)

50g pearl barley

1 Preheat the oven to 170°C/325°F/Gas 3.

2 Use a large casserole big enough to take all of the lamb, and heat the oil over a medium heat. Season the lamb with salt and pepper and add to the oil. Fry to colour all over, until a dark golden brown colour, about 6–10 minutes. Remove the lamb from the casserole, and keep to one side.

3 Add the butter to the oil in the casserole, reduce the heat and cook the carrots for 4–5 minutes with the garlic and thyme. Add the onions, with about 2g salt, and cook for another 4–5 minutes. When everything is nicely caramelised, add the tomato paste and fresh tomato, and cook for another 2–3 minutes.

4 Add the chicken stock and pearl barley, and bring this up to a simmer. Skim off all the scum, and then add the lamb. Bring this back to a simmer, cover with a lid and place into the preheated oven for about 1½–2 hours.

5 When the lamb is cooked, it should be tender and starting to come away from the bone. Serve straight away with some mashed potato and green or runner beans.

ROAST CHICKEN WITH PARSLEY PASTA

THIS MAY SEEM A LABOUR-INTENSIVE WAY OF ROASTING A CHICKEN, BUT THE LEGS DO TAKE LONGER TO COOK TO TENDER, WHICH IS WHY THEY ARE SEPARATED FROM THE BREASTS, WHICH CAN TEND TO DRY OUT.

MEDIUM ~ SERVES 4–6 ~ PREP 15 MINS PLUS SETTING AND CHILLING TIME ~ COOK 1½ HRS

1 chicken, about 1–1.2kg in weight

olive oil

sea salt and black pepper

140g de cecco ziti 0.18 (long macaroni)

a large bunch of fresh flat-leaf parsley

30g unsalted butter

15g plain flour

250ml milk, warmed

20g Parmesan cheese, freshly grated, plus extra

400ml brown chicken stock (see page 155)

cornflour

small sprig of thyme

1 round English lettuce

1 Remove the legs and wings from the chicken. Chop each wing into four and separate the drumsticks from the thighs. Leave the breasts on the bone.

2 Boil a large pan of water, add 1 tablespoon of olive oil and salt, and boil the pasta until tender, about 10–12 minutes. Grease a 30 x 20cm tray, non-stick ideally, with oil on the under-side. Drain the pasta and, while it is still hot, arrange it on the underside of the tray, making sure they are pushed together and in one layer (the starch will make them stick together). Chill.

3 Pick off two-thirds of the parsley leaves, wash and put in a small pan of boiling salted water. Cook until soft, about 3–4 minutes, then drain. Place in a blender with a little of the cooking liquid and purée until smooth. Pass through a fine sieve and chill.

4 Melt 15g of butter in a small pan, add the flour and cook slowly, stirring. Slowly add the milk, stirring all the time. Bring to a slow simmer, then add the cheese and leave to cool a little. Stir in the parsley purée and season. Spread this over the pasta with a palette knife and chill again. While the chicken is roasting, cut the pasta into rectangles and leave at room temperature.

5 Preheat the oven to 200°C/400°F/Gas 6.

6 Season all the chicken pieces. Heat a pan with a little olive oil then add the leg pieces, wings and breast on the bone, and cook a few minutes until golden in colour. Remove from the pan and place the legs in a roasting tray. Roast in the preheated oven for 15 minutes, then add the breast piece, and roast for a further 45–55 minutes.

7 When the chicken is ready, leave it to rest on a cooling wire for 5 minutes, while you grill the pasta under a hot grill until golden. Put the chicken wings back in the roasting tray, add the stock and thyme and bring to a simmer. Reduce by two-thirds and add a little cornflour to thicken.

8 Wilt the lettuce leaves in a saucepan in a little water with salt and half the remaining butter. Pass the sauce through a fine sieve and add the rest of the butter.

9 Divide the pasta between four plates. Take the chicken breasts off the bone and slice widthways, then place on top of the pasta with some of the leg meat. Place the lettuce around and pour on some sauce.

ROAST CHICKEN AND PARSNIP SOUP

YOU CAN MAKE THIS SOUP FROM SCRATCH USING FRESH INGREDIENTS, OR YOU CAN MAKE IT WITH LEFTOVER ROAST CHICKEN AND PARSNIPS. IT'S A LOVELY SOUP TO EAT, AND IS A COMPLETE MEAL IN ITSELF IF YOU HAVE A GOOD BOWLFUL WITH SOME TOAST OR BREAD.

EASY ~ SERVES 6 ~ PREP 10 MINS ~ COOK 35 MINS

1 boneless chicken breast, skinned

450g boned and skinned chicken leg meat, cut into 1cm dice

50ml olive oil

2g fresh thyme leaves

sea salt and black pepper

100g unsalted butter

700g parsnips, peeled and chopped into 1cm pieces, stalks discarded

2 tbsp lemon juice

90g clear honey

100ml double cream

2 litres white chicken stock (see page 155)

1 Preheat the oven to 170°C/325°F/Gas 3.

2 Smear the chicken breast with olive oil and thyme, and season with a little salt and pepper. Place on a tray and bake in the preheated oven for 15 minutes. Remove and leave to cool. Dice into 5mm pieces, and set aside.

3 Warm a pan on a low heat and add the butter. When melted, add the parsnips and 18g sea salt and cook on a low heat, covered, for 5 minutes so the parsnips sweat in the pan, stirring now and again.

4 Add the diced chicken leg meat (not the breast), and cook for a further 5 minutes on the same heat. Stir now and again so that the parsnip and chicken don't colour. Add the lemon juice and honey, cream and stock. Turn the heat up and bring to the boil, then turn down to a simmer and cook for 5 minutes.

5 Turn the heat off and ladle the soup into the blender jug to half full. Purée the soup for 2–3 minutes until you get a very smooth texture. Do the same with the remainder of the soup.

6 Place back into a pan, add the diced chicken breast, and reheat gently to serve.

CHICKEN AND MUSHROOM PIE WITH TARRAGON

YOU CAN EAT THIS PIE HOT OR COLD. IT MAKES A GOOD LIGHT LUNCH WITH A DRESSED SALAD, OR YOU COULD TURN IT INTO A PROPER MAIN COURSE, SERVED WITH VEGETABLES. YOU CAN FREEZE THE PIE IF YOU HAVE TOO MUCH, OR IF YOU WISH TO MAKE A COUPLE AT A TIME.

EASY ~ SERVES 6 ~ PREP 20 MINS ~ COOK 1½ HRS

300g shortcrust pastry (see page 23) or bought puff pastry
2 egg yolks, mixed with 1 tbsp cold water

Filling
8 chicken drumsticks
3 sprigs fresh thyme
sea salt and black pepper
25g unsalted butter
200g onions, peeled and diced
200g button or field mushrooms, brushed and sliced
8g plain flour
200ml double cream
1 tbsp chopped fresh tarragon

1 Place the chicken drumsticks into a pan with the thyme and 2g salt. Just cover with cold water, then place on a high heat, bring to the boil, turn down the heat to a simmer and skim off all the scum. Simmer for 45 minutes then remove the drumsticks and leave to cool for 10 minutes. Pick off all the meat from the bone, and place any skin and bones back into the chicken stock. Cook for a further 15 minutes then leave to cool. Pass this through a fine sieve and then keep 200ml for the recipe (freeze the rest).

2 Melt the butter in a medium pan on a low heat, then add the onion, 1g each of salt and pepper, and cook slowly, covered, for 4 minutes, so the onions sweat and don't colour. Stir now and again. Add the mushrooms and cook slowly for 4 minutes, still with the lid on.

3 Remove the lid and add the flour. Cook for 1 minute, then add the chicken stock gradually, stirring well. Add the double cream, and boil to reduce this liquid by half.

4 Add the chicken and tarragon, cook for 2 minutes then remove from the heat and cool.

5 Preheat the oven to 200°C/400°F/Gas 6, and grease and flour a 20cm pie tin.

6 Line the tin with pastry, fill with the filling, top with the pastry lid. Crimp to seal the edges, and make a couple of little holes in the middle. Egg-wash the pastry, then bake in the pre-heated oven for 30 minutes.

GREEN CHICKEN CURRY

THIS IS THE SORT OF THING I COOK AT WEEKENDS, AND IT'S EASY (AS LONG AS YOU CAN GET THE INGREDIENTS!). THE GREEN CURRY PASTE MAKES MUCH MORE THAN YOU NEED FOR THE RECIPE, BUT IT FREEZES WELL. SERVE THE CURRY WITH FRAGRANT THAI RICE, AND ADD PLENTY OF FRESH CORIANDER TO MAKE THE DISH FRESH AND LIGHT.

EASY ~ SERVES 4 ~ PREP 20 MINS ~ COOK 1¼ HRS

8 chicken thighs

1 small bunch fresh coriander, leaves picked (keep and separate the roots and stalks)

15g fresh root ginger, peeled and finely chopped

8 kaffir lime leaves, crushed

4 lemongrass stalks, bashed and finely sliced

2 small nuggets fresh galangal, peeled and thinly sliced

1 tbsp sesame oil

juice of 2 limes

200ml white chicken stock (see page 155)

250ml coconut milk

1 tsp fish sauce

Green curry paste (makes 280g, freeze the remainder)

2g cumin seeds

1g coriander seeds

50g lemongrass stalks, bashed and sliced

90g Thai (small) shallots, peeled and chopped

40g green chillies, sliced

10g garlic cloves, peeled and sliced

15g fresh root ginger, peeled and chopped

40g fresh coriander roots (see left)

40ml lime juice

1 To make the green curry paste, dry-roast the cumin and coriander seeds in a pan on a medium heat for a minute or two. Place all the paste ingredients, including the toasted seeds, in a coffee or spice grinder and grind to a fine paste, or use a pestle and mortar.

2 Place the chicken thighs in a pan, and cover with cold water. Bring to the boil, then turn the heat down to a simmer and skim off any scum. Add the coriander stalks, ginger, half the lime leaves, lemongrass and galangal, then cook for 1 hour.

3 Remove the chicken from the pan with a slotted spoon and place on a tray. Leave to cool for a

minute, and then remove the meat from the bones. Measure out 200ml of the chicken stock (you can put the rest of the stock into the freezer and use it another time).

4 Place a medium pan on a low heat, add the sesame oil and cook 80g of the curry paste for 1 minute on a low heat. Add the remaining lime leaves, lemongrass and galangal, and the lime juice, and cook to reduce this down until virtually evaporated.

5 Add the chicken stock, coconut milk and fish sauce. Bring this to a simmer and cook for 2 minutes, then add the chicken, and cook for another minute. Sprinkle with the coriander leaves and serve.

CHICKEN WITH WHITE WINE AND MUSHROOMS

ANOTHER BRAISED CHICKEN RECIPE, BUT MUCH MORE TRADITIONALLY FRENCH. SERVE IT WITH STEAMED RICE OR MASHED POTATO (SEE PAGE 66). THIS CAN ALSO BE FROZEN IF YOU WANT TO MAKE MORE THAN FOUR PORTIONS.

EASY ~ SERVES 4 ~ PREP 10 MINS ~ COOK 1¼ HRS

8 chicken drumsticks

sea salt and black pepper

4 sprigs fresh thyme

25g unsalted butter

2 onions, peeled and finely diced

160g button, black-cap or field mushrooms, brushed and sliced

4g peeled and chopped garlic

30g plain flour

200ml white wine

4 tbsp double cream

2g fresh parsley, chopped

1 Place the chicken in a suitable pan and cover with 1.2 litres cold water. Add 2g salt and half the thyme, and turn the heat up to full. Bring to the boil, skim off the scum using a ladle, then turn the heat down to a simmer and cook for 45 minutes.

2 While this is cooking, melt the butter in a separate pan on a low heat. Add the onion, another 2g salt, 4–6 turns freshly milled black pepper and the remaining thyme, and cook for 2–3 minutes without colouring. Add the sliced mushrooms and garlic, and cook for a further couple of minutes without colouring.

3 Add the flour to the onion and mushroom, and cook on a low heat for 2 minutes, then add the white wine. Boil to reduce by half, then add 300ml of the stock that the chicken legs were cooked in and the double cream. Bring this to a simmer, then add the chicken and cook for a further 15 minutes.

4 Add the chopped parsley and serve.

COQ AU VIN

THIS IS A VERY TRADITIONAL FRENCH CHICKEN DISH. IT IS A GREAT COMFORT DISH, AND IS VERY SIMPLE TO PREPARE AND COOK. SERVE IT WITH SOME ROAST OR BRAISED VEGETABLES AND SOME BOILED POTATOES OR MASH (SEE PAGE 66).

EASY ~ SERVES 4 ~ PREP 10 MINS ~ COOK ABOUT 1 HR

8 chicken drumsticks
sea salt and black pepper
25g plain flour
150ml vegetable oil
20g unsalted butter
200g shallots, peeled and chopped

200g button, black-cap or field mushrooms, brushed and sliced
2g fresh thyme leaves
300ml red wine
300ml white chicken stock (see page 155)
4g fresh parsley, chopped

1 Preheat the oven to 180°C/350°F/Gas 4.

2 Place the chicken in a large bowl, season with 6g salt and 4–6 turns freshly milled black pepper, then rub the flour into the chicken. Place the chicken on a clean tray, and keep any excess flour.

3 Heat a casserole on a medium heat, and add the oil. When hot, place the chicken in carefully so as not to splash any of the oil, and cook gently until golden all over, about 5 minutes. Remove from the casserole with a pair of tongs and place on a tray.

4 Add the butter to the casserole, and when melted colour the shallots on a medium heat until golden, about 3–4 minutes. Add the mushrooms and thyme, and cook for a further 2 minutes until the mushrooms are golden as well.

5 Add the leftover flour and cook this, stirring, for 2 minutes, then pour in the red wine and stock. Add half the parsley, then turn the heat up and bring to a simmer, stirring all the time. Add the chicken to this sauce, cover with foil or the lid and cook in the preheated oven for 45 minutes.

6 Add the remaining parsley, and then serve.

CHICKEN CURRY

THIS IS ANOTHER OF MY WEEKEND FAVOURITES (I LIKE CURRIES!). SERVE IT WITH
STEAMED RICE. IF YOU WISH, YOU CAN MARINATE THE DRUMSTICKS IN THE SPICES
FOR A DAY TO IMPROVE THE TASTE OF THE CHICKEN AND THE CURRY.

EASY ~ SERVES 4 ~ PREP 10 MINS ~ COOK ABOUT 1 HR

8 chicken drumsticks
25g unsalted butter
140g onions, peeled and diced
4g garlic cloves, peeled and diced
12g fresh root ginger, peeled and finely chopped
3g medium curry powder
1g powdered turmeric
1g powdered ginger
1g powdered cumin

200ml white chicken stock (see page 155)
20g raisins
20g sultanas
150ml double cream
200ml coconut milk
sea salt and black pepper
80g spring onions, thinly sliced
a small bunch of fresh coriander, leaves picked
200ml natural yoghurt

1 Preheat the oven to 170°C/325°F/Gas 3.

2 Place a casserole on a low heat, and add the butter.
  When melted, add the diced onion, garlic and fresh
  root ginger, and cook until soft without colouring,
  about 2–3 minutes.

3 Add all the powdered spices and cook slowly for
  3 minutes, again without allowing anything to colour.

4 Add the chicken stock, raisins, sultanas, double
  cream, coconut milk, 2g salt, 4–6 turns of freshly milled
  black pepper, and the chicken. Bring this to a slow
  simmer then cover with a lid and cook in the
  preheated oven for 45 minutes.

5 Remove the curry from the oven, and add the spring
  onion, coriander and yoghurt. Simmer for 2 minutes
  and then serve.

ROAST CHICKEN WITH ROAST ARTICHOKES

THE SWEETNESS OF THE ARTICHOKE HEARTS IS GREAT WITH CHICKEN. THE CHICKEN IS ROASTED ON TOP OF THE ARTICHOKES, SO ALL THE FLAVOUR GOES INTO THEM AS THE CHICKEN IS COOKING. SERVE WITH OTHER ROASTED VEGETABLE IF YOU LIKE, OR SOME PLAIN GREENS, AND SOME ROAST POTATOES OR MASH (SEE PAGE 66).

MEDIUM ~ SERVES 4 ~ PREP 20 MINS ~ COOK 1¼ HOURS

1 chicken, about 1.5kg in weight

4 large globe artichokes

200ml olive oil

2 lemons, halved

1 small bunch fresh rosemary, leaves picked, ½ chopped

4g sea salt

1g freshly milled black pepper

Bread sauce

800ml milk

300ml double cream

1 onion, peeled, halved and ½ finely diced

8 cloves

10 black peppercorns

1 bay leaf

2g fresh thyme leaves

25g unsalted butter

2g peeled and chopped garlic

2g sea salt

250g crustless white bread, diced

1 Preheat the oven to 180°C/350°F/Gas 4.

2 For this recipe we want the artichoke hearts only. Cut the stalk off at the bottom close to the base with a sharp knife. Then start to peel the dark green outer leaves away from the outside. The colour of the leaves will change to a paler green. At this point take a sharp serrated knife and remove the top so you have a 3–4cm thick base. Then start to trim the outside, carefully going around the base, cutting away most of the green part. You will have a nice smooth round base. Then take a spoon and scrape out all the centre fuzzy part, the choke. Cut the hearts in half and each half in half.

3 Remove the wishbone from the chicken, as it will help with carving. Place the chicken in a roasting tray, and smear with the oil inside and out. Squeeze the lemons all over and inside the chicken, and place the squeezed halves inside the chicken, along with the chopped rosemary. Put half the salt and pepper inside, and sprinkle the rest over the outside of the chicken. Add the artichoke pieces. Put the roasting tray in the preheated oven and roast the chicken for 30 minutes. Reduce the temperature of the oven to 170°C/325°F/Gas 3.

4 After 30 minutes move the artichokes around in the roasting tray so that they are covered in the juices.

Roast for a further 30 minutes. Cut the chicken where the legs join the body, and add the remaining sprigs of rosemary. Roast for a further 10–15 minutes or so.

5 Meanwhile, prepare the bread sauce. Put the milk and cream into a medium pan. Spike the half onion with the cloves, and add to the milk, along with the rest of the peppercorns, bay leaf and the thyme. Bring to a simmer, and leave to infuse for 15 minutes. Melt the butter in another medium pan on a low heat, then add the diced onion and chopped garlic, and cook for 3–4 minutes until soft without colouring. Pour in the milk through a fine sieve, add the salt, and bring up to a slow simmer. Add the bread and stir regularly so that

it doesn't catch on the pan and burn. Bring this back up to heat, and cook gently for 10 minutes.

6 Remove the chicken from the tray, and leave to rest for 5 minutes. Check to see if the artichokes are ready: they should be soft and slightly golden.

7 Serve the chicken and artichokes with the bread sauce.

MARINATED CHICKEN WINGS

THESE MAKE GREAT FINGER FOOD, BUT IF YOU WANT TO SERVE THESE WINGS TO CHILDREN, OMIT THE CHILLIES. YOU NEED TO START THEM THE DAY BEFORE, AS THE COOKED CHICKEN SHOULD BE MARINATED FOR A DAY. (YOU DON'T HAVE TO LEAVE IT TO MARINATE FOR THIS LONG, IT'S JUST THAT THE FLAVOUR WILL BE BETTER.)

MEDIUM ~ SERVES 6–8 ~ PREP 10 MINS PLUS MARINATING TIME ~ COOK 1¼ HRS

2kg chicken wings

1 x 2.5cm piece fresh galangal

5 kaffir lime leaves

4 lemongrass stalks, bashed and chopped

1 x 2.5cm nugget fresh root ginger, peeled and sliced

a small sprig of fresh thyme

½ garlic bulb

4 shallots, peeled and chopped

4 small green chillies

12 fresh coriander stalks

sea salt

100ml sesame oil

100g sesame seeds, toasted

Sweet and sour marinade

2 garlic cloves, peeled and halved

2 tbsp sesame oil

4½ tbsp dark soy sauce

4 tbsp light soy sauce

200g caster sugar

6 tbsp rice vinegar or white wine vinegar

3 large red chillies, finely chopped

2 tbsp chopped fresh root ginger

1 Place the chicken wings in a medium pan, cover with water, bring to the boil and then turn down to a simmer. Skim off any scum. Add to this the galangal, lime leaves, lemongrass, ginger, thyme, garlic, shallots, green chillies and coriander stalks. Add sea salt to taste and simmer for about 45 minutes until tender. Drain (keeping the stock for another recipe, or freeze.)

2 Meanwhile, for the marinade, gently fry the garlic in the sesame oil for a few minutes, and then add the rest of the ingredients, apart from the chillies and fresh root ginger. Bring to the boil and simmer for 10 minutes, then take off the heat and cool. Mix in the chillies and ginger.

3 Marinate the cooked chicken wings in the sweet and sour marinade for a day (preferably). Remove from the marinade.

4 Preheat the oven to 180°C/350°F/Gas 4.

5 Put a non-stick frying pan on a medium heat, then sauté the cooked and marinated wings in the sesame oil until lightly coloured. Place in the preheated oven for 10 minutes. Remove from the oven, roll in the sesame seeds, and eat while hot. If you have any marinade left over, use this as a dipping sauce.

BROWN CHICKEN STOCK   WHITE CHICKEN STOCK

YOU CAN MAKE LAMB STOCK IF YOU REPLACE CHICKEN BONES WITH MEAT BONES, AND ADD 500G CHOPPED PLUM TOMATOES.

EASY ~ MAKES 3.5 LITRES ~ PREP 15 MINS ~ COOK 4½ HRS

250ml vegetable oil

25g unsalted butter

2kg chicken wings, chopped

300g carrots and 300g onions, peeled and chopped into 1cm pieces

160g celery stick, chopped into 1cm pieces

25g garlic cloves, peeled

100g tomato paste

20g fresh thyme

8g coarse sea salt

4g black peppercorns, crushed

1 Preheat the oven to 200°C/400°F/Gas 6. Put a roasting tray in to heat up.

2 Add the oil, butter and chicken to the tray. Roast for 45–60 minutes until golden brown, stirring occasionally. Place the roasted chicken in a large saucepan.

3 Add the vegetables to the tray and roast for 30–40 minutes until golden, then add the tomato paste and cook for a further 5 minutes.

4 Add the vegetables to the pan with the thyme, salt, peppercorns and 4.5 litres water. Bring to the boil on a high heat, skim off any scum, then simmer for 2½ hours.

5 Turn the heat off and lift out the bones and vegetables. Pass the liquid through a fine sieve into a clean pan. Return to the boil, turn down to a simmer, removing any scum, and cook for 30 minutes. Pass through a fine sieve into a clean container. It is now ready to use, or place in the fridge for 3–4 days or freeze.

THIS IS THE STOCK TO USE FOR BRAISES AND STEWS, OR FOR POACHING OR CASSEROLING CHICKEN. IT CAN BE FROZEN.

EASY ~ MAKES 4 LITRES ~ PREP 15 MINS ~ COOK 1½ HRS

2kg raw chicken carcasses

4.5 litres water

12g sea salt

140g leeks, split and halved

160g celery sticks, halved

300g onions, peeled and quartered

25g garlic cloves, peeled

20g fresh thyme

4g black peppercorns, crushed

1 Place the chicken carcasses, water and sea salt together in a pan, and bring to a simmer. Skim off all the scum that comes to the surface with a ladle, then add the vegetables, thyme and peppercorns. Turn the heat up until it comes back to a simmer, skimming all the time. Continue simmering the stock for 1½ hours, skimming occasionally.

2 Turn the heat off and leave to cool for 30 minutes. Remove the vegetables and carcasses from the stock, so that all you have left is the liquid. This can then be ladled out of the pot and through a fine sieve into a clean container.

3 The stock is now ready for use. If you are not using it straight away, keep in the fridge for no longer than 3–4 days.

DUCK LIVER PARFAIT

THIS IS A POSH PATE, WHICH IS QUITE STRAIGHTFORWARD TO MAKE – IT JUST TAKES RATHER A LOT OF PLANNING AND TIME.

CHALLENGING ~ SERVES 12 ~ PREP 30 MINS PLUS MARINATING AND SETTING TIME ~ COOK ABOUT 1¼ HOURS

250g duck livers, prepared and trimmed

250g fresh duck foie gras (if you cannot get this, double the livers)

½ bottle port

½ bottle Madeira

300ml brandy or Cognac

2 bay leaves

4 sprigs fresh thyme

6 large banana shallots, peeled and very finely diced.

a little vegetable oil

30 smoked bacon rashers

350g butter, melted

350g eggs

3g sea salt

4–6 turns freshly milled black pepper

1　You can start this the day before, which will make your terrine much tastier. Place all the alcohol in a bowl with the bay leaves, thyme and shallots, and leave for a day in the fridge.

2　Leave the livers and foie gras at room temperature for a couple of hours before cooking (the eggs would benefit from this as well).

3　Heat shallots in a pan with the alcohol, and reduce the liquid until the pan is almost completely dry. Remove the thyme and bay leaf.

4　Preheat the oven to 120°C/250°F/a very low gas. Lightly oil and line a terrine mould with clingfilm and then the bacon as described on page 115. Have your butter just melted and at room temperature as well.

5　Place into the blender half each of the duck livers, foie gras and eggs, adding half the shallot mix. Then turn the machine on to full and purée for a minute. Slowly start to add half the melted butter, salt and pepper, then purée again for about 2–3 minutes until smooth. Pass this through a fine sieve, using a ladle to push it through. Then do the same again with the remaining

duck livers, foie gras and eggs (omitting the shallots this time).

6　Mix the two mixtures together when they have been sieved, then mix in the remaining shallots. Taste the mixture for seasoning, then pour into your terrine. Fold over the bacon and then the clingfilm so it is secure.

7　Place the terrine in a deep roasting tray and then into the preheated oven. Pour in enough boiling water to come halfway up the sides of the terrine dish. This will take approximately 45–60 minutes to cook (the middle needs to reach approximately 48°C/118°F).

8　Remove the terrine from the oven carefully and take it out of the tray. Weight down as described on page 115. Leave in the fridge for about 6–8 hours to firm up.

9　Invert the terrine onto a chopping board, and remove the clingfilm. If keeping for later, wrap it in fresh clingfilm and store in the fridge for up to a week. Otherwise slice into 1cm thick slices and serve with toasted brioche, shallot chutney (see page 65) and mixed salad leaves dressed with a walnut vinaigrette (see page 69).

DUCK CONFIT WITH BIG CHIPS, RED WINE SHALLOTS AND SAUCE

CONFIT IS SO FULL OF FLAVOUR, IT NEEDS LITTLE ELSE BY WAY OF ACCOMPANIMENT. BUT THE RED WINE SHALLOTS ARE A GOOD FOIL, AND THE CHIPS ARE JUST A TREAT. THESE CHIPS CAN BE USED WITH MANY OTHER MEAT AND FISH DISHES.

MEDIUM ~ SERVES 4 ~ PREP 20 MINS PLUS MARINATING TIME ~ COOK 2½–3 HOURS

4 duck legs
3 cloves of garlic, peeled and sliced
3g coarse sea salt
2g black peppercorns, cracked
1 medium bunch fresh thyme
2 litres duck fat

Red wine shallots and sauce
16 banana shallots, peeled
1 bottle red wine
500ml brown chicken stock (see page 155)
35g unsalted butter
2g caster sugar

Big chips
2kg large Desirée or King Edward potatoes
1 litre vegetable oil or duck fat
sea salt

1 Place the duck legs in a suitable dish with the sliced garlic, sea salt, black peppercorns and half the thyme, and leave to marinate for a day.

2 Preheat the oven to 85°C/185°F/the very lowest gas possible.

3 Melt the duck fat in an ovenproof pan. Remove the legs from the salt and pepper, and place them in the fat. Cover and put into the very low oven for 2½–3 hours. (You could do this in an uncovered saucepan on top of the stove over a very low heat.)

4 Meanwhile, finely chop up four of the shallots. Take two layers of flesh off the other shallots, as these layers would be too tough for braising. Then chop these layers up as well.

5 Place all the chopped shallot into a pan with the red wine and two-thirds of the remaining thyme. Place this on the heat and reduce by two-thirds, then add the chicken stock and again reduce by two-thirds.

6 Melt 25g of the butter in a frying pan on a medium heat, and add the peeled whole shallots and the rest of the thyme. Slowly colour until golden, about 3–4 minutes, then add the sugar. Turn the heat down a little and cook for another 3–4 minutes. Pass the red wine sauce over these through a fine sieve, pressing really well with a ladle or spoon so you extract as much liquid as you can from the shallot. Bring to a simmer and cook very slowly until the shallots are tender, about 12–14 minutes. Remove them from the heat to wait for the legs to be cooked.

7 Now make the chips. Heat the oil or fat to 160°C/320°F. Peel the potatoes and then cut into 1cm square batons the length of the potato, so they are all the same size. Wash the starch off the potato very well, then place into a pan of slightly salted water. Bring to a rapid boil, then drain and plunge straight away into cold water to stop them cooking any further. Dry them off well and then put them in batches into the hot oil to blanch them, about 2–3 minutes. Drain. Bring the oil back up to 180°C/350°F. Plunge the chips, in batches again, back into the oil and fry until they are golden brown, about 3–5 minutes. Season with sea salt.

8 When the legs are ready, place them in a medium to hot non-stick frying pan on the skin side only, so that it crisps up. Reheat the shallots, adding the remaining butter to the sauce. If you don't want to have chips, then mashed potato (see page 66) would be just as good.

BRAISED DUCK LEGS IN RED WINE SAUCE

THIS IS THE PERFECT DISH FOR A COLD WINTER'S DAY. SERVE WITH SOME GLAZED BABY TURNIPS AND MASH (SEE PAGE 66).

EASY ~ SERVES 4 ~ PREP 15 MINS ~ COOK 2–2½ HOURS

4 duck legs

2g sea salt

30g plain flour

150ml vegetable oil

25g unsalted butter

100g smoked bacon lardons

a small bunch of fresh thyme

1g black peppercorns, finely cracked

25 button onions, peeled

300g button mushrooms, washed and quartered

1 bottle red wine

40g Puy lentils

600ml white chicken stock (see page 155)

1 Preheat the oven to 170°C/325°F/Gas 3.

2 Cut the duck legs through the joint so you have a total of 8 pieces. Place these in a bowl, then add the salt and flour, and rub in well. Put a casserole dish on a medium heat, add the oil and when hot put in the duck legs, dusted free of excess flour (reserve this). Turn over in the pan until golden in colour, about 5 minutes. Remove the legs to a tray.

3 Turn the heat under the casserole to low. Melt the butter then add the lardons, thyme and cracked peppercorns. Cook for a couple of minutes then add the button onions. Turn the heat up a little and move them around the pan as well so they go a golden colour, another 5 minutes. Add the mushrooms next and again cook for 3–4 minutes, then add any remaining flour and stir in and cook for a minute.

4 Add the red wine and reduce this by half at a rapid simmer. Return the duck to the pan.

5 Add the lentils and stock. Bring this back to a simmer, skim off any scum and turn off the heat. Cover with a lid and place into the preheated oven for 1¾–2 hours. Keep an eye on the duck legs, moving them around in the pan now and again. They may need to be topped up with a little liquid towards the end. Serve.

BRAISED HARE LEG WITH SPICES

THIS DISH IS VERY EASY TO MAKE AND IS GREAT FOR THOSE COLD NIGHTS BY THE FIRE. IT NEEDS TO BE MARINATED FOR A DAY BEFORE BRAISING. I WOULD SERVE IT WITH SOME CHOUCROUTE AND BRAISED ONIONS (SEE PAGES 49 AND 54).

EASY ~ SERVES 4 ~ PREP 10 MINS PLUS MARINATING TIME ~ COOK 2½–3 HRS

4 hare legs

sea salt and black pepper

20g plain flour

150ml vegetable oil

30g unsalted butter

4 carrots, peeled and chopped into 1cm dice

100g smoked back bacon, cut into lardons

5 sprigs fresh thyme

10 star anise

1 garlic bulb, split in half

1 tsp black peppercorns, cracked

1 level tsp fennel seeds

2 celery sticks, chopped into 1cm dice

2 onions, peeled and chopped into 1cm dice

5 banana shallots, peeled and chopped into 1cm dice

1 tbsp juniper berries

1 bottle red wine

½ bottle rich port

500ml white chicken stock (see page 155)

1 Season the hare legs with 2g salt and 4–6 turns freshly milled black pepper, then roll in the flour, keeping any excess. Heat a casserole on a medium heat and add the oil. When hot, place in the legs and cook until golden, turning on all sides. This should take no more than 5 minutes. Remove the legs.

2 Turn the heat under the casserole to low, and melt the butter. Add the carrot, bacon, thyme, anise, garlic, peppercorns, fennel seeds, and 2g salt. Cook this until golden and roasted on a medium heat for 5 minutes. Then add the celery, onion, shallot and juniper berries and cook for another 5 minutes until it is all nicely coloured. Add any remaining flour, and cook for a further minute.

3 Pour in the red wine and reduce this by half at a fast simmer, then add the port and chicken stock. Bring this to a simmer, then skim off any scum. Remove from the stove and leave to cool.

4 Put the hare legs into the stock, and leave to marinate for a day in the fridge.

5 Preheat the oven to 170°C/325°F/Gas 3.

6 Place the casserole on the heat and bring back to a simmer. Skim again and then cover with a lid and place in the preheated oven for 2–2½ hours.

VENISON FILLET WITH BEETROOT PUREE AND GRATIN

THIS DISH IS FOR BEETROOT FANATICS. IT'S A GREAT COMBINATION OF FLAVOURS AND BOTH THE VENISON AND BEETROOT ARE GOOD WINTER INGREDIENTS. BEETROOT IS MY FAVOURITE VEGETABLE, AND IT IS VERY VERSATILE, PAIRING WELL WITH MANY THINGS, AND ABLE TO BE COOKED IN MANY WAYS.

MEDIUM ~ SERVES 4 ~ PREP 15 MINS ~ COOK 3–4 HRS FOR THE PUREE

600–800g venison fillet
sea salt and black pepper
100ml vegetable oil
20g unsalted butter

Sauce
1 baked beetroot (see page 38)
250ml brown chicken stock (see page 155)
1 tbsp beetroot purée (see page 38)
squeeze of lemon juice

To serve
1 recipe beetroot gratin (see page 38)
1 recipe beetroot purée (see page 38)

1 When you remove the gratin from the oven, cover it with a sheet of greaseproof paper. Lay another tray on top to compact the gratin, then leave to cool and chill. When chilled, you can cut it into squares with a knife, or into discs with a biscuit cutter.

2 Preheat the oven to 170°C/325°F/Gas 3.

3 Season the venison on all sides with salt and pepper. Put the oil in a hot pan, add the butter, then seal the venison on all sides until golden, about 3 minutes. Place the fillet on a wire rack over a roasting tray in the preheated oven, and cook for about 7–8 minutes for medium-rare (well-done will take about 15 minutes). Leave to rest for 5 minutes.

4 The square or discs of gratin should go into the oven to reheat about 5 minutes before you cook the venison. Warm the purée gently through on top of the stove.

5 To make the sauce, cut the baked beetroot into 5mm dice. Put into a pan with the chicken stock, beetroot purée and lemon juice, and heat gently.

6 Slice the venison into 5mm thick slices. Place a circle of purée in the centre of each plate, put the gratin in the middle, and the venison slices on top. Pour the sauce around.

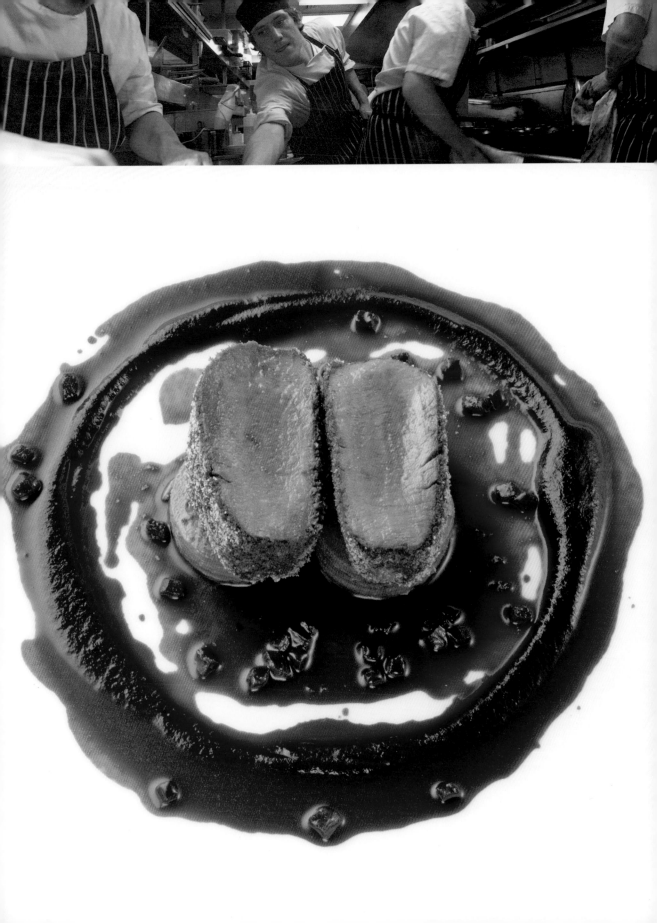

CURED AND MARINATED VENISON WITH QUINCE AND CURRANTS

THERE ARE TWO DIFFERENT WAYS OF PREPARING VENISON HERE, CURED AND AS 'CARPACCIO'. THIS RECIPE REQUIRES ADVANCE PREPARATION.

CHALLENGING ~ SERVES 4 ~ PREP SORRY, BUT IT'S 1½ WEEKS ~ COOK ABOUT 1 HR

Poached quince and vinaigrette

½ bottle red wine

250ml port

350ml orange juice

zest of 1 orange, roughly chopped

8 cloves

1 tbsp juniper berries

150g caster sugar

1 vanilla pod, split (optional)

2 quince

100g raisins (see page 76)

lemon juice

200ml olive oil

500g fillet of venison

Marinade

20g black peppercorns, crushed

5g juniper berries

12 cloves

2g fennel seeds

zest of 3 oranges, roughly chopped

zest of 4 lemons, roughly chopped

100g sea salt

50g caster sugar

To serve

finely grated zest of 1 orange

200g mixed salad leaves

1 To cure the venison, crush all the whole spices, then mix them with the roughly chopped citrus zests, the salt and sugar. Roll the venison fillet in this mixture, and leave it for a day in the fridge.

2 Brush off the salt mix. Halve the fillet widthways, so that you have two equal pieces. Roll one piece in muslin to form a cylindrical shape, tie tightly with string, and then hang the meat in a cool, dry place (this can be outside, as long as you have somewhere dry) for 1½ weeks. Roll the other piece in clingfilm tightly so it has a good cylindrical shape, and then freeze.

3 For the quince, put everything but the quince, raisins, lemon juice and olive oil into a large pan and bring to a simmer. Cut the quince in half and take out the hard core with a teaspoon, then add the flesh to the

pan. If the liquid does not completely cover it, then top up with a little more orange juice. Put a circle of greaseproof paper over the surface of the liquid. Cover and simmer for 45–60 minutes. Add the raisins, and leave everything to cool in the liquor. Put in the fridge for a day, covered, to absorb the flavours (this can be left to marinated for 4–5 days if you wish).

4 After 1½ weeks, the cured hung venison will have dehydrated and shrunk. Unwrap it, and slice it very thinly with a serrated knife.

5 Strain half of the quince liquor into a small pan, and reduce to a syrup. Remove from the heat then add a little lemon juice to counterbalance its sweetness (probably half a lemon). Whisk in the olive oil. This will form the vinaigrette.

6 Take the venison from the freezer, and leave it to defrost for 5 minutes. Slice it about 2mm thick, brush with the vinaigrette, season and sprinkle with a little freshly and finely grated orange zest.

7 To serve, place the defrosted marinated venison slices on each plate. In a bowl, mix the salad leaves with a little of the vinaigrette, then add the dried cured venison. Mix again, and scatter over the plates. Drizzle a little more vinaigrette over everything.

8 Slice the poached quince and place on the plates with the raisins.

Note
Venison is a very healthy meat, as it is low in body fat. This makes a good winter salad, and although it does take a long time to prepare, it's worth it! So for those of you that are health-conscious, this salad is for you.

VENISON MINCE WITH CELERIAC MASH

THIS MAY SEEM SIMILAR TO THE OTHER MINCE RECIPES, BUT IT SHOWS ANOTHER WAY OF COOKING VENISON. THE CELERIAC MASH IS A GOOD ALTERNATIVE TO MASHED POTATO. IT'S ALSO A DISH THAT IS VERY FILLING FOR A SNACK, AND IS A MEAL IN ITSELF.

EASY ~ SERVES 4 ~ PREP 10 MINS ~ COOK ABOUT 1 HR

400g venison mince
150ml vegetable oil
sea salt and black pepper
25g unsalted butter
3 carrots, peeled and cut into 5mm dice
2 onions, peeled and cut into 5mm dice
2g peeled and sliced garlic
150g button mushrooms, sliced

25g plain flour
30g tomato paste
200ml white chicken stock (see page 155)
200ml red wine
40g redcurrant jelly
1 bay leaf
2g each of fresh parsley, thyme and sage leaves
1 recipe celeriac mash (see page 47)

1 Place a casserole on a medium heat, add the oil and when hot, add the mince, 2g salt and 4–6 turns freshly milled black pepper. Seal in the hot oil for 5 minutes until golden. Do not stir the mince straight away as you will cool the pan down too much and the mince will start to boil. Wait a few minutes, and then stir to break down the lumps of meat.

2 Tip the mince into a colander with a bowl underneath to catch the fat. Place the pan back on a medium heat, return the drained oil to the pan and then add the butter. When melted, cook the carrot for 5 minutes and then add the onion and garlic and cook for 5–7 minutes more. When all is golden, add the mushrooms and cook for 2 more minutes.

3 Put the mince back into the pan and stir well, then add the flour and cook for 2 minutes. Stir in the tomato paste, and cook for a minute, then add the stock, red wine, redcurrant jelly, the bay leaf and fresh herbs. Bring this to a simmer, and cook on a very low heat for 30 minutes, stirring now and again.

4 When nearly ready, gently reheat the celeriac mash. Serve the mince and mash together.

ROAST PHEASANT WITH CHESTNUT SAUCE, HONEY PARSNIPS AND PARSNIP PUREE

THIS IS A LOVELY DISH FOR THE WINTER, AND A VERY SEASONAL DISH, WHICH IS EASY TO MAKE. ALL THE FLAVOURS GO VERY WELL TOGETHER, AND I THINK IT'S A NICE DISH TO HAVE ON A COLD SUNDAY NIGHT.

MEDIUM ~ SERVES 4 ~ PREP 20 MINS ~ COOK 30 MINS

2 oven-ready pheasants

sea salt and black pepper

12 fresh chestnuts

1 recipe roast parsnips with honey (see page 46, but without the cumin)

1 recipe parsnip purée (see page 46)

100ml vegetable oil

20g unsalted butter

Chestnut sauce

25g unsalted butter

150g shallots, peeled and finely sliced

4g fresh thyme leaves

75g confit chestnuts in syrup (or fresh, if you can get them), chopped

2 tbsp white wine vinegar

200ml Madeira

600ml white chicken stock (see page 155)

200ml double cream

1 Peel all the fresh chestnuts with a sharp knife and dunk them in boiling water for 30 seconds to blanch them. Peel off their skins and keep for later. Then prepare all your parsnips.

2 For the chestnut sauce, melt the butter in a pan and add the shallots and thyme. Season lightly, put on a lid, and cook for 2–3 minutes until starting to soften. Add the confit chestnuts, replace the lid and cook for another 2–3 minutes. Add the vinegar and Madeira, and stir over the heat for a couple of minutes. Add the stock and cream, bring to the boil and simmer for 10 minutes. Season to taste, then purée in a blender. Pass the purée through a sieve and cool.

3 Preheat the oven to 180°C/350°F/Gas 4.

4 While the parsnips are cooking, place a frying pan on a medium heat, and add the oil and butter. Season the pheasants and place in the pan to seal and colour all over until golden. This should take about 5 minutes.

5 Put the pheasants into a roasting tray, smear with oil and season with salt and pepper. Place in the preheated oven for 8 minutes on each side and then 8 minutes standing up. Cut open where the leg is attached to the body so the legs will be cooked when the breast is.

6 When the pheasants are cooked, take them out and leave to rest for 5 minutes. During this time reheat the sauce, parsnip purée and roast parsnips, and slice the peeled chestnuts thinly on a mandolin.

7 Cut the legs and breasts from the pheasant, and place on a plate. Add the sauce and sliced chestnuts over the meat, with the two types of parsnip to the side.

ROASTED SPATCHCOCK QUAIL WITH A SESAME CRUST

THIS IS A REALLY EASY RECIPE APART, OF COURSE, FROM THE BONING OF THE QUAILS. BUT YOU'LL BE GLAD TO HEAR THAT SOME BUTCHERS WILL DO THAT FOR YOU! THESE COULD ALSO BE COOKED ON A BARBECUE IN THE SUMMER.

MEDIUM ~ SERVES 4 ~ PREP 30 MINS ~ COOK 30 MINS

4 whole quails
100g sesame seeds plus 1 tbsp
40 Thai (small) shallots, peeled
200ml sesame oil
20g unsalted butter
sea salt

4 tbsp clear honey
100ml balsamic vinegar
12 quails' eggs
2g fresh thyme leaves
2g chopped fresh coriander leaves
juice of 1 lime

1 Take the quails one by one, turn them on their backs and cut down the back with a sharp knife. Work your way around the bird making sure that your knife stays close to the bone. When you get close to the legs cut through the main joint so they stay attached. Then you have to go around the breasts: if you do both sides at the same time then you meet in the middle on the breastbone. Then you should cut through both sides along the bone so you have a whole boned-out quail.

2 Preheat the oven to 180°C/350°F/Gas 4.

3 Toast all the sesame seeds in a dry frying pan until lightly coloured then grind 100g of them to fine crumbs in a coffee grinder or spice mill.

4 Put the Thai shallots, half of the sesame oil, the butter and a pinch of salt in a small pan on a medium heat, and lightly colour for 3–4 minutes. Add 2 tbsp of the honey and cook for a minute, then add the balsamic vinegar and reduce until sticky.

5 Bring a pan of water to the boil and cook the quails' eggs for about 2 minutes. Drain, refresh in iced water, and peel.

6 Brush the quail with the remaining honey, season with salt, then sprinkle on the thyme leaves and the ground sesame seeds. Place the little flattened birds in a roasting tray and into the preheated oven for 5–7 minutes, making sure that the legs are cooked.

7 While the quails are cooking, place a small pan on a medium heat and add the remaining sesame oil. Roast the quails' eggs in this until they start to turn golden brown on all sides, a few minutes only, then add the remaining whole sesame seeds and half the coriander. Heat up the shallots, and add the remaining coriander.

8 Take the quail from the oven. Squeeze the lime juice over the quail, and serve with the eggs and shallots.

I LOVE VERY SIMPLE DESSERTS, AND YOU'LL FIND EXAMPLES OF THESE IN THIS CHAPTER, BUT AT THE RESTAURANT I MAKE DESSERTS THAT ARE A BIT MORE COMPLEX.

Some of the desserts I create in the restaurant consist of several elements made from the same fruit: serving a mousse, a sorbet and a jelly, say, all made with apples, figs or oranges. This gives an amazing intensity of flavour. It may seem very complicated, but in many cases you can prepare some of the elements the day before, bringing them all together at the last minute. And of course, you can choose just to serve a mousse or a jelly alone, with a biscuit from the next chapter, which would be much simpler, but still as delicious.

When choosing fruits, season is all-important. Fruits are at their best in their proper season – pears and apples in the autumn, soft fruits in the summer – so try to avoid fruit flown in from abroad as it will probably have been picked under-ripe and will lack the essential fruit flavour.

Ice-cream is the classic dairy dessert for those with a sweet tooth, and there are a few ideas included here. For those who are passionate about chocolate, I have given you various different chocolate desserts (and there are also some chocolate cakes and biscuits in the next chapter). Sometimes a sweet sauce can transform the simplest of cakes or fruit into something very special, and there are several recipes for these at the end of the chapter.

DESSERTS

APPLES · CHERRIES · CHOCOLATE · CITRUS FRUIT · DAIRY · FIGS · MANGOES · PASSIONFRUIT ·
PEARS · PINEAPPLE · PLUMS · PRUNES · RASPBERRIES · RHUBARB · STRAWBERRIES

WHAT TO BUY

APPLES AND PEARS

Most of the apple and pear recipes in this chapter are best made in the autumn, when these two fruits are at the height of their season, but obviously both ingredients can be bought all year round. All apples have different flavours and cooking qualities, and the varieties we see (a few out of very many once grown) most often are Golden Delicious, Granny Smith, Braeburn and Cox's: for juicing and jellies, I use Braeburn and Cox's; for roasting and other cooking, I use Granny Smiths. Bramley apples, which are cooking apples, are the best for baking. There are over 4,000 varieties of pear, and the most used are Comice, Williams, Packham and Conference. Williams pears I use for poaching, and Packham I roast.

CHERRIES

There are two main types of cherry, sweet and sour. Sweet cherries are either red or dark-skinned, whilst the sour are a bright scarlet. The four main varieties of sweet cherries are Bing, Lambert, Rainer and Royal Ann, with extra-sweet Bing being the most popular. Sour cherries are mostly canned or frozen, and Montmorency is the most common variety. The cherry's home-grown season is all too short, from late June through to August only. Cherries are a good natural source of antioxidants,

CITRUS FRUIT

Citrus fruit are obviously not grown here, but they too have their seasons in their countries of origins, and can be better at certain times of year. Seville oranges, for instance, are only around in January/February; blood oranges from December to March. Otherwise, lemons, oranges, limes and grapefruit are available all year round. Most citrus fruits from overseas are picked underripe, to allow for the travel time to our shops. Try to buy organic fruit if you can, as they have a better taste; they are also unwaxed, which is best if you want to use the zest for a marmalade or confit. Citrus fruit

are high in Vitamin C – one lemon alone contains 35% of the recommended daily intake of vitamin C. As well as fruit, the lime trees provides leaves which can be used in cooking (especially good in curries).

FIGS

There are hundreds of varieties of the common fig, and they range in colour from purple-black to yellowish green. The trees can grow up to 15 metres in height and some are dependent on wasps for pollination. I use two types of fig. Those from Italy are dark-skinned, with a deep, pungent fig flavour (for example, Fiorone di ruvo and Negronne). The figs that are green with a powdery white skin (such as Ventura) are slightly less pungent in flavour. They are pretty much available all year round, but are best in the summer and early winter months.

MANGOES

There are around 400 types of mangoes, some green-skinned, some red and some yellow. One variety which is rather close to home for me is Tommy Atkins, but the best are Alphonso and Ataulfo, coming in from India, Pakistan and Thailand, both with yellow skins. In the UK, we spend £22 million a year on this fruit, outselling pineapples. Mangoes all have their own season, and their own flavour. They must be ripe, or they can be tasteless or, even worse sometimes, very fibrous. I find generally that those with a red skin are more fibrous than those with a green skin.

PASSIONFRUIT

There are 55 different types of passionfruit. The purple varieties of passionfruit come from South America and India, have a slightly tart taste and are picked by hand. The yellow varieties come from Australia and Hawaii and the fruit drops to the ground when ripe. These are sweeter than the purple fruits and are mostly used for juicing. Although the plant itself can grow and flower in this country – there is one on the same road as my restaurant – they will never bear fruit because it is not hot enough. The flavour is the most important element, as there is little flesh (and many seeds): it is sweet, strong and full, with a slight sharpness, which is very refreshing if eaten directly from the shell. Buy fruits that look a bit wrinkled, as they are riper; fruits with a smoother skin can be tarter and more acidic in flavour. Passionfruit are rich in Vitamins A, B and C.

PINEAPPLE

Pineapples come from Brazil, Hawaii and the Caribbean, but they can be grown in hothouses in Europe. Hawaiian pineapples have a peak season from April to May; Caribbean fruit have two seasons, December to February, and August to September. The pineapple contains a natural enzyme called bromelin, which prevents the fruit being made into a mousse or jelly, unless the fruit is cooked first. You can tell if a pineapple is fully ripe by looking at the colour of the skin: it will be golden, as opposed to yellowish green. Pineapples are very good for you as they aid digestion and are very rich in dietary fibre and Vitamin C. The sweetest is a variety of golden pineapple developed by Del Monte in Hawaii, and which contains three times more Vitamin C than most pineapples.

PLUMS AND PRUNES

There are over 350 varieties of plum, many of them sadly now unavailable due to lack of demand. The best-known English plum is the Victoria (a light, sweet fruit), followed by Marjorie's Seedling; in France a favourite is the Président. The best English plums – and their relatives such as greengages – are only in season in late summer and early autumn. Imports are always disappointing, as they lack taste and flavour. To make the most of them when they are around, I often make my own prunes from plums: I poach them, then dry them in a very low oven (as I would figs, see page 205). In warmer countries, they would be dried in the sun.

RHUBARB

Rhubarb was originally cultivated in Asia 2000 years ago for its medicinal properties. There is garden rhubarb, and then there is forced rhubarb, or champagne rhubarb, which is grown in darkness and cosseted to a pink, sweet perfection (mostly in what is known as the 'rhubarb triangle' in Yorkshire, around Leeds, Wakefield and Bradford). The forced is what you should use in desserts (such as rhubarb crumble), although the tougher, more fibrous green garden rhubarb makes nice jams and chutney. One thing the French can be jealous about is our British rhubarb!

STRAWBERRIES AND RASPBERRIES

Soft fruits have a very particular season in this country, mainly available towards the middle/end of summer, in July and August. The strawberry is an ancient fruit – and wild strawberries are now being grown for sale – although the larger and plumper cultivated variety we are now familiar with was not sold in London markets until 1830. There are over 40 different types of British raspberries, although only six are commercially grown. Unlike other soft fruit, raspberries grow best in a cold climate, which is why they grow so well here. Please always choose British strawberries and raspberries, which won't have travelled halfway across the world and taste of nothing but water.

DAIRY AND CHOCOLATE

While most of this section of the book contains fruit recipes, you can't have a desserts chapter without featuring cream and chocolate! Cream – whether single, double or whipping – and chocolate – whether dark, light or white – are seen as indulgence foods, particularly chocolate. There is a selection of recipes here which use both cream and chocolate, but I have kept the section very simple, as chocolate can be very tricky to melt and use. Most of the recipes are for home cooking as opposed to the complicated things I might serve you in the restaurant.

ROASTED APPLES WITH CALVADOS, FILO AND APPLE CRISPS AND APPLE SORBET

THIS IS A VERY WARMING, SATISFYING DISH TO EAT. IT HAS MANY TEXTURES, FROM HOT TO COLD, CRISP TO SOFT, AND THE CALVADOS GIVES A GREAT FLAVOUR.

CHALLENGING ~ SERVES 4 ~ PREP 35–40 MINS PLUS COOLING AND FREEZING TIME ~ COOK 2½ HRS

7 Granny Smith apples
50ml lemon juice
300ml water
200g caster sugar plus 4 tbsp
2 vanilla pods, halved, scraped and cut into three
30g unsalted butter, diced
100ml Calvados

Filo crisps
250g caster sugar
150ml water
3 filo pastry sheets
40g unsalted butter, melted
2g powdered cinnamon

1 To start the filo crisps, boil the sugar and water to a caramel, to 180°C/356°F. Pour onto an ovenproof plastic mat. Leave to cool until it has set hard, then place in a blender and grind to a powder.

2 Preheat the oven to 180°C/350°F/Gas 4.

3 Brush one sheet of filo with melted butter and dust with the cinnamon and the sugar powder. Repeat with the other filo sheets, piling them on top of each other. Finish with the sugar powder. Cut the layers into small oblongs, then bake in the oven until golden and crisp, about 15 minutes.

4 Reduce the temperature of the oven to 100°C/212°F/ a very low gas. Peel five of the apples, keeping the peel for the sorbet later (put the peel in a pan with a little lemon juice). Roll the peeled apples in lemon juice to prevent discoloration, and leave to one side.

5 Bring the water to the boil, and add the 200g sugar and the vanilla pods. Simmer for 3 minutes. Slice one peeled whole apple very thinly on a mandolin. Add these slices to the syrup and cook for 2 minutes on a low heat until translucent. Leave to cool, then remove

from the syrup. Place the slices on a plastic mat and bake in the low oven for about 2 hours. When baked, place the slices on a cold surface so they will go crisp.

6 Core and peel the remaining two apples. Chop finely along with the reserved peel, then place in a blender with the syrup (minus the vanilla pods). Add some lemon juice, then purée and pass through a fine sieve. It should be sweet, yet a little sharp. Place this in a sorbet machine to churn or in a metal bowl in the freezer; if the latter, stir now and then until it sets.

7 Preheat the oven to 180°C/350°F/Gas 4.

8 Cut the four whole peeled apples in half, then into three. Cut out the core and seeds. Place an ovenproof sauté pan over a high heat and add the apples. Sprinkle on the rest of the sugar. When it is a light caramel colour, toss the apples around the pan. Add the butter and cook slowly for 5 minutes. Add the Calvados and keep tossing the pan. Place in the oven for 5 minutes until the apples are soft.

9 Arrange a spoonful of sorbet on four plates, with the filo crisps, apple crisps, roast apple and sauce.

VANILLA CREME WITH APPLE JELLY AND GRANITA

A VERY LIGHT AND FRESH DESSERT, IDEAL FOR THE CLIMAX OF A SUBSTANTIAL MEAL.

CHALLENGING ~ SERVES 4 ~ PREP 30 MINS PLUS INFUSING, COOLING AND FREEZING TIME ~ COOK 45 MINS

Vanilla crème

4 egg yolks

80g caster sugar

1 vanilla pod, split and scraped

375ml double cream

125ml full-fat milk

Apple granita

300ml water

200g caster sugar

apple peelings from the juiced apples

50–100ml lemon juice

Apple jelly

1 litre fresh apple juice (from about 15 Granny Smiths or 20 Cox's)

2 vanilla pods, split and scraped

5 gelatine leaves, soaked in cold water

150ml lemon juice

caster sugar (optional)

1 Preheat the oven to 90°C/195°F/the lowest gas.

2 For the vanilla crème, whisk the egg yolks, sugar and vanilla seeds in a bowl until white. Add the cream, milk and vanilla pods, and leave for an hour to infuse. Pass through a fine sieve into a shallow dish: the custard should be about 2cm deep. Lightly blowtorch the top to stop a skin forming, then bake in the oven for about 45 minutes until almost set like a jelly. As soon as it is cooked, leave to cool a little. Divide between four sundae glasses, then place in the fridge to set.

3 Start the jelly by juicing the apples. Peel the apples (save the peel for the granita), then cut into quarters. Remove the cores and seeds, then juice them in a juicer. Skim off all the scum, place the juice in a pan, and bring to a slow heat. All the impurities will come to the surface so skim off the scum. Pass through a fine sieve lined with wet muslin.

4 Add the vanilla, soaked gelatine and lemon juice to the apple juice. Depending on the sweetness of the apples, it may or may not need sugar added. Pass through a fine sieve again and place in a bowl set over ice to almost set. Stir now and again then place into the four glasses. Chill again.

5 Make the granita. Bring the water and sugar to the boil so the sugar melts, about 5 minutes. Leave this syrup to cool. Finely chop all the apple peelings, then place in the freezer for 30 minutes (cold helps apples retain their colour). Put into a blender with the cold syrup, add most of the lemon juice and then purée. Pass through a fine sieve. It should be sweet, yet a little sharp; add more lemon juice if necessary. Place in a ceramic or metal tray in the freezer so it sets hard. When frozen, take a fork and scrape the frozen juice towards you to get the characteristic granita grains. Leave in the freezer. To serve, place the granita on top of the jelly in the glasses.

BAKED STUFFED APPLES WITH BUTTERSCOTCH SAUCE AND CARAMEL MOUSSE

IF YOU ARE ON A DIET, THIS DISH IS NOT FOR YOU, AS IT CONTAINS MAXIMUM CALORIES. . .

MEDIUM ~ SERVES 4 ~ PREP 15 MINS PLUS SETTING TIME ~ COOK 45 MINS

Apple filling
100g unsalted butter

100g caster sugar

50g raisins

50g currants

30g clear honey

finely grated zest of 2 oranges

finely grated zest of 3 lemons

a pinch of powdered ginger

a large pinch of powdered cinnamon

seeds from 1 vanilla pod (save the pod for another recipe)

Caramel mousse
150g caster sugar

300ml hot milk

5 egg yolks

2¾ gelatine leaves, soaked in cold water

350ml double cream, softly whipped

4 large baking apples

20 cloves

1 recipe butterscotch sauce (see page 216)

1 To start the mousse, melt 120g of the sugar to make a dark caramel, about 190°C/374°F, and then add the hot milk and whisk well. Place the remaining sugar in a bowl with the egg yolks, and whisk until white and fluffy. Add the hot milk, and whisk again. Return to the pan and, stirring with a wooden spoon, cook until it thickens enough to coat the back of the spoon.

2 Remove from the heat and add the gelatine. Pass through a fine sieve into a bowl set over ice to cool down. It will start to thicken and begin to set. At this point when nearly set, carefully fold in the whipped cream. Divide between four small bowls, leaving some space at the top, and leave to set.

3 Preheat the oven to 180°C/350°F/Gas 4.

4 For the apples, mix all the filling ingredients together, including the vanilla seeds. Take the cores out of the centres of the apples with a corer. Score around the middle of the peel with a knife. Fill the cavity with the filling, and stud each apple with five cloves. Bake in the preheated oven for 20–25 minutes until the apples are soft and slightly caramelised.

5 When ready to serve, put a baked apple and a mousse in its bowl on each plate. Pour a little of the butterscotch sauce in with the mousse, and pour some more over the apple.

PEARS IN RED WINE WITH VANILLA PARFAIT

THE RED WINE PEARS SHOULD BE MADE A DAY BEFORE SERVING – OR, EVEN BETTER, A COUPLE OF DAYS BEFORE, AS THIS IMPROVES THEIR FLAVOUR. THE PARFAIT CAN ALSO BE MADE IN ADVANCE.

MEDIUM ~ SERVES 4 ~ PREP 15 MINS PLUS FREEZING TIME ~ COOK 40 MINS PLUS INFUSING TIME

8 Packham or Williams pears, peeled

1 recipe vanilla ice-cream or vanilla parfait (see pages 209 or 210)

Red wine poaching liquid

1 litre red wine

300ml port

500ml orange juice

roughly cut peel of 5 oranges

15g cloves

30g juniper berries

20g star anise

40g cinnamon sticks

60g fresh root ginger, sliced

500g soft brown sugar

2 vanilla pods, split and scraped

1 Place all the ingredients for the poaching liquid in a pan and bring to a slow simmer. Cook for 10 minutes.

2 Add the peeled pears and bring back to a simmer. Cover with a sheet of greaseproof paper and then cook for 25–30 minutes until the pears are tender. Leave to cool in the syrup, and then place in the fridge for a day or so.

3 When ready to serve, cut the parfait into 3–5cm cubes and divide between four bowls. Serve with two pears each, plus a little of the strained poaching syrup.

GINGER SAVARINS WITH ROAST PEARS AND GINGER ICE-CREAM

THERE ARE A NUMBER OF ELEMENTS HERE, BUT YOU CAN MAKE THE ICE-CREAM A DAY OR SO IN ADVANCE, POACH THE PEARS THE DAY BEFORE, AND BAKE THE SAVARINS AT THE LAST MINUTE, DURING WHICH TIME YOU CAN ROAST THE PEARS.

MEDIUM ~ SERVES 4 ~ PREP 30 MINS PLUS FREEZING TIME ~ COOK JUST OVER 1 HR

Roast pears

1 litre water

440g caster sugar

peeled zest of 2 lemons

2 x 20g nuggets fresh root ginger, peeled and thinly sliced

3 vanilla pods, split and scraped

4 Williams or Packham pears, peeled

75g unsalted butter

1 recipe ginger ice-cream (see page 209)

Savarins

225g unsalted butter

225g caster sugar

5 eggs

175g plain flour

100g ground almonds

3 tbsp powdered ginger

3 tbsp candied ginger from a jar, chopped

1 You need to poach the pears before roasting them, and this is best done the day before serving them. Place the water, 400g of the caster sugar, the lemon zest, half the ginger and 1 vanilla pod in a pan and bring to a simmer. Cook for 10 minutes, then add the peeled pears. Cover with a sheet of greaseproof paper and cook for 20–25 minutes at a simmer until just tender. Leave to cool in the syrup, whole, until you want to use them. Drain and quarter the pears, and remove the cores.

2 The next day, to serve your dessert, preheat the oven to 180°C/350°F/Gas 4. Butter and flour four small savarin moulds or a ring mould.

3 For the savarins, place the butter and sugar in a small kitchen aid or mixer bowl, and cream together until white and fluffy, about 5 minutes. Then add the eggs, one by one, and mix for a further 3 minutes. Add the flour and ground almonds together slowly on a low speed. Then at the end add the gingers,

and pipe the mix into the prepared moulds. Bake in the preheated oven for 12 minutes. Remove from the moulds.

4 Meanwhile, roast the pears. Heat a large non-stick frying pan on a high heat, and add 50g of the butter. When it is golden brown, add the pears, the remaining vanilla pods and ginger, and roast these for 5 minutes, tossing them now and again until slightly coloured. Add the remaining sugar and it will caramelise to a golden brown. Cook for another 3–4 minutes until well coloured, then add the remaining butter, which you have diced, and stir this in, watching the coloration. Then add 100ml of the strained pear syrup, and cook for another 2 minutes.

5 Serve the hot pears with their sauce, with a scoop of the cold ice-cream and a savarin. (Remember to take the ice-cream out of the freezer some 10 minutes in advance to soften a little.)

SPICED PEARS WITH HONEY MADELEINES AND CHOCOLATE AND CINNAMON SAUCE

POACHED PEARS WITH CHOCOLATE IS QUITE A CLASSIC DISH, BUT HERE I HAVE ADDED JUST A LITTLE FLAVOUR TWIST. THE PEARS CAN BE SERVED COLD OR HOT, BUT THE SAUCE AND THE MADELEINES SHOULD BE WARM.

MEDIUM ~ SERVES 4 ~ PREP 20 MINS PLUS COOLING ~ COOK 40 MINS

8 Packham or Williams pears, peeled

To serve
1 recipe chocolate and cinnamon sauce
(see page 217)
1 recipe honey madeleines (see page 251)

Poaching liquid
2.5 litres water
1.5kg caster sugar
15g cinnamon sticks
15g star anise
10g cloves
8g juniper berries
30g fresh root ginger, peeled and sliced
1 x 5g piece mace
2 vanilla pods, split and scraped
roughly cut peel of 3 oranges
roughly cut peel of 4 lemons
250ml lemon juice
200ml Cognac

1 Place all the ingredients for the poaching liquid into a pan, bring to a slow simmer, and cook for 10 minutes.

2 Add the peeled pears and bring back to a simmer. Cover with a sheet of greaseproof paper and then cook for 25–30 minutes until the pears are tender. Leave to cool in the syrup, and then place in the fridge for a day.

3 Serve the pears hot or cold, with the hot chocolate and cinnamon sauce and the madeleines.

BAKED PLUM TART WITH ALMONDS AND CREME PATISSIERE

THIS IS A DISH YOU COULD MAKE THE DAY BEFORE, AND THEN SERVE IT HOT OR COLD WITH SOME FRESHLY MADE CUSTARD, PERHAPS ONE FLAVOURED WITH A LITTLE POWDERED CINNAMON (SEE PAGE 214).

MEDIUM ~ SERVES 4 ~ PREP 35 MINS PLUS RESTING AND COOLING TIME ~ COOK 1HR

8 ripe plums
1 recipe crème pâtissière (see page 216)
80g palm sugar, grated (or dark brown muscovado)

Sweet shortcrust pastry
300g unsalted butter, softened
200g caster sugar
1 vanilla pod, split and scraped
3 eggs
500g plain flour
2 egg yolks, beaten with 1 tbsp water

Frangipane
125g unsalted butter
125g caster sugar
2 eggs
125g ground almonds
20g plain flour
1 tsp powdered cinnamon
50g flaked almonds, toasted

1 For the pastry, cream the butter, sugar and vanilla seeds in a mixing bowl until white. Beat in the eggs, one by one. Add the flour, creaming it in until it all comes together. Wrap the pastry in clingfilm and place in the fridge to rest for 30 minutes. Meanwhile, grease and flour a tart tin 23cm in diameter and 2.5cm deep, with a removeable base.

2 Make your crème pâtissière. When cooked, place in a bowl, cover with clingfilm and leave to cool a little.

3 Dust your work surface with flour and roll out the pastry to 5mm thickness. Line the tart ring with the pastry, making sure that you get into the corners. Place the pastry-lined tart ring into the fridge to chill and rest for about 30 minutes.

4 Preheat the oven to 180°C/350°F/Gas 4.

5 For the frangipane, cream the butter and sugar in a bowl together until white. Beat in the eggs, one by one, and then fold in the ground almonds and flour, followed by the cinnamon and almonds.

6 Place the crème pâtissière in the bottom of the pastry case. Spoon the frangipane on top. Cut the plums in half and push into the frangipane, cut-side down. Sprinkle with the grated palm sugar.

7 Bake in the preheated oven for about 45 minutes until golden brown. You may have to turn the heat down by 10 degrees halfway through if it starts colouring too much.

POACHED MERINGUE WITH PRUNES AND COGNAC CUSTARD

THIS WAS ONE OF MY FAVOURITE PUDDINGS AT SCHOOL, POACHED PRUNES WITH BIRD'S CUSTARD. I'VE REFINED IT A LITTLE SINCE THEN. . .

MEDIUM ~ SERVES 4 ~ PREP 45 MINS PLUS MARINATING TIME ~ COOK 1 HR

500g pitted prunes

1 recipe Cognac custard (see page 214)

Prune poaching liquid

500g soft brown sugar

500ml water

5g cinnamon sticks

4g vanilla pods, split and scraped

200ml Cognac

Poached meringues

600ml milk

100ml Cognac

2 vanilla pods, split and scraped

250g caster sugar

200g egg whites

fine sea salt

1 tsp white wine vinegar

1 Place all the prune poaching liquid ingredients together in a pan, and bring to the boil. Add the prunes and poach for 30 minutes at a slow simmer. Remove from the heat, and leave the prunes in the liquor for a day if you can. Drain the prunes, reserving the liquid.

2 Have your custard made before, and then you can put your prunes into it to warm through and also to marinate. Cover with clingfilm to keep them warm.

3 For the meringues, place the milk in a shallow pan and gently heat with 50ml of the Cognac, one of the vanilla pods plus its seeds, and 50g of the sugar. Leave this to infuse whilst you make your meringue.

4 Place the egg whites into a mixer bowl, and start to whisk. When they get a little fluffy, add a pinch of salt and the vinegar. Then slowly start to add the remaining caster sugar in a steady stream until it is all used, beating all the time.

5 Add the remaining vanilla seeds and Cognac to the infused milk.

6 To make the meringues, use two large spoons, and moisten the ends in the hot milk. Take a spoonful of the meringue in one spoon, shape with the other, then drop this quenelle (or mound) into the warm milk when it is a nice shape. Do this quickly with as many other quenelles as the pan will take at one time. They will take about 4–5 minutes to cook, turning them over halfway.

7 As they are cooked, remove from the milk with a slotted spoon and place on a cloth, or straight away into serving bowls. Pour the custard and prunes over the meringue, and serve 200ml of the prune poaching juices with them.

SPICY PLUM FRITTERS WITH LEMON RICE PUDDING

IF YOU LIKE, YOU COULD PUREE SOME RED WINE-POACHED PLUMS FROM THE RECIPE ON PAGE 186 TO GO WITH THE FRITTERS AND RICE PUDDING. THE FRITTERS WOULD ALSO BE VERY GOOD WITH AN ICE-CREAM.

MEDIUM ~ SERVES 4 ~ PREP 25 MINS PLUS SITTING AND SETTING TIME ~ COOK 40–50 MINS

8 ripe plums
500ml vegetable oil
caster sugar
powdered cinnamon

Lemon rice pudding
85g pudding rice
600ml milk
1 vanilla pod, split and scraped
roughly cut peel of 2 lemons
75g caster sugar
2½ gelatine leaves, soaked in cold water
finely grated zest of 2 lemons
150ml double cream

Fritter batter
15g fresh yeast
300ml warm bottled spring water
15g caster sugar
125g plain flour
170g strong flour
finely grated zest of 1 lemon
1 tsp sea salt
1 tsp powdered cinnamon
a large pinch of powdered ginger
a large pinch of five-spice powder

1 For the rice pudding, put the rice, milk, vanilla pod, roughly cut lemon peel and sugar into a pan and cook slowly on a low heat for about 35–40 minutes.

2 Remove from the heat and leave to cool for a minute then remove the vanilla pod and lemon peel. While the pudding is still warm, mix in the soaked gelatine and the finely grated lemon zest. Cool to room temperature. Whisk the double cream until semi-whipped. Fold this into the rice, and put the mixture into a greased ring mould. Leave to set for 45 minutes, during which time you can make your fritter batter.

3 Crumble the yeast into the water and sugar and leave for 10 minutes. Place all the batter ingredients into the mixer, and then slowly add the yeasty water. Whisk in

the mixer for 10 minutes until you have a shiny batter. Cover the bowl with clingfilm and leave for 2 hours.

4 Heat the deep-frying oil to 190°C/375°F. Cut the plums in half and discard the stones. Coat each half in batter, and then deep-fry for 3–4 minutes, turning halfway through cooking. Remove with a slotted spoon and dredge with caster sugar and cinnamon.

5 Serve the fritters with the rice pudding. If you wish, drizzle with puréed poached plums (see page 186).

POACHED PLUMS WITH CINNAMON MOUSSE

THE POACHED PLUMS CAN OBVIOUSLY BE SERVED BY THEMSELVES, BUT THE ADDITION OF THE CINNAMON MOUSSE BRINGS ADDED FLAVOUR.

MEDIUM ~ SERVES 4 ~ PREP 25 MINS PLUS INFUSING TIME ~ COOK 35 MINS

12 plums
1 recipe red wine poaching liquid (see page 204)

Cinnamon mousse
250ml single cream
250ml milk
25g cinnamon sticks
120g egg yolks
100g caster sugar
12g gelatine leaves
400ml whipping cream, lightly whipped

1 Simmer the poaching liquid as described on page 204, then add the plums and poach for about 25 minutes. Leave to cool in the liquid for a day.

2 For the mousse, bring the single cream and milk to a simmer with the cinnamon, then leave to stand for 15–20 minutes.

3 Mix the egg yolks with the sugar and whisk together until creamy and white. Add the cinnamon-infused milk, stirring constantly with a wooden spoon, and then cook, still stirring, until the mixture thickens enough to coat the back of the spoon. Add the gelatine and then pass through a fine sieve into a bowl. Place this over ice. When cool, fold in the whipped cream.

4 Have ready four tall highball or sundae glasses. Chop the plums in half, removing the stones. Put half of them in the bottom of the glasses then top up with the mousse. Put the rest of the plums on top.

CHERRY CLAFOUTIS

START THIS RECIPE THE DAY BEFORE, AS THE BATTER NEEDS TO MATURE AND REST, THEN JUST PUT IT ALL TOGETHER AT THE LAST MINUTE AND BAKE.

EASY ~ SERVES 4 ~ PREP 10 MINS PLUS RESTING TIME ~ COOK 20–25 MINS

500g stoned and picked cherries, washed and well dried
a little unsalted butter

Batter
15g strong plain flour
70g ground almonds, very lightly toasted
100g caster sugar
250ml double cream
120g eggs
60g egg yolks
1 vanilla pod, split and scraped

1 Sift the flour and ground almonds into a large bowl, then stir in the sugar. Beat the cream, eggs and egg yolks together with the vanilla seeds, and stir into the flour and sugar. Whisk well to obtain a smooth paste. Add the vanilla pod, then leave to rest for a day in the fridge before using.

2 Preheat the oven to 180°C/350°F/Gas 4, and grease a shallow 20cm round ovenproof dish with a little butter.

3 Spoon the batter into the greased ovenproof dish, stir in the cherries, and bake in the preheated oven for 20–25 minutes. Serve hot.

APPLE PUREE

THIS CAN BE USED AS BABY FOOD IF YOU OMIT A LITTLE OF THE SUGAR. YOU COULD ALSO SERVE IT WITH GREEK YOGHURT FOR BREAKFAST.

EASY ~ MAKES 420g ~ PREP 10 MINS ~ COOK 15 MINS

500g Braeburn or Cox's apples, peeled, cored and diced
1 vanilla pod, split and scraped
4 tsp lemon juice
150ml water
30g caster sugar

1 Put all the ingredients into a pan, cover and gently cook for 10 minutes. Remove the lid and slowly cook for a further 5 minutes.

2 You can either leave this as a chunky purée or place in a blender and purée until fine, then pass through a fine sieve.

I SPEND MOST OF MY TIME IN THE RESTAURANT
KITCHEN MAKING QUITE COMPLICATED AND
CREATIVE DISHES, SO WHEN I'M AT HOME
I PREFER TO COOK AND EAT MORE SIMPLY.

LEMON TART WITH LEMON SORBET

THIS VERY SIMPLE DESSERT CAN BE MADE THE DAY BEFORE, ALTHOUGH IT DOES TASTE BEST ON THE DAY AND THE PASTRY WILL BE CRISPIER.

EASY ~ SERVES 4 ~ PREP 20 MINS PLUS RESTING AND COOLING ~ COOK 1 HR

1 x 23cm baked sweet pastry case (see page 182)

Lemon filling
finely grated zest and juice of 6 lemons
300g caster sugar
300ml double cream
9 eggs, beaten and sieved

Lemon sorbet
600ml lemon juice
finely grated zest of 5 lemons
450ml water
300g caster sugar

1. Make the sorbet first. Put all the ingredients in to a pan, bring to the boil and skim. Leave to infuse for a day. Churn in a sorbet machine. Alternatively, place in a bowl in the freezer, stirring every 20 minutes.

2. On the day of serving, preheat the oven to 170°C/325°F/Gas 3.

3. For the lemon filling, put the lemon juice, zest and sugar in a pan and bring to the boil. Boil the cream in a separate pan, then add to the juice. Remove from the heat, cool a little, then add the eggs, and whisk well. Pass through a fine sieve.

4. Pour the lemon filling into the pre-baked pastry case and bake in the preheated oven for 30–40 minutes.

5. Serve a wedge of tart with a couple of scoops of sorbet on the side.

Variation
You could enhance this dish by making and adding some lemon jelly or a lemon marmalade (see pages 191 and 192).

LEMON CURD WITH LEMON RICE AND JELLY

BECAUSE OF THE CITRUS FLAVOURS, THIS DESSERT IS VERY LIGHT AND REFRESHING.

MEDIUM ~ SERVES 4 ~ PREP 15 MINS PLUS SETTING AND CHILLING ~ COOK 30 MINS

1 recipe lemon rice pudding (see page 184)

Lemon curd
75g egg yolks
3 eggs
160g caster sugar
250g unsalted butter, melted
juice and finely grated zest of 6 lemons

Lemon jelly
juice and finely grated zest of 8–10 lemons
130g caster sugar
400ml mineral water
4 gelatine leaves, soaked in cold water

1 For the lemon curd, cream the egg yolks, eggs and sugar together in a bowl. Add the butter, lemon juice and zest, transfer to a pan, and whisk together on a low heat until the mixture comes to a simmer and thickens. Cook for a further 2–3 minutes, then pass through a fine sieve into a bowl. Cover with clingfilm and place in the fridge to chill.

2 For the jelly, boil the lemon juice, lemon zest, sugar and water together for 1 minute and then remove from the heat. Mix in the gelatine until melted, then leave to cool. When cool, pour into the bottom of four large Martini or sundae glasses, and leave to set.

3 Meanwhile make your rice pudding as described on page 184.

4 When the jelly has set, put some curd on top of the jelly and then leave in the fridge for another 5 minutes. Place the rice on top. Chill and serve.

Variation
You can re-use many of the elements here in different ways: the lemon curd in pancakes (see page 192), with your breakfast toast or tea-time crumpets; the rice pudding with plum fritters (see page 184); and the jelly with a simple fruit salad or the lemon sorbet on page 190.

LEMON PANCAKES WITH MARMALADE AND LEMON CURD

THIS IS A MORE REFINED VERSION OF YOUR SHROVE TUESDAY PANCAKES WITH SUGAR AND LEMON JUICE. MAKE THE PANCAKE BATTER THE DAY BEFORE SO THAT IT IS RESTED. THE LEMON CURD NEEDS TO BE MADE AT THE LAST MINUTE SO THAT IT IS STILL WARM.

MEDIUM ~ SERVES 4 ~ PREP 15 MINS PLUS RESTING TIME ~ COOK 30 MINS

Pancake batter
100g plain flour
caster sugar
a pinch of sea salt
50g eggs
250ml milk
25g unsalted butter, melted
1½ tsp vegetable oil
finely grated zest of 2 lemons

1 recipe lemon curd (see page 191)
1–2 lemons

Lemon marmalade
juice and rind of 5 grapefruit
juice and rind of 5 oranges
juice and rind of 8 lemons
350g caster sugar

1 Make the pancake batter up to a day in advance; it cooks better if it has been rested. Mix the flour, 10g sugar and the salt together in a bowl, then make a well in the centre. Mix the eggs, milk, melted butter and 1½ teaspoon oil together, then add to the well. Whisk the flour in gradually and well so that there are no lumps. Pass this through a fine sieve, then stir in the lemon zest. Store in the fridge.

2 Make the lemon curd as described on page 191, then place in a bowl, cover with clingfilm and keep it warm.

3 For the marmalade, cut the citrus rind, free of all pith, into fine strips. Blanch in boiling water for 1 minute, and drain well. Pour all the juices into a pan and boil to reduce by half. Add the strips of rind and the sugar, and cook to a syrup, about 30 minutes.

4 Preheat the oven to 180°C/350°F/Gas 4.

5 To cook the pancakes, heat a non-stick 20–24cm frying pan on a low heat. Add a dash of oil, and when this is hot, add a ladleful, or enough of the pancake batter to thinly cover the base of the pan. Swirl the batter around the pan to cover the whole base, and then cook the pancake for 1 minute on each side. Turn out of the pan and sprinkle with a little caster sugar straight away. Place on a tray. Make more pancakes in the same way, aiming for 2–3 per person. Keep covered until all are ready.

6 Spread each pancake with some of the marmalade, then fold the pancakes in half. Put a spoonful of curd on each half, and then fold in half again. Place these little triangular pancakes into the preheated oven for 2–3 minutes.

7 When serving, squeeze a little lemon juice on each pancake.

Variation
You can make chocolate pancakes simply by omitting the citrus zest, and adding 1 tablespoon of good-quality cocoa powder to the batter.

PIMMS GRANITA WITH ORANGE JELLY

IN THIS NICE, REFRESHING SUMMER DESSERT, USING SPARKLING WATER SLIGHTLY
CHANGES THE TEXTURE OF THE GRANITA. ADDING FRESH CITRUS FRUIT WITH LOTS
OF MINT GIVES SOMETHING THAT IS PERFECT FOR A HOT SUMMER'S DAY.

EASY ~ SERVES 4 ~ PREP 30 MINS PLUS FREEZING AND SETTING TIME ~ COOK 10 MINS

Orange jelly

600ml orange juice

100g caster sugar

juice of 1 lemon

5½ gelatine leaves, soaked in cold water

Orange salad

4 oranges, peeled and segmented

4 blood oranges, peeled and segmented

2g fresh mint, finely chopped

about 50–100ml Pimms

Granita

100ml each of orange juice, lime juice, lemon juice
and pink grapefruit juice

250g caster sugar

400ml Perrier water

1 vanilla pod, split and scraped

about 200ml Pimms

1 For the granita, put the juices, sugar, water and vanilla
   into a pan and bring to a simmer. Add the Pimms to
   taste, depending on what strength you would like.
   Cool, then pour into a suitable container and place
   in the freezer so that it sets hard. When it is almost
   set, scrape with a fork to get the characteristic granita
   granules.

2 For the jelly, place all the ingredients apart from the
   gelatine in a small pan, and bring to a simmer.
   Remove from the heat and add the gelatine. Stir to
   melt, then pass through a fine sieve into four glass
   bowls. Chill in the fridge to set.

3 For the salad, mix the orange segments in a bowl with
   the mint. Add a little Pimms to taste. Leave to infuse for
   a while.

4 To serve, spoon the salad on top of the jelly when the
   latter has set. Place the granita on top.

Variation

If blood oranges are not in season, you can use
grapefruit instead.

POACHED STRAWBERRIES WITH MINT AND CHAMPAGNE

THIS IS A VERY BRITISH COMBINATION – ENGLISH STRAWBERRIES SERVED WITH SCOTTISH SHORTBREAD BISCUITS (SEE PAGE 244).

MEDIUM ~ SERVES 4 ~ PREP 15 MINS PLUS RESTING AND COOLING TIME ~ COOK 30 MINS

1kg strawberries, washed, trimmed and halved

600ml water

2 vanilla pods, split and scraped

250g caster sugar

juice and zest of 1 lemon

1 small bunch fresh mint

Champagne sabayon

8 egg yolks

150g caster sugar

160ml champagne

500ml double cream, lightly whipped

To serve

1 recipe Scottish shortbread biscuits (see page 244)

1 To poach the strawberries, place the water, vanilla pods, sugar and lemon juice in a pan, and bring to a simmer. Cook for about 5 minutes, then add the strawberries. Bring back to a simmer and then remove from the heat, and leave to cool in a metal bowl, still in their liquor. When cool, place in the fridge to chill.

2 After a couple of hours, finely chop the mint and mix in with the strawberries.

3 For the sabayon, place the egg yolks, sugar and champagne in a metal bowl and place over a pan of slowly simmering water (the bowl must not touch the water). Whisk this mix for about 8–12 minutes so that it cooks in the gentle heat and starts to thicken – you should be able to draw a line through the sabayon and it will remain. Keep whisking off the heat until it cools, then fold in the whipped cream.

4 Serve the strawberries in bowls, with the sabayon to the side or spooned on top, together with the shortbread biscuits.

STRAWBERRY PARFAIT AND MOUSSE WITH FRESH STRAWBERRIES

THIS RECIPE IS ANOTHER GOOD EXAMPLE OF ONE FRUIT BEING USED IN SEVERAL DIFFERENT WAYS – FRESH, AS ICE-CREAM AND AS A MOUSSE. IT'S A LIGHT DESSERT, BUT YOU MUST USE REALLY RIPE FRUIT. TO MAKE THE PUREE, SIMPLY BLEND HULLED STRAWBERRIES UNTIL SMOOTH.

MEDIUM ~ SERVES 4 ~ PREP 20 MINS PLUS SETTING AND FREEZING TIME ~ COOK 10 MINS

550g strawberries, washed and hulled
juice of 1 lemon
100g caster sugar

Strawberry mousse
300g strawberry purée
3 gelatine leaves, soaked in cold water
300ml double cream, lightly whipped

Strawberry parfait
500g strawberry purée
100g caster sugar
juice of 1 lemon
2 egg whites
300ml double cream, lightly whipped

1 For the parfait, cook the strawberry puree, 75g of the sugar and the lemon juice to a temperature of 120°C/250°F. This will reduce down to a slightly sticky texture, about 10 minutes.

2 Make a meringue with the egg whites and remaining sugar by whisking them together until they form semi-soft peaks. Fold these carefully into the reduced strawberry purée and then fold in the whipped cream very lightly. Pour this into a greaseproof-lined tray to a depth of 2cm, and put in the freezer for 1½ hours.

3 For the mousse, warm a small proportion of the strawberry purée, and add the soaked gelatine. When melted, mix with the remaining purée, and place in a bowl set over ice. When it is nearly set, after about 12–15 minutes, fold in the cream.

4 Place the mousse into the bottom of four sundae glasses and then leave to set in the fridge.

5 Take 500g of the fresh strawberries, and blend to a purée with the lemon juice and sugar. Slice the remaining strawberries. When the strawberry parfait is set, cut into 5–8cm squares.

6 Put some of the sliced strawberries on top of the mousse, and divide the parfait cubes between the plates. Pour the strawberry coulis over the top of each portion.

VANILLA BAVAROIS WITH FRESH RASPBERRIES

A BAVAROIS IS A COOLED SET CUSTARD. IT MAKES FOR A SIMPLE SUMMER DESSERT, ESPECIALLY WHEN ACCOMPANIED BY FRESH RASPBERRIES.

MEDIUM ~ SERVES 4 ~ PREP 20 MINS PLUS COOLING AND SETTING TIME ~ COOK 15 MINS

Bavarois
250ml double cream
250ml milk
3 vanilla pods, split and scraped
120g egg yolks
100g caster sugar
12g gelatine leaves, soaked in cold water
400ml whipping cream, whipped

800g fresh raspberries
60g caster sugar
juice of 1 lemon

1 To start the bavarois, put the cream and milk into a saucepan. Split the vanilla pods, and scrape in the seeds. Add the pods as well, and bring to a slow simmer. Remove from the heat and leave to stand for 15 minutes to infuse.

2 Whisk the egg yolks and sugar together until pale white and fluffy, then pour in the vanilla and cream mixture, stirring all the time with a wooden spoon. Cook over a gentle heat, still stirring, until it thickens enough to coat the back of the spoon, then take off the heat.

3 Add the soaked gelatine to the mixture, allow to melt, and then pass through a fine sieve into a large deep bowl set over ice.Stir and now and again. When cooled and nearly set, fold in half the cream, followed by the rest. Place in the fridge to set.

4 Take 200g of the fresh raspberries, place them in a blender and purée until fine. Add the sugar and lemon juice, then pass through a fine sieve into a bowl to chill. (This is a raspberry sauce or coulis, useful in quite a few other desserts.)

5 To serve, warm and moisten a couple of tablespoons in hot water and make quenelles (or mounds) from the mousse. Put two per person in four bowls. Sprinkle in the raspberries, and then pour the raspberry sauce over.

PASSIONFRUIT CURD WITH PASSIONFRUIT JELLY AND SPONGE FINGERS

THIS IS A GOOD DESSERT FOR CHILDREN, AS THEY LIKE JELLY AND SPONGE FINGERS. INSTEAD OF SERVING THEM SEPARATELY AS I SUGGEST HERE, YOU COULD LINE THE MOULDS WITH HALVED SPONGE FINGERS AND THEN FILL THE LINED MOULDS WITH THE CURD AND JELLY.

MEDIUM ~ SERVES 4 ~ PREP 40 MINS PLUS SETTING TIME ~ COOK 15 MINS

4 passionfruit
1 recipe passionfruit curd (see page 199)
1 recipe sponge fingers (see page 244)

Passionfruit jelly
100ml orange juice
400g passionfruit pulp (from about 8 fruit)
150ml water
100g caster sugar
3½ gelatine leaves, soaked in cold water

1 For the jelly, place all the ingredients apart from the gelatine into a pan and bring to a simmer. Cook for 10 minutes then remove from the heat. Add the gelatine, allow it to melt, and then purée in a blender for a minute. Pass through a fine sieve. Place this in a bowl over ice until it has nearly set.

2 Meanwhile, divide the passionfruit curd between four large Martini glasses or medium ramekins. Place the nearly set jelly onto the curd. Cut the passionfruit in half and scoop out the pulp on top of each portion.

3 Serve the sponge fingers with the jelly and curd.

PASSIONFRUIT PAVLOVA

YOU COULD SERVE THIS CLASSIC PAVLOVA WITH SOME VANILLA CUSTARD (SEE PAGE 214).

MEDIUM ~ SERVES 4 ~ PREP 25 MINS PLUS COOLING TIME ~ COOK 1¼ HRS

Pavlova
8 egg whites
a pinch of fine sea salt
500g caster sugar
4 tsp cornflour
2 tsp white wine vinegar
1 vanilla pod, split and scraped

Passionfruit curd
400g passionfruit pulp (from about 8 fruit)
120g egg yolks
150g eggs
120g caster sugar
150g unsalted butter, melted

1 For the passionfruit curd, put all the ingredients except the butter into a pan, and combine with a whisk. Bring gently to the boil, then simmer until it thickens, about 2–3 minutes. Whisk in the melted butter. Place in a clean bowl, cover with a sheet of clingfilm and leave to cool.

2 Preheat the oven to 150°C/300°F/Gas 2, and line two baking sheets with greaseproof paper.

3 For the pavlova, whisk the egg whites and salt together until stiff, then slowly add the sugar, little by little, whisking all the time, followed by the cornflour, vinegar and vanilla seeds.

4 Divide the pavlova mixture between the two sheets, spooning it into rough rectangles of 20 x 10cm, and about 2.5cm thick. Bake in the preheated oven for 45–60 minutes, then leave to cool in the turned-off oven. Turn out onto a cooling wire and carefully peel off the paper.

5 When the pavlovas are cool, place one of them on a large plate. Spread with all of the curd, and then put the other pavlova on top.

Variation
You could also serve this with a passionfruit sauce. Put the flesh and seeds of 6 passionfruit into a pan with 150g caster sugar and the juice of 1 lemon. Bring to a slow simmer, cook for 5 minutes, then add 1 teaspoon of arrowroot that you have slaked in a little water. Cook for 2 minutes, then pass through a fine sieve.

POACHED RHUBARB WITH ITALIAN MERINGUE AND CREME PATISSIERE

ITALIAN MERINGUE MIGHT LOOK A LITTLE MORE COMPLICATED, AS IT USES A SUGAR SYRUP, BUT IT ISN'T REALLY. YOU'LL NEED AN ELECTRIC MIXER, OR YOU COULD USE AN ELECTRIC HAND WHISK.

CHALLENGING ~ SERVES 4 ~ PREP 40 MINS PLUS COOLING TIME ~ COOK 1¾ HRS

2kg forced rhubarb, trimmed
600ml water
200g caster sugar
2g fresh mint leaves, finely cut

To serve
1 recipe crème pâtissière (see page 216)
400ml whipping cream, lightly whipped

Italian meringue
350g caster sugar
100ml water
200g egg whites
1 vanilla pod, split and scraped

1 Preheat the oven to 110°C/210°F/Gas ¼, and put an ovenproof plastic mat or some greaseproof paper on a baking sheet.

2 For the meringue, put the sugar and water in a pan together and boil to a temperature of 120°C/250°F.

3 In a mixer, whisk the egg whites up for 2–3 minutes then, still whisking, add the melted sugar, carefully and gradually pouring it into the bowl, between the whisk and the side of the bowl. Whisk for a further 10 minutes, adding the vanilla seeds. Keep the pod for later.

4 Spoon the meringue mix onto the mat or paper into eight oblongs, 8cm long, 4cm wide and 1cm thick. Bake in the preheated oven for about 1 hour. They should be crisp when you take them out of the oven. Leave to cool.

5 Next, make the crème pâtissière as described on page 216, then gently fold in the lightly whipped cream.

6 For the rhubarb, cut half the rhubarb into 8cm batons, and the rest into rough chunks. Keep them separate. Put the water, sugar and vanilla pod from the meringue into a suitable pan, and cook gently for 10 minutes. Add the rhubarb batons to this stock and poach at a simmer for about 10 minutes until tender. Remove with a slotted spoon, draining well, and place on a tray.

7 Place the remaining rhubarb in the stock and cook until soft, about another 10 minutes. Drain very well, then reduce the stock by half. Place the rhubarb in a bowl, and mash it up with a fork.

8 Cool the stock, then chill it and add the mint.

9 Place some mashed rhubarb on each plate, then put a meringue sheet on top. Pipe the cream along the length of the meringue and then top with some rhubarb batons. Pipe more cream on top, and put the other meringue piece on. Spoon the mint-flavoured poaching liquor around. Serve with the remaining cream.

RHUBARB FOOL

IT MAY BE SLIGHTLY UNUSUAL TO HAVE GELATINE IN A FOOL, BUT RHUBARB CAN BE QUITE WET ONCE IT IS COOKED, AND WOULD MAKE THE TEXTURE TOO SLOPPY.

EASY ~ SERVES 4 ~ PREP 10 MINS PLUS COOLING AND SETTING TIME ~ COOK 5–10 MINS

1kg forced rhubarb, trimmed and roughly chopped
1 vanilla pod, split and scraped
200g caster sugar
juice of 1 lemon
2½ gelatine leaves, soaked in cold water
400ml double cream, whipped

1 Put the rhubarb, vanilla pod and seeds, sugar and lemon juice in a pan and bring to a slow simmer. Cook for 5–10 minutes with a lid on until soft. Remove from the heat.

2 Squeeze the gelatine dry and add to the rhubarb. When it has melted, place in a bowl over ice so it cools and sets a little.

3 Mix the whipped cream into the rhubarb, and then divide between 4 tall glasses. Leave to set in the fridge.

Note
Serve the fool with sponge fingers or shortbread (see page 244).

RAVIOLI OF MANGO AND COCONUT RICE PUDDING

THIS LIGHT AND REFRESHING DESSERT HAS A THAI INFLUENCE, COMBINING MANGO, COCONUT AND LIME, ALL OF WHICH WORK VERY WELL TOGETHER.

EASY ~ SERVES 4 ~ PREP 15 MINS ~ COOK 25–30 MINS

2 large ripe mangoes

Lime syrup-sauce
100ml water
100g caster sugar
juice and finely grated zest of 4 limes

Coconut rice pudding
300ml milk
300ml coconut milk
1 vanilla pod, split
100g pudding rice

1 For the syrup-sauce, place the water, sugar, lime zest and juice into a saucepan, bring to the boil and then simmer for 5 minutes. Cool and chill.

2 For the coconut rice pudding, put everything in another saucepan and slowly cook for 20–25 minutes until tender, stirring every now and again with a wooden spoon. Remove from the heat, cool and chill.

3 Peel the mangoes, then slice very thinly using a mandolin or sharp knife. You should end up with 12 long oval slices. Dice the mango trimmings, cleaning flesh from the stones, and stir this into the rice.

4 Place three mango slices on each plate, with a dollop of rice pudding on each slice. Put another slice of mango on top, and drizzle the syrup-sauce around.

MANGO RICE, CUSTARD AND JELLY

THIS IS ANOTHER OF MY DESSERTS WHICH USES ONE FRUIT IN A NUMBER OF DIFFERENT WAYS. IT WOULD MAKE A GREAT DESSERT FOR A KIDS' BIRTHDAY PARTY.

MEDIUM ~ SERVES 4 ~ PREP 20 MINS PLUS INFUSING, SETTING AND CHILLING ~ COOK 1 HR

Mango custard
4 egg yolks
80g caster sugar
2 vanilla pods, split and scraped
400ml double cream
100ml milk
½ large ripe mango, peeled

Mango purée jelly
2 large ripe mangoes, peeled
juice and zest of 2 limes
100g caster sugar
2 gelatine leaves, soaked in cold water

Mango rice
40g pudding rice
250ml milk
200ml double cream
40g caster sugar
1 vanilla pod, split and scraped
2 gelatine leaves, soaked in cold water
½ large ripe mango, peeled

1 Preheat the oven to 90°C/195°F/the lowest gas.

2 For the custard, whisk the egg yolks, sugar and vanilla seeds in a bowl until white. Add the cream, milk and vanilla pods, and leave this for 30 minutes to infuse. Pass through a fine sieve. Dice the mango and mix into the custard mix. Put into an ovenproof baking dish 2cm deep, and bake in the preheated low oven for about 1 hour. When it is cooked, it will look almost set, like a jelly. Chill in the fridge until set.

3 Make your rice while you wait for this to set. Mix the rice, milk, cream, sugar and vanilla pod in a pan, then bring to a slow simmer and cook for about 20–25 minutes, stirring every now and again with a wooden spoon.

4 For the mango purée jelly, chop the mangoes and place into a pan with the lime juice, lime zest and sugar. Bring to a slow simmer and cook just for 5 minutes. Add the gelatine, place in a blender and purée until fine. Pass through a fine sieve into a bowl set over iced water.

5 When the rice is ready, melt the gelatine into it. Dice the mango and mix this into the rice. Place this on ice to cool.

6 Place half the mango purée jelly into the bottom of four sundae glasses. Place half of the rice on top of the purée. Spoon the custard in next, with more rice, and then top with the rest of the purée, or make as many layers as you wish. Chill.

POACHED FIGS WITH RED WINE JELLY

THIS DISH IS GOOD IN SUMMER OR WINTER, WHENEVER GOOD FIGS ARE AVAILABLE. IT'S ALSO A USEFUL DISH FOR FIGS WHICH ARE SLIGHTLY UNDER-RIPE, A LITTLE BIT FIRM AND NEED AN INJECTION OF FLAVOUR.

EASY ~ SERVES 4 ~ PREP 10 MINS PLUS MARINATING AND SETTING TIME ~ COOK 30 MINS

Poaching liquor and jelly

1 bottle red wine

½ bottle port

2 cinnamon sticks

3 vanilla pods, split and scraped

1 tbsp cloves

15 juniper berries

8 star anise

juice and zest of 3 oranges

juice and zest of 2 lemons

400g caster sugar

10 gelatine leaves, soaked in cold water

12 figs

1 recipe crème pâtissière (see page 216)

200g crème fraîche

1 tsp powdered cinnamon

1 tsp five-spice powder

1 For the poaching liquor, place the wine and port together in a pan with the cinnamon sticks, vanilla, cloves, juniper, anise, the citrus juice and zest and the sugar, and boil to reduce by half, about 20 minutes.

2 Add the figs, put a sheet of greaseproof paper on top, and bring to a simmer. Poach for about 10–12 minutes until slightly soft, then leave to cool. Place in the fridge for a day to marinate.

3 Remove the figs from the poaching liquid. Now transform the liquid into a jelly. Pass it through a fine sieve, then warm up a little of it. Add the soaked gelatine leaves and melt. Pour into a bowl over ice so that it begins to set, then chill in the fridge.

4 Mix the crème pâtissière and crème fraîche with the cinnamon and five-spice powder.

5 Slice the figs. In four small glass bowls (so that you can see the layers), layer up the figs, spiced cream and red wine jelly alternately. Make sure that the red wine jelly is set enough to sit on the crème pâtissière. Chill.

BAKED FIG BRULEE WITH A FRESH FIG PUREE

THIS BASIC CREME BRULEE RECIPE CAN BE USED IN A NUMBER OF DIFFERENT WAYS, WITH FRUITS OTHER THAN FIGS TO FLAVOUR IT – TRY BLACKBERRIES, RASPBERRIES OR STRAWBERRIES.

MEDIUM ~ SERVES 4 ~ PREP 40 MINS PLUS INFUSING TIME ~ COOK 1¾ HRS PLUS DRYING, COOLING AND FIRMING TIME

12 poached figs (see page 204)
caster sugar

Basic crème brûlée

150g caster sugar
8 egg yolks
3 vanilla pods, split and scraped
250ml milk
750ml double cream

Fresh fig purée

500g figs, chopped
300ml port
300ml red wine
200g caster sugar
juice of 4 lemons
½ cinnamon stick

1 Preheat the oven to 100°C/212°F/a very low gas.

2 First, dry out the poached figs slightly. Place them on a heatproof plastic mat or a baking tray and bake in the low oven for 3 hours. If you don't wish to do this, that's fine – serve the ordinary poached figs. The dehydrating just intensifies the figs' flavour.

3 For the basic brûlée, place the sugar, egg yolks and vanilla seeds in a bowl, and whisk until white and fluffy, about 5 minutes. Add the milk and cream, and then give it a good whisking to mix thoroughly. Add the vanilla pods, and leave for 1 hour to infuse.

4 Reduce the temperature of the oven to 90°C/195°F/ the lowest gas.

5 Now make your purée. Place all the ingredients in a pan, place on a medium heat, and bring to a simmer. Reduce until most of the liquid has evaporated, about 30 minutes, then remove the cinnamon. Purée in a

blender and pass through a fine sieve. This should be sweet and sharp, so it may need a little more sugar or lemon depending on the ripeness of the figs.

6 Place the dehydrated or confit figs into an ovenproof baking dish. Remove the vanilla pods, whisk your brûlée mix up again, and then pass this through a fine sieve on to the figs. Use a blowtorch to just sear the surface of the brûlée, which stops too much of a skin forming. Place into the preheated low oven and bake for about an hour until almost set. Put into the fridge to cool and firm up, for a good 1½ hours.

7 Remove the brûlée from the fridge, and dab the surface with paper towel to remove any moisture. Sprinkle the whole thing with caster sugar – about 4 tablespoons – and set a blowtorch on it, turning the surface into a dark caramel.

8 Serve spoonfuls of the brûlée with spoonfuls of the fig purée.

FIG TARTS WITH CINNAMON ICE-CREAM

YOU COULD ALSO MAKE ONE LARGE TART INSTEAD OF FOUR SMALL: USE A 23CM TIN WITH A REMOVEABLE BASE, AND BAKE AT 180°C/350°F/GAS 4 FOR 45 MINUTES.

MEDIUM ~ SERVES 4 ~ PREP 15 MINS PLUS RESTING AND FREEZING TIME ~ COOK 30–45 MINS

16 figs
1 recipe cinnamon ice-cream (see page 209)
½ recipe crème pâtissière (see page 216)
400g bought puff pastry
icing sugar
powdered cinnamon

1 Make both the ice-cream and the crème pâtissière in advance. Keep the former frozen until about 10 minutes before serving; the latter chilled.

2 Preheat the oven to 200°C/400°F/Gas 6.

3 Roll out the puff pastry to 3–4mm thick then cut out four large circles with a 15cm round cutter (or you could use a china bowl). Put on a baking sheet, cover and leave to rest for 20 minutes.

4 Spread the puff pastry with the crème pâtissière. Slice the figs and layer these in a ring starting from the middle of each pastry circle until you get almost to the edge. Dust these well with icing sugar all over, as well as with a little cinnamon. Bake in the preheated oven for 20–25 minutes.

5 Eat the hot tarts straight away with a scoop of the cold ice-cream.

Variations
If you like, or don't have the time to make ice-cream, make a sweetened mascarpone flavoured with cinnamon instead. Simply place 300g mascarpone cheese in a bowl, add 80g caster sugar, 1 teaspoon of powdered cinnamon, and the seeds from 1 vanilla pod, and beat with a wooden spoon for 3–4 minutes.

ROAST PINEAPPLE AND SORBET

RAW PINEAPPLE IS NICE ENOUGH, BUT I REALLY LIKE THE FLAVOUR OF ROASTED
PINEAPPLE, ESPECIALLY WHEN ACCOMPANIED BY A SORBET MADE FROM THE SAME FRUIT.

EASY ~ SERVES 4 ~ PREP 15 MINS PLUS FREEZING TIME ~ COOK 30 MINS

2 pineapples
225g caster sugar
400ml water
2 vanilla pods, split and scraped
juice of 2 lemons
50g unsalted butter, chilled and chopped
100ml Calvados

1 Peel the pineapples. Slice one of them into long,
equal-sized batons of about 10 x 1.5cm, keeping all
the trimmings. Chop up the other pineapple roughly,
and mix with the trimmings of the first pineapple.

2 For the sorbet, put 200g of the sugar and the water in
a pan with 1 vanilla pod, and bring slowly to the boil
to melt the sugar. Put the chopped pineapple and
trimmings into this, bring to a simmer, cover with a lid,
and cook gently for 10 minutes. Drain, reserving the
syrup. Place the poached pineapple into a blender
with the juice of 1 lemon and 200ml of the syrup, and
blend to a fine purée. Pass through a fine sieve. Place
in a sorbet machine to churn or pour into a container
and place into the freezer; if you do the latter, you
will have to stir the mixture now and again until it has
set firm.

3 Heat a large frying pan on a medium heat, and add
the butter. When it has melted, add the pineapple
batons with the remaining vanilla pod. Sprinkle with
the remaining sugar. Move the batons around the
pan, turning them until they are golden and
caramelised all over, about 10–15 minutes

4 Add the Calvados and reduce to a syrup, then
add 250ml of the stock syrup. Continue cooking
the pineapple until it is soft, about 10 minutes.
Remove from the pan, and quickly reduce the
sauce until thick.

5 Serve the pineapple batons with their sauce and
the sorbet.

CINNAMON ICE-CREAM

GINGER ICE-CREAM

TO MAKE A SIMPLE VANILLA ICE-CREAM, SIMPLY LEAVE OUT THE CINNAMON STICKS AND POWDERED CINNAMON.

EASY ~ SERVES 4 ~ PREP 10 MINS PLUS FREEZING ~ COOK 20 MINS

300ml milk
300ml double cream
2 vanilla pods, split and scraped
2 cinnamon sticks
6 egg yolks
250g caster sugar
1 tsp powdered cinnamon

1 Place the milk and cream in a pan with the vanilla pods (not the seeds) and cinnamon sticks. Heat this gently over a low heat until it starts to steam, without even reaching a simmer. Remove from the heat and leave to infuse for 15 minutes.

2 Mix the egg yolks in a large bowl with the sugar, vanilla seeds and powdered cinnamon, then whisk for 3–4 minutes. Pour in the infused milk and the spices, and whisk together.

3 Place back in the pan over a gentle heat, stirring with a wooden spoon, for 5–8 minutes until the mixture thickens enough to coat the back of the spoon. Pour this through a sieve into a clean bowl straightaway to cool down. Leave at room temperature for 5 minutes, stirring now and again, then place in the fridge to cool. Leave the vanilla pods and cinnamon sticks in the mixture.

4 Place the cooled custard mixture in an ice-cream machine or in the freezer to set. If you are just using your freezer, the ice-cream will take longer to set; keep stirring every 10 minutes or so until it has frozen.

THIS WOULD BE GREAT WITH THE ROAST PEARS ON PAGE 179, OR A STEAMED TREACLE SPONGE PUDDING.

EASY ~ SERVES 4 ~ PREP 10 MINS PLUS FREEZING TIME ~ COOK 20 MINS

500ml milk
250ml double cream
1 tsp powdered ginger
2 vanilla pods, split and scraped
6 egg yolks
100g caster sugar
100g stem ginger in syrup from a jar, diced

1 Place the milk, cream, ginger powder and vanilla pods in a pan and heat gently over a low heat until it starts to steam, without even reaching a simmer. Remove from the heat and leave this for 15 minutes to infuse.

2 Place the egg yolks in a bowl with the sugar, vanilla seeds and stem ginger (and a little of the ginger syrup if you like), and whisk really well for 3–4 minutes. Pour in the infused milk and whisk well for 1 minute.

3 Now cook to thicken, cool and freeze exactly as described in the recipe for cinnamon ice-cream (see left).

LIME PARFAIT

VANILLA PARFAIT

THIS IS GOOD CUT INTO 6CM SQUARES, SERVED WITH A LIME SAUCE. THE SYRUP ON PAGE 201 (WITH RAVIOLI OF MANGO) WOULD BE GOOD. YOU CAN HALVE THE RECIPE IF YOU LIKE.

MEDIUM ~ SERVES 8 ~ PREP 20 MINS PLUS FREEZING TIME ~ COOK 15 MINS

200g caster sugar
juice and finely grated zest of 10 limes
18 egg yolks
600ml double cream, semi-whipped

1 Put the sugar and lime juice in a pan, and heat slowly to melt, then cook to 120°C/248°F, the soft ball stage.

2 While waiting for this, whisk the egg yolks in a mixer bowl until light and fluffy. Add the hot sugar carefully, pouring it in between the beater and the side of the bowl, still whisking.

3 Add the lime zest and whisk the mixture until cool. Fold in the semi-whipped cream, put in a greaseproof-paper-lined container so that it is at least 2cm deep, and freeze. Cut into squares after 3 hours.

THIS PARFAIT USES THE SAME INGREDIENTS AS A VANILLA ICE-CREAM, EXCEPT THAT THE CREAM IS WHIPPING RATHER THAN DOUBLE, WHICH HELPS TO GIVE THE PARFAIT ITS MOUSSE-LIKE QUALITY.

EASY ~ SERVES 4 ~ PREP 10 MINS PLUS INFUSING, COOLING AND FREEZING TIME ~ COOK 10 MINS

2 vanilla pods, split and scraped
250ml milk
150g egg yolks
200g caster sugar
400ml whipping cream

1 Scrape the seeds from the vanilla pods onto a saucer. Put the milk and the vanilla pods (not the seeds) into a pan, and bring to a simmer. Remove from the heat and leave to infuse for 30 minutes.

2 Cream the egg yolks and sugar together in a bowl, then add half the vanilla seeds. Whisk until light and fluffy, then add the warm milk. Cook this on a gentle heat, stirring with a wooden spoon, until the mixture thickens enough to coat the back of the spoon, about 2–3 minutes. Tip into a large bowl to cool.

3 Whip the cream lightly with the remaining vanilla seeds, and then add to the cooled custard. Place this into a 2.5cm deep tray that is lined with greaseproof paper. Place in the freezer, where it will take a couple of hours to set.

GRAPEFRUIT PARFAIT

YOU COULD SERVE THIS, CUT INTO 8CM
SQUARES, WITH SOME FRESH GRAPEFRUIT
SEGMENTS. AS WITH THE LIME PARFAIT, YOU
CAN HALVE THE RECIPE IF YOU LIKE.

MEDIUM ~ SERVES 8 ~ PREP 20 MINS PLUS FREEZING TIME ~
COOK 15 MINS

150g caster sugar
juice of 5 grapefruit
18 egg yolks
finely grated zest of 2 grapefruit
450ml double cream

1 Put the sugar and half the grapefruit juice in a pan,
and heat slowly to melt, then cook to 120°C/248°F, the
soft ball stage.

2 Meanwhile, in a mixer, whisk the egg yolks and the
remaining juice to a light sabayon. Add the hot sugar
carefully, pouring it in between the beater and the
side of the bowl, still whisking.

3 Add the grapefruit zest and whisk the mixture until
cold. Fold in the whipped cream, put in a greaseproof-
paper-lined container so that it is at least 2cm deep,
and freeze.

BRIOCHE PAIN PERDU

USE A SLIGHTLY SWEETENED BREAD,
SUCH AS BRIOCHE, FOR THIS RECIPE AS
IT WILL IMPROVE THE FLAVOUR.

EASY ~ SERVES 5 ~ PREP 15 MINS ~ COOK 45 MINS

unsalted butter
5 eggs
3 egg yolks
250g caster sugar
2 vanilla pods, split and scraped
400ml double cream
400ml milk
6 slices brioche, about 1.5cm thick
2 tbsp raspberry coulis (see page 197)

1 Preheat the oven to 170°C/325°F/Gas 3. Lightly butter
a 1 litre ceramic dish, and put it in a roasting tray.

2 Beat the eggs, yolks, sugar and vanilla seeds with a
whisk until pale. Add the cream and milk, then whisk
well again, and pass through a fine sieve.

3 Dip the brioche into the coulis to cover both sides,
and then arrange in the prepared dish in the roasting
tray. Pour the egg and cream mixture into the dish on
top of the brioche. Pour boiling water into the roasting
tray to come halfway up the sides of the dish. Bake in
the preheated oven for 45 minutes until set like a jelly.

4 Serve at the table, spooning it out of the dish, and
accompany it with some vanilla ice-cream or custard
(see pages 209 and 214).

Variation
You can put fruit into this, and change the flavour of
the fruit coulis as well.

SPICED BRULEE WITH PALM SUGAR

THIS BRULEE IS GIVEN AN INTERESTING FLAVOUR BY USING PALM SUGAR.

MEDIUM ~ SERVES 4 ~ PREP 10 MINS PLUS INFUSING AND COOLING TIME ~ COOK 50 MINS

375ml double cream
125ml full-fat milk
2 cinnamon sticks
10 star anise
20g liquorice root, sliced
½ tsp cloves
a small piece of fresh root ginger, sliced
2 vanilla pods, split and scraped
75g palm sugar, finely grated
5 egg yolks
caster sugar

Coffee syrup
100g instant coffee granules
200ml water
125g caster sugar
lemon juice

1 Put the cream and milk into a pan, and add all the spices, up to and including the vanilla pods (not the seeds). Heat until warm, remove from the heat, and leave to infuse for 15–20 minutes.

2 Whisk together the palm sugar, egg yolks and vanilla seeds. When the cream mixture has cooled, whisk it into the yolk mixture. Leave for a day in the fridge. Mix again, then pass through a sieve to remove the spices.

3 Preheat the oven to 90°C/195°F/a very low gas.

4 Put four ramekins of about 6cm in diameter and 4cm deep in a baking tray, and fill them with the brûlée mix. (I actually use metal rings lined with a double thickness of foil in the restaurant; I can remove these for serving). Pour boiling water into the tray around the ramekins, enough to come three-quarters of the way up the sides. Put the tray into the low preheated oven, and cook for 40 minutes, until they are almost set but still wobble a little. When ready, put them in the fridge to cool for a good 30 minutes.

5 For the syrup, put all the ingredients in a pan, bring to the boil, and boil to reduce by at least two-thirds to a thick syrup. Pass through a sieve to remove any gritty bits of coffee granule. Add enough lemon juice to take the edge off the sweetness. Leave to cool.

6 Place the ramekins on plates and sprinkle caster sugar over the tops. Caramelise with a blowtorch until the tops are dark golden brown. Serve with some of the coffee syrup.

VANILLA CUSTARD

COGNAC CUSTARD

THIS IS GOOD WITH PASSIONFRUIT
PAVLOVA, AND MANY OTHER FRUITS,
SUCH AS RASPBERRIES, STRAWBERRIES,
PLUMS, PRUNES, ETC.

EASY ~ SERVES 4 ~ PREP 5 MINS PLUS INFUSING TIME ~
COOK 15 MINS

300ml milk
250ml double cream
2 vanilla pods, split and scraped
5 egg yolks
100g caster sugar

1 Warm the milk and cream together with the
  vanilla pods (not the seeds) until it begins to steam,
  without even reaching a simmer. Remove from the
  heat and leave to infuse for 10 minutes.

2 Cream the egg yolks with the sugar and vanilla
  seeds, then pour on the hot milk. Return to the
  pan and gently cook, stirring with a wooden spoon,
  until the custard thickens enough to coat the back
  of the spoon.

3 Pass through a fine sieve into a bowl set over ice to
  stop the cooking.

Variation
This can also be used as the basis of a vanilla
ice-cream.

THIS CUSTARD IS VERY INTENSE IN
FLAVOUR, AND IS GOOD WITH MERINGUES
AND PRUNES, SIMPLE POACHED PRUNES,
AND CHRISTMAS PUDDING.

EASY ~ SERVES 4–6 ~ PREP 5 MINS PLUS INFUSING TIME ~
COOK 10 MINS

500ml milk
250ml double cream
2 vanilla pods, split and scraped
6 egg yolks
150g caster sugar
100ml Cognac

1 Make this exactly as the vanilla custard (see left),
  stirring in the Cognac at the last minute.

GINGER CUSTARD

CARAMEL CUSTARD

THIS IS GOOD WITH THE MADELEINES ON PAGE 251, AND WOULD GO WELL WITH THE SPICED BRULEE ON PAGE 212 OR THE ROASTED APPLES ON PAGE 174.

EASY ~ SERVES 4–6 ~ PREP 5 MINS PLUS INFUSING TIME ~ COOK 10 MINS

300ml milk
250ml double cream
1 vanilla pod, split and scraped
4 egg yolks
100g caster sugar
½ nugget stem ginger from a jar, finely chopped

1 Cook exactly as the vanilla custard (see left), then add the chopped ginger.

THIS IS A GOOD SAUCE FOR ROAST APPLES, OR YOU CAN TURN IT INTO ICE-CREAM.

MEDIUM ~ SERVES 4 ~ PREP 20 MINS ~ COOK 30 MINS

500ml milk
250ml double cream
75g caster sugar
120g egg yolks

Caramel
125g caster sugar

1 Place the milk and cream on to heat until it begins to steam, without even reaching a simmer.

2 Cream the caster sugar and egg yolks together until pale.

3 Put the sugar in a pan and heat to melt and colour to a dark caramel on a high heat.

4 Pour the milk and cream onto this. It will bubble up, but carry on whisking vigorously until well mixed. Pour this mix onto the egg yolks, whisking as well.

5 Return to the pan on a medium heat and cook, stirring with a wooden spoon, until it thickens enough to coat the back of the spoon. Pass through a fine sieve, into a bowl set over ice to stop the cooking.

SWEET SAUCES

CREME PATISSIERE

Crème pâtissière, or pastry cream, is useful for any number of desserts and pastries, and can be flavoured in different ways. For instance, for a coffee pastry cream, simply add 15g instant coffee powder to the milk at the beginning.

EASY ~ SERVES 4 ~ PREP 10 MINS PLUS COOLING TIME ~ COOK 10 MINS

300ml milk
1 vanilla pod, split and scraped
4 egg yolks
60g caster sugar
40g plain flour

1 Put the milk and vanilla pod into a pan, and bring up to a slow simmer. Cream the egg yolks and sugar together with a whisk until white. Add the flour and stir well, then pour on the hot milk and whisk well.

2 Place back on the stove on a medium heat and, stirring with a wooden spoon, bring it up to a simmer. It will start to thicken. Cook for 3–4 minutes, stirring, then pass through a fine sieve into a bowl. Cover with a sheet of clingfilm and leave to cool.

THICK CARAMEL SAUCE

This sauce can be used to accompany roasted fruit and fruit crumbles.

MEDIUM ~ SERVES 4 ~ PREP 10 MINS ~ COOK 10 MINS

250g caster sugar
250g double cream

1 Put the sugar in a pan, and heat to melt and make a dark caramel, about 190°C/374°F. At the same time, heat the cream in another pan to a simmer.

2 Whisk the hot cream into the caramel – it will spit – until it is well incorporated. Pass through a fine sieve.

BUTTERSCOTCH SAUCE

Great with baked apples (see page 177), an apple pie or sponge.

EASY ~ SERVES 4–6 ~ PREP 3 MINS ~ COOK 5 MINS

150g caster sugar
300ml double cream
100g unsalted butter, diced

1 Cook exactly as for caramel sauce (see above), but stir in the butter at the last moment.

CHOCOLATE SAUCE

This can be used with ice-creams or poached pears, chocolate pancakes with chocolate mousse inside them – any way you like, really.

EASY ~ SERVES 4 ~ PREP 5 MINS ~ COOK 15 MINS

800ml water
200g caster sugar
150g cocoa powder
250g unsalted butter, diced
300g good dark chocolate, broken into pieces

1 In a large pan, bring to a simmer the water, sugar and cocoa powder, then remove from the heat.

2 Add the butter and melt, stirring, then add the chocolate last, and stir until it melts. Serve hot.

CHOCOLATE AND CINNAMON SAUCE

This is delicious with spiced pears (see page 180), but it would also be good with chocolate pancakes and chocolate fondant (see pages 192 and 218).

EASY ~ SERVES 4 ~ PREP 5 MINS ~ COOK 10 MINS

170ml double cream
170ml full-fat milk
2g powdered cinnamon
250g dark chocolate, finely chopped

1 Bring the milk and cream to the boil with the cinnamon.

2 Pour over the chopped chocolate, and stir until the chocolate melts and you get a shiny, smooth emulsion. Serve hot.

COFFEE SAUCE

This would be good with the coffee mousse on page 220, but also with ice-cream.

EASY ~ SERVES 4 ~ PREP 10 MINS ~ COOK 10 MINS

200ml single cream
100ml milk
2 tsp instant coffee powder
250ml espresso coffee
3 egg yolks
30g caster sugar

1 Bring the cream, milk, coffee powder and coffee to the boil.

2 Whisk the egg yolks with the sugar in a bowl until pale and white, then pour in the milk and cream, stirring continuously.

3 Return to the heat and cook gently, stirring with a wooden spoon, until the mixture thickens enough to coat the back of the spoon. Pass through a fine sieve.

HOT CHOCOLATE FONDANT

CHOCOLATE MARQUISE

This is a very simple chocolate dessert. If you want, you could serve it with some vanilla parfait and chocolate sauce (see pages 210 and 217). You could chop the parfait and drop a cube of it into the runny centre of the fondant.

EASY ~ SERVES 4 ~ PREP 15 MINS ~ COOK 15–18 MINS

125g dark chocolate, broken into pieces
125g unsalted butter, diced
150g caster sugar
3 large eggs
35g plain flour

1 Preheat the oven to 200°C/400°F/Gas 6. Lightly butter four cups or ramekins, and then sprinkle with caster sugar.

2 Melt the butter and chocolate together gently in a pan. Beat the eggs and sugar together, then mix in the flour. Mix the flour mixture and the chocolate mixture together.

3 Pour into the prepared moulds, and bake in the preheated oven for 10–12 minutes only, so that the centre is still runny.

This is a denser version of chocolate mousse.

MEDIUM ~ SERVES 4 ~ PREP 10 MINS PLUS SETTING TIME ~ COOK 10 MINS

200g good dark chocolate, broken into pieces
2 eggs
2 egg yolks
80g clear honey
300ml double cream, semi-whipped (optional)

1 Whisk the eggs and egg yolks together until very light. Pass through a fine sieve in to a bowl.

2 Meanwhile, boil the honey to a temperature of 120°C/250°F, and melt the chocolate. Mix these together carefully, then mix into the egg mixture.

3 Fold in the cream if you want a lighter marquise. Place in a large bowl or in four little pots and then chill to set.

COFFEE MOUSSE

CHOCOLATE MOUSSE

SERVE THIS MOUSSE WITH SOME COFFEE SAUCE (SEE PAGE 217).

EASY ~ SERVES 4–6 ~ PREP 15 MINS PLUS SETTING TIME ~ COOK 15 MINS

6 egg yolks

150g caster sugar

3 tbsp instant coffee powder

300ml milk

600ml double cream

250ml espresso coffee

3 gelatine leaves, soaked in cold water

1 Whisk the egg yolks and sugar with 1 tablespoon of the coffee powder for a minute. At the same time, heat the milk and half the cream on a low heat with the remaining instant coffee and the espresso.

2 Add the warm cream to the egg yolks and sugar, and whisk well. Place this back over heat and cook, stirring with a wooden spoon, until the mixture thickens enough to coat the back of the spoon.

3 Add the gelatine to the cream, and allow to melt, then pass through a fine sieve. Put over ice, stirring every now and again until almost set.

4 Lightly whip the remaining cream, and gently fold it into the mixture. Place in four little coffee pots or ramekins or a large bowl and chill to set. Serve with coffee sauce.

YOU CAN SERVE THIS MOUSSE IN A VARIETY OF WAYS: PLAIN, OR WITH SOME CHOCOLATE SAUCE (SEE PAGE 217), OR YOU COULD SPOON IT INSIDE CHOCOLATE PANCAKES (SEE PAGE 192), AND SERVE THE SAUCE WITH THIS AS WELL.

MEDIUM ~ SERVES 4 ~ PREP 20 MINS PLUS SETTING TIME ~ COOK 20 MINS

150g dark chocolate, broken into pieces

300g unsalted butter

150g cocoa powder

8 egg yolks

200g caster sugar

50ml espresso coffee

400ml crème fraîche, whisked to smooth

1 Put the chocolate, butter and cocoa powder in a pan on a low heat, gently melt, and whisk together well.

2 In another bowl, either by hand, or in a machine, whisk the egg yolks until light and fluffy. Put the sugar in a pan, and gently heat to melt, then heat to 120°C/248°F, the soft ball stage. Pour this onto the yolks between the whisk and the side of the bowl, whisking all the time. The yolks will thicken into a sabayon and go white and fluffy.

3 Add the melted chocolate mixture to the yolks, and mix before adding the shot of hot coffee. Mix this into the chocolate mix and leave to cool. When cool, stir in the crème fraîche.

4 Place into four pots or glasses, or one larger container, and chill.

CINNAMON TRUFFLES

WE MAKE ALL OUR OWN CHOCOLATES AND TRUFFLES AT THE RESTAURANT, AND SERVE THEM AFTER DINNER. WE USE VALRHONA CHOCOLATE, WHICH IS 70 PER CENT COCOA SOLIDS.

EASY ~ SERVES 4 ~ PREP 15 MINS PLUS INFUSING AND SETTING TIME ~ COOK 15 MINS

370g good dark chocolate, broken into pieces
500ml double cream
2 cinnamon sticks
10g powdered cinnamon
cocoa powder, for dusting

1 Bring the cream to the boil with the cinnamon sticks and powder, then remove from the heat and leave to infuse for 15 minutes.

2 Add the chocolate, and stir over a low heat to melt. Pass through a fine sieve on to a greaseproof paper-lined tray, 2cm deep. Place in the fridge to set.

3 When set – it won't be rock hard – either cut into simple squares or, using a Parisian scoop, make small balls. Roll in cocoa powder, and chill.

EARL GREY CHOCOLATE TRUFFLES

A LOVELY CHOCOLATE TO HAVE AFTER DINNER WITH COFFEE OR TEA. VERY SIMPLE TO MAKE.

EASY ~ SERVES 8 ~ PREP 10 MINS ~ COOK 20 MINS

370g dark chocolate, broken into pieces
500ml double cream
4 sachets Earl Grey tea

1 Bring the cream to a simmer with the tea, then leave to infuse for 15 minutes. Pass through a fine sieve into another pan.

2 Stir in the chocolate and heat gently until the chocolate has melted. Pass through a fine sieve onto a greaseproof paper-lined tray, 2cm deep. Place in the fridge to set.

3 Shape as for the cinnamon truffles (see left).

AT THE RESTAURANT WE
MAKE BETWEEN TWELVE
AND FIFTEEN BREADS DAILY. IN
THIS CHAPTER I'VE INCLUDED
SOME OF MY FAVOURITES,
WHICH ARE ALSO THE
SIMPLEST TO MAKE.

You have several choices too, whether to make the doughs into plain or fancier breads or rolls. I have also given you some recipes for my favourite home-made cakes and biscuits.

I think there is nothing better on a lazy Sunday afternoon than to have an indulgent slice of cake with a cup of tea. Although British cooking was once famous for its cake-making, in the last few decades we seem to have lost this ability, so I hope the selection featured here might tempt you back into the cake-baking kitchen. Some of the biscuit recipes I include in this chapter could be served with coffee or tea, but many of them are also the perfect accompaniment to a dessert.

BAKING

BISCUITS · BREADS · BRIOCHE · CAKES · CIABATTA · COOKIES · FOCACCIA ·
FRUIT CAKE · MUFFINS · PIZZA · SCONES · SHORTBREAD · TEA CAKES

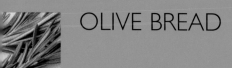

OLIVE BREAD

THE FLAVOUR OF THIS BREAD WILL BE VASTLY IMPROVED IF YOU USE GOOD-QUALITY OLIVES, RATHER THAN THOSE PRESERVED IN BRINE. YOU COULD USE THIS DOUGH TO MAKE A ROLLED AND STUFFED BREAD SIMILAR TO THE ROAST RED PEPPER BREAD ON PAGE 230. USE TAPENADE TO SPREAD INSTEAD OF RED PEPPER PUREE.

EASY ~ MAKES 1 LOAF OR 18–20 ROLLS ~ PREP 40 MINS PLUS RISING TIME ~ COOK 10–35 MINS

25g fresh yeast
185ml warm water
500g strong white flour
8g salt
80ml olive oil
170g each of stoned black olives and green olives, roughly chopped

To finish
olive oil
18–20 small sprigs fresh rosemary (optional)

1 Stir the yeast into the warm water and leave for 15 minutes. Whisk a little.

2 Place the flour, salt and olive oil into a mixer bowl, turn the mixer to slow speed, and then slowly add the yeasty water. Mix for 2 minutes. Turn the speed up to medium, and mix for a further 8 minutes. In the last 2 minutes, add all the olives so they are well broken down.

3 Turn the dough out onto a floured surface and knead for 5 minutes. Place in an oiled bowl and leave to rise for 1–1½ hours in a warm place with a damp cloth over it.

4 Turn the dough out and roll into a long rectangle. Spread with the olive mixture, then roll up into a long sausage and cut into 2.5cm pieces. Place straight onto an oiled baking tray 4cm apart or place into greased, floured metal ramekins. Alternatively, shape into one large loaf and place on an oiled baking tray. Brush the tops of the loaf or rolls with olive oil.

If you wish, press a small rosemary sprig into the top of each roll, or all over the surface of the single loaf. Leave to rise for 1 hour, covered with a damp cloth.

5 Preheat the oven to 220°C/425°F/Gas 7.

6 Bake the rolls in the preheated oven for 10–12 minutes, the loaf for 30–35 minutes. Cool on a wire rack.

ROAST HONEY GARLIC FOCACCIA

YOU COULD MAKE A PLAIN FOCACCIA WITH THIS DOUGH, OF COURSE, BUT THE FLAVOURINGS ADD LOTS OF INTEREST. IT'S A GREAT BREAD TO TAKE ON PICNICS, OR TO SERVE AT BARBECUES – IT'S GOOD FOR DIPPING INTO MEAT JUICES.

MEDIUM ~ MAKES 1 LARGE LOAF ~ PREP 50 MINS PLUS RISING TIME ~ COOK 1 HR

30g fresh yeast
350ml warm water
1 tsp caster sugar
1kg strong white flour
15g fine salt
150ml olive oil
150ml white wine

Flavourings
25g unsalted butter
4 fresh rosemary sprigs
2 garlic bulbs, cloves separated and peeled
5g coarse sea salt
2 tbsp clear honey
100ml balsamic vinegar
2g fresh thyme or rosemary leaves, chopped

1 Cook the flavourings first. Place a sauté pan on a medium heat and add the butter and half the rosemary. When the butter has melted, add the garlic and 1g of the sea salt. Cook for 10 minutes, tossing the pan now and again, so the garlic is evenly coloured. Then add the honey and cook for a further 3–4 minutes so that it starts to caramelise. Then deglaze with the balsamic vinegar. Turn the heat down and reduce the liquid until it is all sticky.

2 To make the bread dough, sprinkle the yeast into half the warm water with the sugar, and then whisk for a minute to dissolve. Leave for 15 minutes. Whisk a little.

3 Place the flour and salt in a bowl, then make a well in the centre and pour in the yeasted mix. Draw some of the flour over to cover the water and then cover with a cloth and leave for 20 minutes in a warm place.

4 Add the olive oil and white wine to the well, then draw in the flour and stir in the remaining water. Bring to a dough with your hands, and knead for 5 minutes.

Place in the mixer on a medium speed and work in half of the garlic and thyme leaves.

6 Place the dough in a well-oiled bowl, cover with a damp cloth and leave to rise in a warm place until doubled in size, about 1¼ hours.

7 Turn out the dough onto a floured surface, knock back and knead for 5 minutes, then leave to rest for 10 minutes.

8 Flour the dough, work surface and rolling pin. Roll out the dough to form a large round circle or oblong 2.5cm thick. Cover and leave to rise for 45 minutes.

9 Preheat the oven to 220°C/425°F/Gas 7.

10 Use your fingertips to press into the surface of the dough to form dimples. Brush with a little extra olive oil, then stick small rosemary sprigs in all over, and scatter with the rest of the garlic and herbs. Sprinkle on the remaining sea salt, then bake in the preheated oven for 30–45 minutes. Cool on a wire rack.

CIABATTA

THIS IS ANOTHER SIMPLE WHITE BREAD, WHICH COMES FROM ITALY. YOU HAVE TO START IT THE DAY BEFORE, THOUGH. I LOVE IT GRILLED WITH SOME OLIVE OIL AND PARMA HAM. YOU COULD MAKE ROLLS WITH THE DOUGH: ROUGHLY TEAR INTO ABOUT 20 PIECES, AND BAKE FOR 10–12 MINUTES.

EASY ~ MAKES 4 LOAVES ~ PREP 30–45 MINS PLUS RISING TIME ~ COOK 30 MINS

Starter
6g fresh yeast
300ml warm water
90ml warm milk
8g caster sugar
300g Italian 00 plain flour

Dough
8g fresh yeast
500ml warm water
150ml olive oil
14g sea salt
700g Italian 00 plain flour

1 For the starter, sprinkle the yeast into the warm water and milk with the sugar, then leave for 15 minutes. Whisk lightly, then mix in the flour to form a loose batter. Cover with a damp tea-towel and leave for 12 hours.

2 For the dough, sprinkle the yeast into the warm water, and leave for 15 minutes. Put this and the starter, plus 100ml of the olive oil and the salt, into the mixer, and mix well. Add the flour and beat well for 5 minutes: it will become springy and come away from the side of the bowl.

3 Cover the dough with a damp cloth and leave to rise until it has almost trebled in size, about 25 minutes in a warm place.

4 Do not knock the dough back. Flour two baking sheets and your hands. Divide the dough into four with a dough scrape. Place on the baking sheets with well-floured hands and stretch to form long rectangles. Dust the dough with extra flour. Then neaten and plump up the dough by running your fingers under the dough. Leave to rise, uncovered, for 20 minutes.

5 Preheat the oven to 220°C/425°F/Gas 7.

6 Dust the loaves with 00 flour and bake in the preheated oven for 30 minutes. Brush on the remaining olive oil, and cool on a wire rack.

SIMPLE WHITE BREAD

PIZZA DOUGH

MAKING BREAD AT HOME IS ONE OF THE MOST SATISFYING THINGS YOU CAN DO. IT TAKES NO MORE TIME THAN IT MIGHT TAKE TO GO OUT AND BUY A LOAF.

EASY ~ MAKES 2 LOAVES OR ABOUT 20 ROLLS ~ PREP 30 MINS PLUS RISING TIME ~ COOK 8–20 MINS

20g fresh yeast
550ml warm water
5g caster sugar
1kg strong white flour
15g sea salt

1 Dissolve the yeast in the warm water then add the sugar and leave for 15 minutes. Whisk a little.

2 Place the flour into a mixer bowl along with the salt, then turn the machine on to slow. Slowly start to add the yeasty liquid to the flour then, when it comes together, turn the speed up to medium and beat for 8–10 minutes.

3 Turn the dough out onto a floured surface and knead for 5 minutes. Place in a floured bowl and cover with a damp cloth. Leave to rise for around 45–60 minutes in a warm place.

4 Knock the dough back and shape into two loaves or about 20 rolls. Place on a tray and leave to rise: 20 minutes for small rolls, 30 for the loaves.

5 Preheat the oven to 220°C/425°F/Gas 7.

6 Bake the rolls in the preheated oven for 8–10 minutes, and the loaves for 15–20 minutes.

THERE IS NOTHING NICER THAN A HOME-MADE PIZZA. THE COOKING MAKES THE KITCHEN SMELL GOOD, YOU CAN CHOOSE ANYTHING YOU LIKE TO PUT ON TOP.

EASY ~ MAKES 4 PIZZA BASES ~ PREP 20 MINS PLUS RISING TIME ~ COOK 12–20 MINS

12g fresh yeast
a pinch of caster sugar
330ml warm water
500g strong white flour
60ml olive oil
8g sea salt

1 Stir the yeast and sugar into the warm water in a large mixing bowl, and leave to stand for 15 minutes. Whisk a little.

2 Place the flour, oil and salt in a mixer bowl, turn on to a slow speed, and slowly add the yeasty liquid. Turn the speed up to medium and beat for about 8 minutes.

3 Place the dough on a floured surface and knead for 2–3 minutes. Put into an oiled bowl, cover with a damp cloth and leave to rise for 45 minutes in a warm place.

4 Preheat the oven to 220°C/425°F/Gas 7. Put two baking sheets in the oven to heat up, or some baking stones.

5 Turn the dough onto a floured surface and cut into four. Roll out to make the pizza bases, thin or thick, depending on your taste. Garnish with your choice of ingredients, and bake on the preheated sheets thinner pizzas for about 12 minutes, thicker 15-20 minutes.

ROAST RED PEPPER BREAD

THE RED PEPPER PUREE RECIPE GIVEN HERE MAKES MORE THAN THE 400G NEEDED IN THE RECIPE. BUT IT CAN BE FROZEN OR BE USED AS THE BASE FOR A GAZPACHO, AS A BASE ON A PIZZA, AS A PASTA SAUCE…

MEDIUM ~ MAKES 15 ROLLS OR 2 LOAVES ~ PREP 1 HR PLUS RISING TIME ~ COOK 1 HR

50g fresh yeast
1 tsp caster sugar
200–300ml warm water
1.1kg strong white flour
30g sea salt
400g roasted pepper purée

Red pepper purée (makes about 1kg)
10 red peppers
200ml olive oil
2 large sprigs fresh rosemary
8 large sprigs fresh thyme
½ garlic bulb, peeled
2g sea salt

1 Preheat the oven to 200°C/400°F/Gas 6.

2 For the red pepper purée, halve the peppers, cut the cores out and discard the seeds. Place the olive oil in a roasting tray and into the oven. When it is hot, throw in the peppers first, and then everything else. You will then need to cook this for about 40 minutes until all the ingredients are well roasted. Leave in a bowl covered with clingfilm for about 2 hours. Remove the rosemary stalks and any thyme twigs, then place in a blender and purée to a coarse texture.

3 To start the bread, stir the yeast and sugar into the warm water and leave for 15 minutes. Whisk a bit.

4 Place the rest of the bread ingredients into a mixer bowl along with two-thirds of the measured red pepper purée. Turn the machine on to a medium speed. Add the yeasty water in a steady stream, and it will all come together. Leave the machine running for 15 minutes.

5 Tip the dough out onto a floured surface, and knead it for 5 minutes. Place into a lightly floured bowl to rise, cover with a damp cloth, and leave in a warm spot for about 30 minutes.

6 Tip it out onto a floured surface, and roll out in to an oblong shape, 2cm thick, 25cm wide and 50cm long. Spread the remaining purée onto the dough. Working from the long side, roll this up into a long roll shape. Now either cut the long roulade in half and put into two floured 450g loaf tins; cut the roulade into 2.5cm thick rounds and lay horizontally on a greaseproof paper-lined tray, or flour about 15 dariole moulds and put the bread in these. Whatever you decide, they will then need another 20 minutes of rising.

7 Preheat the oven to 220°C/425°F/Gas 7.

8 Bake the rolls in the preheated oven for about 8-10 minutes, the loaves for 15–20 minutes. When they are ready, place on a wire rack to cool, and brush the tops with olive oil.

ONION AND BACON BRIOCHE

YOU CAN MAKE THIS INTO ONE LARGE LOAF, WHICH WILL TAKE ABOUT 45 MINUTES TO BAKE. WHETHER BREAD OR ROLLS, THIS IS A GOOD ACCOMPANIMENT FOR A PATE, AND I LIKE IT VERY MUCH AS A BREAKFAST TOAST.

EASY ~ MAKES ABOUT 15 ROLLS ~ PREP 30 MINS PLUS RISING TIME ~ COOK ABOUT 50 MINS

110g finely cut bacon lardons
390g unsalted butter, softened
100g onions, peeled, finely diced
a pinch of fresh thyme leaves
40g fresh yeast

125ml warm milk
60g caster sugar
500g strong white flour
325g eggs
15g sea salt

1 Cook the bacon in 15g of the butter until just soft, then add the onion dice with the thyme leaves. Cook for 8–10 minutes with the lid on until soft. Remove the lid and cook for a further 2 minutes, then leave to cool, keeping all the fat from the cooking.

2 Crumble the yeast into the warm milk, stir in the sugar, and leave for 15 minutes.

3 Place the flour in the mixer bowl with the eggs and salt, then mix to a batter on a slow speed. Add the milk and yeast and beat for 5–8 minutes, then add the bacon and onion and their juices. Beat for 2–3 minutes.

4 Turn the dough out onto a floured surface and knead for 5 minutes. Place in a lightly floured bowl, cover with a damp cloth, and leave to rise in the bowl in a warm place for 1½ hours.

5 Knock back the dough. Cut it into 35g pieces – you should get about 15 – and then roll into balls. Place on a floured baking sheet or into small, floured dariole moulds. Leave to rise for another 30 minutes.

6 Preheat the oven to 220°C/425°F/Gas 7.

7 Bake in the preheated oven for 35 minutes. Cool on a wire rack.

TEA CAKES

MALT LOAF CAKE

IT'S A SHAME, BUT NOT MANY PEOPLE MAKE THINGS LIKE THIS ANY MORE. BUT THERE IS NOTHING NICER THAN A HOT TEA CAKE, TOASTED AND SERVED WITH BUTTER AND JAM.

IF YOU LEAVE THIS CAKE UNGLAZED, IT IS DELICIOUS TOASTED WITH HONEY.

EASY ~ MAKES 22 TEA CAKES ~ PREP 30 MINS PLUS RISING TIME ~ COOK 8–10 MINS

EASY ~ MAKES 1 LOAF ~ PREP 20 MINS PLUS RISING TIME ~ COOK 50 MINS

1kg plain flour
100g caster sugar
3½ tsp mixed spice
7g sea salt
70g fresh yeast
600ml milk
70g unsalted butter, melted
115g sultanas
115g raisins
55g currants

15g dried yeast
15g caster sugar
125ml warm water
400g plain flour
1 tsp sea salt
100g sultanas
1 tbsp treacle
25g unsalted butter
4 tbsp malt extract

Sugar glaze
60g icing sugar
4 tbsp water

1 Place the flour, sugar, spice, salt and yeast in a mixer bowl, and pour on the milk a little at a time. Add the melted butter, and knead in the machine on a medium speed for 10 minutes until smooth.

2 Add the fruit to the mixture, mix in well, and leave to rise for 45 minutes, covered with a damp cloth.

3 Knock back the dough and divide it into three. Roll each piece into a sausage and cut each one into seven. Roll into balls, and then squash a little. Cover with a damp cloth and leave to rise for another 30–40 minutes.

4 Preheat the oven to 200°C/400°F/Gas 6.

5 Bake the risen tea cakes in the preheated oven for 8–10 minutes. Serve immediately or leave to cool.

1 Place the yeast, sugar and water together in a bowl, and leave for 10 minutes to ferment. Whisk a little.

2 Place the water mixture into a mixer bowl with the flour, salt and sultanas, and slowly mix. Melt the treacle and butter on a low heat, then add this to the dough along with the malt extract.

3 Turn the dough out onto a floured surface, and knead for 5 minutes. Shape into a rectangular loaf and place in a greased 1kg loaf tin. Cover with a damp cloth and leave to rise for 1–1½ hours.

4 Preheat the oven to 180°C/350°F/Gas 4.

5 Bake in the preheated oven for about 45 minutes. To check it is cooked, stick a skewer in; if it is dry, the loaf is ready. Turn out onto a wire rack, and leave to cool.

6 Put the icing sugar and water in a small pan, and bring to the boil. Pour over the cake.

CHOCOLATE FUDGE SPONGE

THIS SPONGE, WHICH IS BAKED IN A SWISS ROLL TRAY, CAN BE CUT INTO SQUARES OR ANY OTHER SHAPE, AND EATEN COLD OR WARM, PERHAPS WITH SOME HOT CHOCOLATE SAUCE (SEE PAGE 217).

EASY ~ MAKES 2 THIN CAKES~ PREP 25 MINS ~ COOK 20 MINS

140g unsalted butter
225g plain flour
450g caster sugar
3 large eggs
a pinch of bicarbonate of soda
100g good cocoa powder
300ml full-fat milk
85g good dark chocolate, melted

1 Preheat the oven to 160°C/325°F/Gas 3. Grease and flour two Swiss roll tins or other trays (they must be about 2cm deep). Line the trays with greaseproof paper.

2 Cream the sugar and butter together in a mixing bowl until light, either by hand using a wooden spoon, or in a mixer.

3 Add one egg at a time, on a slower speed if using the machine, then add the sieved flour, bicarbonate of soda and cocoa powder. Using a whisk now, whisk in the milk and melted chocolate.

4 Pour into the prepared baking tray and bake in the preheated oven for 20 minutes. Turn the sponge out onto a wire rack to cool.

Variation
The sponge can also be rolled up, like the classic Swiss roll, with chocolate mousse inside (see page 220).

BANANA CAKE

THIS IS A FAVOURITE WITH CHILDREN AND ADULTS ALIKE. I'VE ALWAYS LOVED BANANA CAKE. IT'S VERY QUICK TO MAKE, AND GREAT FOR AFTERNOON TEA.

EASY ~ MAKES 1 CAKE ~ PREP 20 MINS ~ COOK 45 MINS

3 medium bananas, peeled and chopped
85g unsalted butter
175g caster sugar
1 egg
225g plain flour
4 tsp baking powder
1 tsp sea salt

1 Preheat the oven to 180°C/350°F/Gas 4, and grease and flour a 450g loaf tin.

2 Purée the banana in a liquidiser. Cream the butter and sugar together until light and fluffy, then mix in the egg, flour, baking powder, salt and banana purée.

3 Spoon into the prepared tin, and bake in the preheated oven for 45 minutes. Turn out on to a wire rack, and leave to cool.

A WELL-COOKED SIMPLE MEAL CAN BE JUST
AS GOOD AS AN EXTRAVAGANT DINNER.

FIG MUFFINS

BLUEBERRY MUFFINS

MUFFINS ARE GOOD FOR TEA OR BREAKFAST, AND WITH SOME DESSERTS. THESE MUFFINS HERE ARE IDEAL WITH THE FIG PUD ON PAGE 204.

MEDIUM ~ MAKES 10–12 ~ PREP 15 MINS PLUS FIG POACHING TIME ~ COOK ABOUT 20–25 MINS

140g unsalted butter, softened
140g caster sugar
140g eggs, beaten
150g white self-raising flour
a large pinch of bicarbonate of soda
a pinch of fine sea salt
¼ tsp five-spice powder
a large pinch of powdered ginger
70g poached figs (see page 204), puréed
2 whole figs, chopped

1 Preheat the oven to 180°C/350°F/Gas 4, and line a 12-hole muffin tray or individual metal dariole moulds with greaseproof paper, or butter and flour them.

2 Beat the butter and sugar until fluffy and white, then add the eggs little by little.

3 Sift the flour, bicarbonate of soda, salt and spices into the eggs, then mix in the fig purée and the chopped figs. Divide the mixture between the muffin trays.

4 Bake in the preheated oven for 20–25 minutes.

BEING FRUIT FLAVOURED, THESE ARE MY FAVOURITE – GREAT FOR BREAKFAST.

EASY ~ MAKES 10–12 ~ PREP 15 MINS ~ COOK 20–25 MINS

120g unsalted butter
225g caster sugar
2 eggs
285g plain flour
2 tsp baking powder
1 tsp powdered cinnamon
100ml soured cream
finely grated zest of 1 lemon
125g blueberries

1 Preheat the oven to 180°C/350°F/Gas 4, and line a 12-hole muffin tray or individual metal dariole moulds with greaseproof paper, or butter and flour them.

2 Beat the butter and sugar until fluffy and white, then add the egg little by little.

3 Sift the flour, baking powder and cinnamon into the egg mixture, then beat in the cream and lemon zest. Fold the blueberries in lightly. Divide the mixture between the muffin trays.

4 Bake in the preheated oven for 20–25 minutes.

BANANA AND WHITE CHOCOLATE MUFFINS

POPPY SEED AND RASPBERRY MUFFINS

THIS AND THE FOLLOWING MUFFIN RECIPE WERE GIVEN TO ME BY MY BROTHER ROBERT, WHO IS A CHEF IN NEW YORK. THEY ARE SCRUMMY.

EASY ~ MAKES 15–20 ~ PREP 25 MINS ~ COOK 20–25 MINS

200g unsalted butter
100g granulated sugar
90g light brown sugar
2 small eggs
330g plain flour
2 tsp baking powder
½ tsp bicarbonate of soda
½ tsp fine sea salt
100ml soured cream
1 tsp vanilla extract
2 large bananas, peeled and mashed
160g white chocolate chips

1 Preheat the oven to 180°C/350°F/Gas 4, and line 1–2 12-hole muffin trays or individual metal dariole moulds with greaseproof paper, or butter and flour them.

2 Beat the butter and sugars until fluffy and white, then add the eggs little by little.

3 Sift the flour, baking powder, bicarbonate of soda and salt into the egg mixture, and fold in lightly. Then add the cream, vanilla and banana. Fold the chocolate chips in lightly. Divide the mixture between the muffin trays.

4 Bake in the preheated oven for 20–25 minutes.

THESE MUFFINS HAVE A GREAT COMBINATION OF FLAVOURS.

EASY ~ MAKES 20–25 ~ PREP 20 MINS ~ COOK 20–25 MINS

115g unsalted butter
230g caster sugar
5 medium egg yolks
1 tbsp vanilla extract
230ml soured cream
35g poppy seeds
315g plain flour
1 tsp bicarbonate of soda
½ tsp baking powder
a large pinch of fine sea salt
3 medium egg whites
¼ tsp cream of tartar
200g fresh raspberries

1 Preheat the oven to 180°C/350°F/Gas 4, and line 1–2 12-hole muffin trays or individual metal dariole moulds with greaseproof paper, or butter and flour them.

2 Beat the butter and half of the sugar until fluffy and white, then add the egg yolks little by little. Mix in the vanilla, cream and poppy seeds.

3 Sift the flour, bicarbonate of soda, baking powder and salt into a bowl.

4 In a separate bowl, whisk the egg whites with the remaining sugar and the cream of tartar to a meringue texture. Fold this into the egg yolk mixture, then fold in the flour. Fold in the raspberries lightly. Divide between the muffin trays.

5 Bake in the preheated oven for 20–25 minutes.

CHOCOLATE FUDGE CAKE

THIS IS A MUST FOR CHOCOLATE LOVERS, PERFECT FOR A TEA AT THE WEEKEND, AND IT'S A GOOD CAKE TO MAKE FOR SOMEONE'S BIRTHDAY.

EASY ~ MAKES 1 CAKE ~ PREP 30 MINS PLUS CHILLING TIME ~ COOK 50 MINS

110g unsalted butter
110g caster sugar
2 eggs
2 tbsp golden syrup
30g ground almonds
110g self-raising flour
a pinch of sea salt
30g good cocoa powder

Icing

110g granulated sugar
110ml milk
140g good dark chocolate, broken into pieces
55g unsalted butter
2 tbsp double cream

1 Preheat the oven to 180°C/350°F/Gas 4. Grease and line an 18cm cake tin with greaseproof paper.

2 Cream the butter and sugar and whip until light and fluffy. Add the eggs, along with the syrup and ground almonds. Sift the flour, salt and cocoa powder together and fold into the butter mixture. Spoon this into the prepared cake tin, and bake in the preheated oven for 40 minutes. Leave in the tin for a while, then turn out on to a wire rack, and leave to cool.

3 To make the icing, place the sugar and milk in a pan and heat to dissolve the sugar. Bring up to the boil and then simmer for 8 minutes. Take the pan off the heat, add the chocolate and allow to melt. Then add the butter and cream and stir together until everything has melted. Place the icing in the fridge to chill until thick enough to spread.

4 Cut the cake in half horizontally, then place a third of the icing in between the layers and the rest on top.

Variation

If you wish, make double the quantity of the cake and icing. Sandwich all four cakes together and cover with icing. You could even serve with chocolate sauce (see page 217).

STEM GINGER CAKE

THIS IS ONE OF MY FAVOURITE CAKES TO EAT, AND I PARTICULARLY LIKE IT WHEN STILL WARM FROM THE OVEN. IT CAN BE ICED OR EATEN AS A DESSERT CAKE AS WELL.

EASY ~ MAKES 1 CAKE ~ PREP 25 MINS PLUS COOLING TIME ~ COOK 50 MINS

230g self-raising flour
1 tsp bicarbonate of soda
1 tbsp powdered ginger
1 tsp powdered cinnamon
1 tsp powdered allspice
110g unsalted butter, diced
110g black treacle
110g golden syrup
110g dark brown sugar
280ml milk
45g stem ginger from a jar, chopped
1 egg, beaten

1 Preheat the oven to 180°C/350°F/Gas 4, and grease and line a 900g loaf tin.

2 Sift the flour, bicarbonate and spices into a bowl. Add the diced butter and rub in until the texture is like fine breadcrumbs.

3 Melt the treacle and syrup in a small pan, then leave to cool to room temperature. In another pan melt the sugar in the milk, then add the ginger. Mix this into the flour, followed by the treacle and the egg.

4 Pour into the prepared cake tin and bake in the preheated oven for 45 minutes. Cool on a wire rack.

CARROT CAKE

A CLASSIC CAKE, WHICH IS PERFECT FOR TEA. YOU CAN SERVE IT PLAIN, BUT YOU CAN ALSO ICE IT IF YOU LIKE, USING THE SUGAR GLAZE ON PAGE 234.

EASY ~ MAKES 2 CAKES ~ PREP 20 MINS ~ COOK 30–40 MINS

500g plain flour
2 tbsp baking powder
2 tbsp baking soda
2 tsp powdered cinnamon
½ tsp sea salt
400g caster sugar
500ml vegetable oil
5 eggs
700g peeled and grated carrot
100g raisins
100g sultanas

1 Preheat the oven to 180°C/350°F/Gas 4. Grease and line two 450g loaf tins.

2 Sift together the flour, baking powder, soda, cinnamon and salt. In a large mixing bowl beat the sugar, oil and eggs together until light and fluffy, then add the grated carrot. Add the sifted ingredients, followed by the dried fruit.

3 Spoon into the prepared tins and bake in the preheated oven for 30–40 minutes. To test if done, push a skewer in; if it comes out dry, the cakes are ready. Cool on a wire rack.

RICOTTA CAKE

THIS CAKE IS BEST SERVED STRAIGHT FROM THE OVEN, WITH SOME ICE-CREAM.

EASY ~ MAKES 1 CAKE ~ PREP 15 MINS PLUS SOAKING TIME ~ COOK 40 MINS

80g sultanas
100ml Marsala wine
750g ricotta cheese
1 vanilla pod, split and scraped
6 eggs
3 tbsp cornflour
290g caster sugar

1 Soak the sultanas in the Marsala for 2 hours.

2 Preheat the oven to 170°C/325°F/Gas 3, and grease a 25cm square baking tray.

3 Put the ricotta, vanilla seeds, eggs, cornflour and sugar in a food processor and purée until smooth. Add the sultanas and their liquid, and mix.

4 Spoon the mix into the greased tray, filling to the top. Bake in the preheated oven for 40 minutes. Cool on a wire rack.

Variation
You can make small cakes as well, in muffin trays – they will take 30 minutes to cook. This would also make a nice pud for the kids if made with apple juice instead if Marsala (although the alcohol does cook out, just leaving the flavour).

FRUIT CAKE

THIS IS A CLASSIC FRUIT CAKE, WHICH COULD BE USED AS A CHRISTMAS OR BIRTHDAY CAKE.

EASY ~ MAKES 1 CAKE ~ PREP 20 MINS PLUS SOAKING TIME ~ COOK 2½ HRS

225g sultanas
225g raisins
225g currants
225g unsalted butter, softened
225g caster sugar
5 eggs, beaten
225g strong plain flour
5g baking powder
50g mixed candied peel
finely grated zest of 1 lemon

1 Soak the dried fruit in water for an hour, then drain and dry on a cloth.

2 Preheat the oven to 170°C/325°F/Gas 3, and grease and line an 18cm cake tin, 9cm deep.

3 Cream the butter and sugar together until pale, then add the eggs a little at a time. Fold in half the flour with the baking powder, then add the soaked dried fruit, candied peel, lemon zest and the rest of the flour.

4 Spoon this mix into the prepared tin and make a slight depression in the middle. Bake in the preheated oven for 2½ hours. To test that it's cooked through, pierce with a skewer in the middle of the cake, which should come out dry.

5 Turn out of the tin onto a wire rack. When cold, store in an airtight container.

SPONGE FINGERS

SHORTBREAD BISCUITS

THESE SPONGE FINGERS ARE GOOD WITH THE PASSIONFRUIT CURD ON PAGE 199, OR SIMPLY WITH A COUPLE OF SCOOPS OF HOME-MADE ICE-CREAM.

EASY ~ MAKES ABOUT 40–50 FINGERS ~ PREP 20 MINS PLUS COOLING TIME ~ COOK 20 MINS

4 eggs, separated
50ml water
200g caster sugar
70g plain flour
150g ground almonds

1 Preheat the oven to 170°C/325°F/Gas 3, and put a piece of greaseproof paper on a heavy baking sheet.

2 Whisk the egg yolks with the water and 150g of the sugar in a metal bowl over a pan of hot water. The bowl should not touch the water, and the heat should be low. When the eggs have thickened to a sabayon, take off the heat to cool.

3 Whisk the egg whites and the remaining sugar together until they are firm. Fold in the sabayon, and then very carefully fold in the sieved flour and ground almonds.

4 Pipe the mixture onto the greaseproof paper-lined tray into fingers 1cm wide and 6cm long.

5 Bake in the preheated oven for about 10 minutes. When they come out of the oven, sprinkle with caster sugar and then cool on a wire rack.

A CLASSIC RECIPE. YOU COULD ADD THE FINELY GRATED ZEST OF ½ LEMON TO THE MIXTURE BEFORE BAKING. DELICIOUS WITH THE STRAWBERRIES ON PAGE 194.

EASY ~ MAKES 12–16 BISCUITS ~ PREP 20 MINS PLUS RESTING TIME ~ COOK 40 MINS

220g unsalted butter
110g caster sugar
220g plain flour
110g rice flour

1 Beat the butter until soft, then add the sugar and beat until pale and creamy.

2 Sift the flours together then add to the butter, and lightly mix. Divide this in half.

3 Place a 15cm flan ring on a baking tray and press one-half of the paste into the ring, forming a neat circle. Remove the ring. Crimp the edges of the paste circle, and prick the centre lightly with a fork. Mark the shortbread into 6–8 wedges, and sprinkle with a little extra caster sugar. Do the same with the remaining shortbread paste. Leave both to rest in the fridge for 30 minutes.

4 Preheat the oven to 170°C/325°F/Gas 3.

5 Bake in the oven for 40 minutes until a pale biscuit colour, then leave to cool on a wire cooling rack.

FLAPJACKS

I USED TO EAT A LOT OF FLAPJACKS WHEN I WAS A KID, AND HAVE ALWAYS LOVED THEM. YOU COULD VARY THEM A LITTLE BY ADDING SOME DRIED FRUIT.

EASY ~ MAKES 16 BISCUITS ~ PREP 20 MINS ~ COOK 35 MINS

170g unsalted butter
110g demerara sugar
55g golden syrup
225g rolled oats

1 Preheat the oven to 180°C/350°F/Gas 4, and grease a 30 x 15cm baking tin.

2 Melt the butter in a pan, then add the sugar and syrup, and heat through. Remove from the heat and add the oats.

3 Spread the mix into the prepared tin, and bake in the preheated oven for 30 minutes until golden brown.

4 Remove from the oven and mark immediately into 16 bars. Leave to cool.

SCONES

FOR A FRUIT SCONE, ADD 30G DRIED FRUIT; FOR A CHEESE SCONE, ADD 30G GRATED CHEESE, OMITTING 30G OF THE BUTTER AND ALL THE SUGAR.

EASY ~ MAKES ABOUT 15 SCONES ~ PREP 30 MINS TIME ~ COOK 7 MINS

225g plain flour
1 tbsp baking powder
½ tsp sea salt
55g unsalted butter
30g caster sugar
150ml milk

To finish
1 egg yolk, beaten, or extra flour

1 Preheat the oven to 220°C/425°F/Gas 7.

2 Sift the flour with the other dry ingredients into a bowl, then rub in the butter and stir in the sugar. Make a deep well in the middle, then pour in the milk and mix in with a palette knife.

3 On a floured surface knead the dough very lightly until it is just smooth. Roll out to 2.5cm thick, then cut into small rounds.

4 Brush the tops with beaten egg yolk or dust with flour, and bake in the preheated oven, towards the top, for 7 minutes. Cool on a wire rack.

TO ME, HOME AND FAMILY REVOLVE
AROUND THE KITCHEN TABLE. I REMEMBER
VIVIDLY THE FAMILY MEALS MY MOTHER
COOKED — SHE EVEN MADE THE BREAD.

FLORENTINES

BUTTER BISCUITS

THESE CHOCOLATE-COATED TREATS ARE
CLASSIC ITALIAN BISCUITS.

THESE ARE SOFT-TEXTURED BISCUITS,
WHICH KIDS WOULD LOVE.

EASY ~ MAKES 20 BISCUITS ~ PREP 25 MINS PLUS
SETTING TIME ~ COOK 10 MINS

55g unsalted butter
55g caster sugar
2 tsp clear honey
55g plain flour
45g candied peel, chopped
45g glacé cherries, chopped
45g blanched almonds, chopped
85g good dark chocolate, melted

1 Preheat the oven to 180°C/350°F/Gas 4. Grease and
flour two baking sheets.

2 Melt the butter with the sugar and honey, then take
off the heat. Add the flour, peel, cherries and almonds,
and mix thoroughly.

3 Drop 2 teaspoons of the mix at a time onto the baking
sheets, leaving plenty of space in between, as they will
spread when they cook.

4 Bake in the preheated oven for 8–10 minutes, then
leave to cool on a wire rack.

5 When cold, spread the flat side of each biscuit with
melted chocolate. When it is nearly set, mark it with
wavy lines.

EASY ~ MAKES 30 BISCUITS ~ PREP 20 MINS ~
COOK 12 MINS

300g unsalted butter
200g icing sugar
100g eggs, beaten
400g plain flour
finely grated zest of 1 lemon

1 Preheat the oven to 170°C/325°F/Gas 3. Grease and
flour two baking sheets.

2 Cream the butter and sugar together, then add the
eggs, flour and lemon zest. Mix thoroughly, then spoon
into a piping bag fitted with a star nozzle. Pipe the
mixture onto the trays in fingers of about 8 x 1cm.

3 Bake in the preheated oven for 12 minutes, watching
carefully, then leave to cool on a wire rack.

HONEY SNAPS

YOU CAN EAT THESE DELICIOUS SNAPS
WITH ICE-CREAM.

EASY ~ MAKES 30 BISCUITS OR 10 BASKETS ~ PREP 20 MINS ~
COOK 12 MINS

125g unsalted butter
225g clear honey
1 tsp bicarbonate of soda
250g plain flour
170g caster sugar

1 Preheat the oven to 180°C/350°F/Gas 4, and grease
   a baking sheet.

2 Place the butter and honey in a pan and melt, then
   add the bicarbonate of soda and stir in. Remove
   from the heat, add the flour and sugar, and beat
   really well.

3 Place tablespoons of the mix on the greased baking
   sheet, spaced well apart, and bake in the preheated
   oven for 10–12 minutes. For baskets, make the
   individual biscuits a little larger, 2–3 tbsp each. Cool
   on a wire rack.

Variation
You could also make slightly larger biscuits into baskets
to hold ice-cream or a mousse. While still warm from
the oven, and working quickly, remove individually
from the tray with a fish slice, and allow to shape over
the bottom of a tea-cup.

MANHATTAN COCONUT COOKIES

WITH COCONUT AS WELL AS
CHOCOLATE CHIPS, THESE WOULD BE
PERFECT FOR A CHILDREN'S TEA PARTY.

EASY ~ MAKES 20–30 BISCUITS ~ PREP 20 MINS PLUS
COOLING AND CHILLING TIME ~ COOK 10 MINS

500g icing sugar
500g desiccated coconut, lightly toasted
225g egg whites
250g unsalted butter, melted
250g chocolate chips

1 Place the sugar and coconut in a bowl then add the
   egg white and mix together. Add the butter and mix,
   and then when the butter is cool, add the chocolate
   chips. Place in a container and chill for 20 minutes.

2 Preheat the oven to 180°C/350°F/Gas 4.

3 When the mixture is set hard, roll it into balls of about
   2–3cm in diameter. Place on a baking sheet, and
   bake in the preheated oven for 10 minutes. Cool on
   a wire rack.

ALMOND AND ORANGE TUILES

ALMONDS AND ORANGE GO VERY WELL TOGETHER, AND WILL MAKE A CRISP BISCUIT FOR TEATIME THAT IS A LITTLE DIFFERENT FROM YOUR AVERAGE DIGESTIVE. . .

EASY ~ MAKES 20 ~ PREP 10 MINS PLUS RESTING TIME ~ COOK 5 MINS

100ml orange juice
finely grated zest of 2 oranges
250g caster sugar
200g nibbed almonds, toasted
65g strong white flour
135g unsalted butter, melted

1 Warm the juice, zest and sugar together in a pan to melt the sugar, then stir in the almonds, flour and melted butter. Place this in the fridge to rest for 30 minutes.

2 Preheat the oven to 180°C/350°F/Gas 4.

3 Spread some of the mixture onto a plastic mat into round discs 10–12cm in diameter. Bake in the preheated oven for 5 minutes until golden brown.

4 Remove from the oven and quickly, using a spatula or fish slice, place on to a rolling pin to curl. Remove when they are cold and crisp.

5 Repeat steps 3 and 4 until the mixture is finished.

VANILLA TUILES

YOU WILL HAVE TO MAKE THESE TUILES IN BATCHES. YOU COULD MAKE CHOCOLATE TUILES BY SUBSTITUTING 20G OF THE FLOUR WITH GOOD COCOA POWDER.

EASY ~ MAKES ABOUT 20 LARGE TUILES ~ PREP 20 MINS PLUS RESTING TIME ~ COOK 5 MINS

100g plain flour
100g icing sugar
1 vanilla pod, split and scraped
40g clear honey
100g egg whites
100g unsalted butter, melted

1 Mix the flour, sugar and vanilla seeds, then add the honey and egg whites. Whisk well together, then pour in the butter, whisk again, and leave to rest for 30 minutes.

2 Preheat the oven to 180°C/350°F/Gas 4.

3 Spread some of the mixture on to a plastic mat into round discs 10–12cm in diameter. Bake in the preheated oven for 5 minutes until golden brown.

4 Remove from the oven and quickly, using a spatula or fish slice, place on to a rolling pin to curl. Remove when they are cold and crisp.

5 Repeat steps 3 and 4 until the mixture is finished.

CHOCOLATE CHIP COOKIES

I THINK THESE ARE BEST JUST EATEN STRAIGHT FROM THE OVEN, WHEN THE CHOCOLATE IS STILL RUNNY.

EASY ~ MAKES 15–20 BISCUITS ~ PREP 20 MINS ~ COOK 15 MINS

200g unsalted butter

150g soft light brown sugar

a few drops of vanilla essence

2 egg yolks

250g self-raising flour

50g good cocoa powder

200g chocolate chips

2 tbsp milk

1 Preheat the oven to 180°C/350°F/Gas 4, and grease a baking sheet.

2 Cream the butter, sugar and vanilla together, then beat in the egg yolks. Sieve the flour and cocoa powder, then add to the mix, followed by the chocolate chips and milk. Mix well.

3 Place heaped tablespoons onto the greased tray and bake in the preheated oven for 15 minutes. Cool on a wire rack.

HONEY MADELEINES

THIS MIX IS BEST MADE THE DAY BEFORE YOU COOK. DELICIOUS WITH POACHED PEARS (SEE PAGE 178).

MEDIUM ~ MAKES AT LEAST 24 LARGE MADELEINES ~ PREP 15 MINS ~ COOK 30 MINS

280g unsalted butter

390g eggs

200g caster sugar

30g demerara sugar

60g clear honey

270g plain flour

8g baking powder

a pinch of sea salt

finely grated zest of 1 lemon and 1 orange

1 Preheat the oven to 180°C/350°F/Gas 4, and grease and flour a couple of madeleine trays.

2 Place the butter on a gentle heat and cook to a beurre noisette, a nut-brown-colour. Pass through a fine sieve straightaway into a bowl.

3 Whisk the eggs in the mixer bowl until light.

4 Meanwhile, place the sugars and honey in a pan and cook to the soft ball stage, 120°C/248°F. Add this to the whisked eggs in a steady stream, still whisking.

5 Fold in the flour, baking powder, the salt and noisette butter. All this should take no more than 5 minutes, whisking all the time, from start to finish. Pour the mix into the madeleine trays then bake in the preheated oven for 12 minutes. Cool on a wire rack.

MY WORK IS A JOY, IT IS MY LIFE, IT KEEPS
ME HAPPY. I HAVE FOUND MY TRUE
VOCATION. IT IS NOT A JOB, MORE A
FEELING OF BELONGING.

INDEX